S
Within I

WITHIN LIVING MEMORY SERIES

Other Counties in this series include:

Bedfordshire
Hertfordshire
Northamptonshire

Shropshire
Staffordshire
Surrey

Somerset Within Living Memory

Compiled by the Somerset
Federation of Women's Institutes from notes
sent by Institutes in the County

Published jointly by
Countryside Books, Newbury
and the SFWI, Taunton

First Published 1992
© Somerset Federation of Women's Institutes 1992

COUNTRYSIDE BOOKS
3, Catherine Road,
Newbury, Berkshire

ISBN 1 85306 204 9

Cover design by Mon Mohan
Produced through MRM Associates Ltd, Reading
Typeset by Acorn Bookwork, Salisbury
Printed in England by J.W. Arrowsmith Ltd, Bristol

Contents

Acknowledgements

Somerset Federation of Women's Institutes would like to thank all W.I. members who supplied material for this project through their local Institutes.

Unfortunately we were not able to include extracts from every submission; to do so would have meant some duplication of content, and of course we had to take into account the total amount of space available in the book.

But all the contributions, without exception, were of value: deciding the shape and content of the book. We are grateful for them all.

The cover photograph was kindly supplied by Mrs Cary of Pylle W.I. Our thanks are also due to Pip Challenger and to Pat Taylor who provided the delightful line illustrations for the book.

Ann Mumford
Co-ordinator

Foreword

Somerset is a large irregularly shaped County with an attractive coastline, a few major towns but mainly villages and hamlets scattered along the roads or nestling among the hills, each a complete community. Life must have vastly changed since the early days of the century. It is these changes and people's memories of their way of life that this book seeks to record.

How often do we hear 'Do you remember when___?', then listen to stories of the harshness of life, strict daily routine or simple pleasures of life during the First World War, the so-called Roaring Twenties, depressed Thirties, wartime Forties or the re-building and re-adjustment of the Fifties. I've always thought it is wrong to let the way of life of everyday folk pass beyond recall. An instance of this was my own grandfather, a farmer, who used a wealth of herbal remedies to treat many ailments both for his farm workers and the animals. One certainly relieved my whooping cough, but none were ever recorded and so are now lost forever.

Now, in print, our collection of memories is recorded to be read not only by us, the present generation and our children but also by those yet to be born.

The Women's Institutes around the County have researched the contents, using their usual skills and ingenuity to seek out stories and memories of the older folk. We thank them all for their help and hope they and many others will enjoy our delve into the past.

F. Middleditch
County Chairman

TOWN & COUNTRY LIFE

LIFE IN THE VILLAGES
AND TOWNS

It is not so very long since the lamplighter travelled the streets of
Taunton at dusk and at dawn, and children played hopscotch in the
road, untroubled by traffic. Glimpses of Somerset's towns and villages before the 1950s show a way of life which had changed little
from their Victorian predecessors. Everyone seemed to know everyone else and local characters and eccentrics had their place and were
often regarded with tolerance and affection. It seemed a world
impervious to change, where the old feudal customs could still be
taken for granted and the Squire receive a curtsey or a doff of the cap as
he rode by. But change was coming, heralded by the first telephones
and motorised transport. And lest we tend to see the past in too golden a
light, there are reminders too of the poverty of those who needed to
rely upon local charity to survive, and the odour of the workhouse
which still clung to the old people's hospital in the 1950s.

TAUNTON IN THE 1930s

'My family, father, mother, two brothers and I, came to Taunton in
June 1930. Dad was the Deputy Manager at the Ministry of Labour on
the corner of Wood Street and Bridge Street (since demolished when
Wood Street was widened). Having no car, Dad rode his bicycle to
work. Most people travelled to work by bus, bicycle or walked. The
bus fare from Clifford Avenue to the Parade was twopence adults and
a penny children.

Dad had an upstairs office overlooking Bridge Street. The large
window opened onto a flat roof. When the summer Carnival was
held in the 1930s, we sat on chairs on this flat roof to watch the
procession go by. Some participants had collection bags on long sticks
which they held up for our contributions.

We lived in Clifford Avenue (then under construction). The next
houses were being built and the rest of the field was still under
cultivation. Horse-drawn reapers and binders were brought to harvest the corn and as it was cut the rabbits ran out – they made a tasty
dinner. We used to have rides on the horses. Whitmore Road, parallel
to Clifford Avenue, was a hay meadow. After the hay was cut, we

10

had picnics in the field and sometimes the friends in Clifford Avenue organised their own sports afternoon in the field.

Mother bought the main family groceries from a Co-op store in Greenway Avenue, near St Andrew's church. Once a week an assistant from the shop came to our house and sat at the dining room table with his order book. He wrote down all the items that Mother wanted. Two or three days later a cart came from the shop and delivered the groceries in a cardboard box.

The milkman came along the road twice a day with a churn in a horse-drawn cart. He had metal measures for half pint, one pint and one quart. Customers took out their jugs to be filled. The baker also came in a horse-drawn cart with a roof sheltering the bread. Sammy Dawe came periodically with his honing machine. He sharpened knives, scissors and shears.

Clifford Avenue was lit by gas lamps. In the evening the lamplighter rode along the road on his bicycle carrying a long wooden pole with a hook on the end. As he rode past each lamp he pulled the switch to turn the light on. In the morning he rode along the road again to switch the lights off.

On passing the scholarship in 1933, I attended Bishop Fox's Girls Grammar School, then in Staplegrove Road. A great deal of pride was felt in being able to wear the Bishop Fox's uniform. Some classrooms were in the main school and some were over the road in Weir Lodge. There were tennis courts and netball pitches at the school, but the hockey and rounders pitches were at the playing fields in Kingston Road, where the present Bishop Fox's school stands. For swimming we walked from the school to the baths in St James Street. For Speech Day in September the whole school walked to the County Hotel, where the Speech Day was held in the ballroom at the rear. Parents also attended. School Certificates gained at the exams in the summer were also presented on Speech Day.

In the 1930s the area where Musgrove Park Hospital now stands was called Manor Fields. Bertram Mills Circus came there periodically, preceded by a parade through the town. Sir Alan Cobham also came to Manor Fields. They displayed planes and held competitions. There were comic turns and opportunities for the public to ride in an aeroplane.'

BURNHAM ON SEA IN THE 1920s

'When, at the age of six, I moved with my family from Dorset to Burnham on Sea, my first impression from the train was of rows and rows of red brick houses, very different from the warm stone of our Dorset village.

11

I remember taking part in a concert given for relief of the flood victims at Athelney. Until the big new artificial drain (now a fisherman's paradise) was built across the moors, it was possible to travel on the old S and D railway, with fields on both sides covered in flood waters – a strange sight. From the peat moors came turf and we used to buy turfs at Burnham for fuel.

Seventy years ago, little ships (one was called the *Julia*) came across from South Wales with coal, and sometimes a timber-laden ship from Sweden would be waiting for a pilot to take it up to Bridgwater or Highbridge. The confluence of the rivers Parrett and Brue meant that there were some nasty currents at their mouths. Most years, someone drowned there, so we children were forbidden to go to the end of the jetty.

There was an old railway carriage at the end which served as the Seamen's Mission. Punch and Judy came in the summer, and Freddy Fay, his wife and daughter Erin performed daily on their little outdoor stage on the sands. Very often there was a fierce wind and when the sand was dry, it whirled about in a spiteful manner, and stung bare legs. In wet weather, there was a lot of sticky mud.'

WIVELISCOMBE IN THE 1930s

'At one time Wiveliscombe could proudly boast that there was no need to go elsewhere to shop. Everything could be bought in this small town, which possessed upwards of 64 shops covering a variety of goods, products and trades. In addition to these could be added five blacksmiths and at least 28 public houses. The number of shops has reduced dramatically over the years to approximately 17, and the hitherto thriving public house trade now only supports five pubs in the locality.'

WILLITON IN THE 1930s

'In the 1930s there were very few cars in Williton, but still some of the old Brooke Bond tea vans, with their solid rubber tyres and disc wheels, travelling along slightly crab-wise. There was an occasional privately owned small bus or charabanc in the summer, grinding on their way with smoking exhaust.

There were tricycles, including the Walls Ice Cream ones, with two wheels at the front and a large container filled with ice-cream and painted with the slogan "Stop Me and Buy One" painted on it.

There were bicycles galore, including the tradesmen's bikes, ridden by errand boys. Butcher Langdon's, with a large carrier over the front wheels, was filled with joints of meat being delivered to customers' houses.

Sometimes the visiting scissor grinder came on his bicycle and would sharpen your scissors or knives in the street by propping up his wheel and pedalling away to turn a grindstone over the front wheel. There were many horse-drawn vehicles, such as Jones' bread cart, filled with loaves of bread and cakes to be delivered around the district, and Bulpin's milk float, with its large churn, from which the milk was dipped and poured into jugs people had left on their doorsteps.

Old Mrs Fowler from Bob Lane had her hand cart and collected fish from the railway station to sell around Williton. Jim Chidgey, with his green baize apron, was busy sweeping the streets and pavement by hand and filling his hand-cart.'

WATCHET IN THE 1930s

'Life in Watchet in the 1930s was pleasant and it was a good place to grow up in, a close-knit society where everyone knew each family. Teachers, clergy, doctors, bank managers and tradesmen all took a keen interest in local activitites.

The public hall in Harbour Road was in great demand, a meeting place for the WI, whist drives, dances and the Dramatic Society, and it was used almost every evening. The cosy cinema was a great attraction and was the first in the district when opened at the top of Swain Street. Later it became Van Heusen's shirt factory. A thriving golf club on Cleeve Hill meant that most activitites took place in or around the town.

The Territorial Army held summer camps at Doniford under canvas, later joined by the RAF for gunnery practice and flying training in light aircraft, eventually setting up a permanent camp at what is now St Audries' Holiday Camp. This was used until the outbreak of the Second World War. The association with the service personnel resulted in many successful marriages, with people moving to various parts of the world but always happy to return to Watchet in retirement.'

BRIDGWATER IN THE 1940s

'Where we lived at Bridgwater the river Parrett was just across the road and at night, particularly during high tides, we could see the lights of the ships making their way up river. They appeared to come so close as to be sailing right into the front garden before negotiating the very sharp bend at that point in the river.

I remember crossing that river via the Town Bridge and stopping to watch an old man fishing in a dinghy below. He put what looked like a long handled mop over the side of the boat. He waited for a while before, with one swift movement, he lifted the mop out of the milk chocolate-coloured water and dropped it into the boat. The mop head was engorged and wriggled with dozens of eels which had been making their run up river from the Bristol Channel. The old man's method never failed.

I also have the impressionable recollection of a nine year old of a visit to the old covered market at the top of the town. There one could purchase day-old chicks at one penny each and carry them home cheeping in brown paper bags to put under a broody hen.'

STAPLEHAY BEFORE 1914

'Looking back to 1912, Staplehay was very much a village. We had our own bakery, butcher, cabinet maker, undertaker, dressmaker, and two cobblers who kept our shoes in good repair. The landlord of the Crown Inn, Mr Vincent, could often be seen standing outside in his large beige green apron bidding the passerby "a very good day to you". We only had two car owners in the district – Mr Wakefield, a banker at Amerd House, and Mr Sale, an antiques dealer in London who lived at Quintons. Col Wodday lived at Canonsgrove, he drove a carriage and pair, and sometimes a "four in hand". At the Manse, the Rev Bishop's eldest daughter ran a small school for beginners. We also had Band of Hope concerts twice a year in the school room when local people entertained.'

COMBWICH BETWEEN THE WARS

'Combwich derived its name from the legendary witch Dame Withycombe who lived in a cottage near the village. Symon's field used to be a great place for snowball fights between the "Uprounders" from one end of the village and the "Overlongers" from the other end and for skating after a hard frost.

Children were sometimes allowed by the kindly blacksmiths, Mr Quick and Jim, to blow the big bellows while they heated and hammered the iron shoes for a horse and there was not a child in the village who did not have an iron hoop made by Mr Quick for a penny.

The appetising smell of delicious fresh bread came from Mr Hunt's bakery and deliveries were made by horse and cart.

Further along the road from the bakehouse, there is still a hook where customers at the Baker's Arms tied their horses. The village bus ran on Monday, Wednesday and Saturday – one shilling return to

14

Bridgwater – deliveries and shopping undertaken by owner/driver Wallace Bailey for threepence. The last bus home on Saturday was the "Merry bus" at 10 pm, and Wallace had to take care not to exceed 15 mph or he was sharply reprimanded by his sister Ada, who sat beside him.

One-armed postman, Mr Patch delivered the mail for 40 years, walking first to Bere Manor, then round the village, across to Otterhampton and Steart, and back along the river bank.

The water supply for villagers who did not have their own wells, was the pump opposite the Ship Inn.

Apple orchards where the Wassail Ceremony was an annual event, have disappeared to make way for houses on Ship Lane, School Lane, Riverview and Martin's Close.

Ferry crossings could be made, rowed by Mr Pane in his little boat, from the White Horse on the Pawlett side of the river to the Anchor on the Combwich side, where the high wall was the scene of fierce competition at "Fives", for the regulars to the two pubs. Back in the 19th century on a misty evening, the horses pulling a stage coach bolted and plunged into the river. All on board were drowned and it is said that on many misty nights, the coach can be seen and the victims' cries heard again.

The deep fishing ponds that provide such a pleasant outlook for a modern housing estate, are the result of the clay extraction for the old brick and tile works.

Lofty Cornish used to go down the river with the tide to dig sand for tile making and the men of the village learned to swim tied by a rope to his "flattener". They were not considered proficient until they could swim the river·at full tide.

Ships like *Fanny Jane*, *Sunshine* and *Irene* sailed between Comb-wich, Bristol, Wales and Ireland carrying bricks and returning with cargoes of coal which was unloaded in tall baskets, carried on the men's shoulders, up the skids to the wharves across the road.'

CHEWTON MENDIP BETWEEN THE WARS

'In the centre of the village was the Chewton Mendip Co-op Society shop, a co-operative of village people, with next to it the post office. Further down in Lower Street could be found the Cornelius's bicycle shop and a sweetshop.

Annie and George Gane sold sweets and also bicycles. They wouldn't have electricity even when it was available, so at the beginning of the winter they bought half cwt of candles to light the shop. It was just too bad when, as sometimes happened, they ran out of candles! Mabel Cornelius did a milk round, selling the milk from her son Cecil's cows in cans and quarter and half pint measures. Her husband kept horses for landaus and carts to transport people to Hallatrow station. After her husband's death Mabel Cornelius sold and repaired bicycles from Spring Cottage.

There was also, a wheelwright's, carpenter's and undertaker's, while further up near the Folly was a butcher's. At one time a seamstress lived in one of the little cottages at Kingshill. People from this part of the village didn't usually venture up to Bathway where there was another shop (the present post office) selling drapery and groceries and where hobnail boots at five shillings a pair hung from the ceiling. Also at Bathway was the business of Mr Charlie Wookey – foundry, undertaker's and wheelwright's. He made farm carts and wooden vans and Mrs Hayes remembers an oak stool for turning cheeses and a milking stool which cost half a crown. Uphills the farriers at Nedge would make you a set of shoes for four shillings and sixpence in the 1920s. You could even buy a car made in the village. The Chewton Mendip Motor Works originally based at the Bathway foundry site later moved to Cutlers Green where the Mendip Car was produced.'

STAPLEGROVE BETWEEN THE WARS

'Traders within Staplegrove catered for the needs of the majority of residents. The Rendall family served Staplegrove with its requirements for meats for the table. Animals were slaughtered on the premises on a Monday afternoon. Delivery to customers was made over a wide area, earlier by horse and two-wheeled butcher's cart, and later by motor van. Tuesday was the day for the rendering of fats into lard, Thursday was "faggot" day. The aroma on both days made us, as children, walk around the area of the butcher's emulating the advert of the "Bisto Kids".

Groceries and sundry supplies were on offer at the Staplegrove Stores, owned successively by the Knight and Endicott families. Most needs could be supplied, which saved families living locally a trip into town. As children, in the 1920s, we bought our bars of "Black Jack" there at four for a penny, or liquorice boot-laces at the same ratio, and of course broken biscuits.

Mr Alfred Stowell was the village cobbler or "snob". He plied his trade in a shed in his back garden (it's still there) next to the Staplegrove Stores. He would sole and heel a pair of men's boots for five shillings or ladies shoes for three shillings. Near to the church, Mr William Millett (parish clerk and verger) also plied this trade and he catered for the parishioners in his vicinity.

Bread could be obtained on the doorstep either from Norton Mills, the Co-operative Society, Locks, or Pauls. Milk also was delivered to the door, twice each day, by Mr Hallett from Tanyard or Mr Shattock. The former had his horse and dairy cart with the large brass churn, Mr Shattock rode his bicycle carrying two pails of milk on the handlebars. Fish also was delivered to the door twice each week by Mr Norris, who came with his cycle with fore and aft carriers and two large wicker baskets. He would rest his board on one of the lidded baskets and fillet fish in the street. He also delivered the Sunday papers.

Mr T. Marks of Greenway Road Garage served the needs of motorist and cyclists. He was there to supply the carbide for acetylene lamps, an occasional tyre and tube and, if needs be, a new bicycle. The accumulator for the wireless he would charge for sixpence. Mr Marks also operated a taxi service and a small charabanc for outings, used by church organisations quite frequently in the summer.

Residents in the Staplegrove area going into Taunton to shop would either walk or cycle, though on a wet day they could make use of the local bus service. This need was supplied by Mr Hanks of Bishops Lydeard or Mr Withers of Bagborough. Both ran a scheduled service; the fare for adults from Mr Rendall's shop to the Parade in Taunton in the 1930s was one penny.

The Staplegrove Inn (known to the locals as "The Flying Horse") was managed by many landlords over this period, Whitecross, Davey, Symons and Down. Being quite near to the village hall, it was used by the people attending local dances and social functions, as it is to the present day.'

COSSINGTON IN THE 1930s

'I was born in 1927 in the village inn, which was kept by my grandfather. Later we moved to a small holding on the border of Cossington and Chilton Polden. At the age of eight I went to live with my grandmother in the village, in the cottage where she was born and raised ten children. The toilet was at the top of a long garden, and we used candles and lamps for lighting, and the old black range for cooking. We had no radio and I used to read to my grandmother. Once a week a fish and chip van came around, and I had a penny-worth of chips. I joined the church choir and once a year we went to the rectory for tea. The rector's wife always made coffee ice-cream which was a treat.

The coal was delivered by the Symes family from Chilton Polden, who used to collect the coal from the station at Cossington with a horse and cart. As children we used to hang onto the back of the cart and have a ride.

17

War broke out, and evacuees came to live with us. Home Guards and ARP groups were formed. There was a searchlight battery set up in the old quarry. Some bombs were dropped locally, also a couple of planes crashed nearby. The iron railing, gates and a shell from the First World War which was used as a war memorial were taken away to be used for scrap metal.

For the Queen's Coronation in 1953 we all went down to the school to watch it on TV and then went to a tea at the village hall. We were the second people to have a TV and rows of children used to sit in our house to watch it.'

CASTLE CARY IN THE 1930s

'Water ran down by the side of the main street in Castle Cary, as it does now in the city of Wells. By the horse pond one could see, perhaps, someone collecting water from the chute, while two swans swam majestically on the pond or waddled clumsily over the pavement.

I arrived in Castle Cary in about 1939, to teach eight year olds. As the school was opposite the church, we used to hear the passing bell tolling when there was a funeral – one stroke for each of the deceased's years. When war came the junior school was requisitioned for ATS quarters and the children were given space in the new school being built at Ansford. How nice it was to sit in pastel-coloured classrooms instead of the usual pea-green or buff.

Shops stayed open until 9 pm on Saturdays, 8 pm on Fridays and 7 pm on other days, except, of course, on Sundays, when no shops were open. The milkman called twice every day and the grocer called on one day for orders which were delivered two or three days later. Many shops closed if a funeral was to pass by, and the houses along the street drew their blinds.

Curfew was sounded every night during the winter at eight o'clock, right up to the beginning of the war when it was discontinued. It was never resumed after the war.'

ODCOMBE IN THE 1940s

'At Odcombe Miss Harris ran the post office and Mrs Dunstan sold home-made faggots from one of the two village shops. Mr Merchant sold newspapers, Mr Roberts repaired bicycles, and Mr Rodber the blacksmith also cut hair. Mr Pearce ran a pony and trap carrier service and on his twice daily journeys to Yeovil carried gloves made at home by many village housewives. One village character had a donkey pulling a bin on wheels and carted away the contents of "toilet buckets" etc.

The Masons Arms and Odcombe Inn were in lower Odcombe and the Rising Sun in Dray Road. The latter two had men's and ladies' skittle teams and darts were popular. Whist drives, WI meetings etc were held in a hall above the Rising Sun's skittle alley, and concerts and lantern shows in the chapel schoolroom. Apart from a few car owners, villagers walked, cycled or used the bus service.'

COMBE FLOREY IN THE 1950s

'Combe Florey was a very small village but there was a church and a chapel, a school, a station with a stationmaster and a porter, a market, a pub and a village hall where the farmers used to eat on market days. There was also a small boys prep school. The boys used to come to church on Sundays and occasionally to read the lesson. They looked very nice in their grey uniform.

There was a WI, a Youth Club and a flourishing cricket team. There were two cinemas within easy reach and we used to go quite often. There was a Dramatic Society with a moderate amount of talent. We joined forces with a neighbouring village and held dances in the village hall. We had the Exmoor Travelling Library call every other week. A village tea followed by a big party in the evening was held to celebrate the harvest, and a well supported Flower Show was an annual event. There was a Dog Show held at the local foxhound kennels and there were many Hunt Balls in the area. All this took place in a scattered community of some 200 people during the 1950s.'

LYDEARD ST LAWRENCE 1900–1960

'At Christmas, before the First World War, the lady of the manor at Lydeard St Lawrence allowed each child to choose a present from the village shop worth sixpence for the five to ten year olds and one shilling for those aged eleven to 14 years. These presents were taken to the school and distributed by the lady at the end of the Christmas term (the lord of the manor always read both lessons in church). This continued for many years. Before the Second World War each knew his place in village life. With the changes in society which that war brought about earlier social divisions have become blurred.

Up to the First World War, transport was limited to walking, cycling, horse and trap and train from Crowcombe station one and a half miles away. Between the wars a frequent bus service to and from Taunton was established and was well used by the community.

However, with greater car ownership the service was reduced and by 1960 the majority of village residents had become car owners.

Before the Second World War shire horses were hard at work on local farms and at the hay and corn harvests casual work from villagers was much in demand. Schoolchildren picked and sold mushrooms, blackberries and also whortleberries from the Quantock Hills. Milk was delivered by a local farmer. Eggs, cream and butter were all bought from nearby farms. From the early years of the century there have been two general shops and a bakery in the village. At first bread was delivered by horse and trap and when the baker invested in a van, he good-naturedly became a general carter and with his loaves, delivered everything from corsets to paraffin to outlying districts. The village post office has been in the care of three generations of the same family for over 50 years and before that was a shop selling bread, groceries and drapery. Before the Second World War a policeman lived in the village, also a District Nurse from Wales who married the postmaster.

THE VILLAGE STREET

'Growing up in Broadway in the 1930s I remember the village street far quieter than today; there were very few cars, buses or motorcycles and not many farmers had tractors, instead there was the plod, plod of the cart-horse. This meant children could play safely in the street, whipping tops or trundling hoops. Hopscotch squares marked with chalk on a dry road would remain for several days, children happily hopping from one square to another. Children walked to and from the village school without fear for their safety.

There were regular deliveries of meat, bread, groceries and coal, a lot by horse-drawn carts, with a few tradesmen having motor transport. Boys on bicycles were a familiar sight making local deliveries; this was a quick and cheap way of obliging the customer. Paraffin was delivered regularly as many were dependent on this for lighting and cooking. The van bringing this also carried pots and pans and many other household wares and the driver would buy for a few pence rags and rabbit skins. The housewives congregated around the various delivery vehicles to make their purchases and this provided a good opportunity for the exchange of village news and gossip. All a far cry from the dash to the supermarket of the 1990s.'

'As a boy of seven I was evacuated from Dagenham to Henton which, despite the war, was a quiet village. Sounds then were individual and distinctive. If I walk through the village now, sometimes I think I still hear some of those sounds, even though they have all long since gone. At Threeways, for instance, the dull, short swish of a wood plane or the rasp of a saw as Tom and Arch Gibbs, local builders and undertakers, worked to make a coffin. No "flatpacks" in those days. By Bleadney chapel you could still hear them but Roger and I would then be listening for a far more fascinating sound for two seven year old boys. There were only a few graves around the front of the chapel but one in particular had a large flat tombstone on it with a small round hole in the middle, about one inch in diameter. If you dropped a little stone through the hole you would hear it plop onto something a few feet down. Roger and I were convinced it had landed on the coffin.

The Picadilly Inn must have been unique in its time for, along with so many of the other houses in the village, it did not have its own well. The sound of Mrs Horsington's bucket as she carried water from the Laurels opposite was as familiar in Mill House as was the sound of our own bucket when we got drinking water from the same source.

Gully House, where I lived for most of the war, was like so many of the cottages, it had neither electricity nor water. From the garden the most common sound was that of Mrs Lizzie William's water pump, that had probably had its last spot of oil during the First World War and would still have been creaking away today had mains water not arrived in the late 1950s.'

CURTSEY TO THE SQUIRE

'The large landowners had a great influence on village life at East Coker in the early years of the century. When the Squire rode through the lanes on horseback, which he did regularly, he expected the girls to curtsey and the boys to doff their caps. Trouble for parents if they did not! This same landlord could (and did) evict a man from his cottage on his land for taking employment in a local webbing factory when labour was slack on the land. In the late 1800s a little chapel was built on Long Furlong lane to serve the inhabitants of Burton and Skinners Hill as the landowners had a bitter quarrel with the lord of the manor and had forbidden his employees to attend the parish church.'

'At Goathurst, of course, we had the lord of the manor, Lord Wharton, and if you were lucky enough to meet him in the park when you were picking sticks, occasionally you might meet him and he'd give you sixpence. We used to look forward to seeing Lord Wharton. Lady Wharton, she didn't come out so much, sometimes she used to come out with him, but usually it was him and his son on their own. He had a son John and a daughter Elizabeth, and if you met them you might be lucky and get a sixpence, which was good. They had their walking sticks which would open up and they used to sit down on them sometimes.'

'Shapwick used to be self contained, having a shop, post office, baker, butcher, mill, milkman, lime kiln and a few blue lias stone quarries for building. Everyone knew everyone else. If there was a stranger in the village all knew it. If you lived near an elderly person and her milk was left on the doorstep or her curtains stayed shut late into the morning, you investigated as a matter of course to see if they were alright.

The village was owned by two families, the Warrys at Shapwick House and the Strangways at the Manor. The Strangways had their own little entrance door to the church which no one else dare use. They sat in pews near the altar while the Warrys sat in the front seats in the body of the church. In my grandmother's day when anyone in the village met someone from the big houses, the women had to curtsey and the men take off their hats and bow.'

'Barrington's oldest inhabitant, born in 1905, has seen extraordinary changes in the life of the village. After her childhood in Wales she was taught dressmaking and returned to Barrington as a sewing maid at Barrington Court, which was being restored by Colonel and Mrs Lyle.

The establishment had an indoor staff including a butler and a pantry boy, a cook, a kitchen and scullery maid, five housemaids, an elderly nurse who did sewing as her charges were growing up, and Doris aged 18. She attended to the ladies' clothes, putting them out for dinner and, after the dinner gong had sounded, putting day garments away or sending them to the laundry in the grounds. The outdoor staff included a head gardener, ten gardeners, two chauffeurs and a handyman, plus a man in charge of the beagles, under

Capt Beaucham, Colonel Lyle's adjutant during the First World War.

The church was generously supported. A new heating system was installed and the oil lamps were replaced when electricity came to the village. Mrs Lyle and her daughters made tapestry kneelers for the chancel. When Barbara Lyle was married, steps were built to replace the slope from the road. The 'family' had a special pew and the staff had to attend morning service.

Although Colonel Lyle was strict (boys had to doff their caps and stand to attention) he was very generous. Villagers could use his bus, a converted ambulance, twice a week to go to Taunton. He bought the staff tickets for performances at the County Hotel. A cricket pitch was made. Dancing classes were taken by Joan Lyle at the school and there was a children's party with presents at Christmas.'

'Nynehead Court, and nearly all the village, was owned by the Sanford family but they rented the Court to a Major and Mrs Stobart who, at Christmas, gave the village children a party at the Court or a trip to the pantomime in Taunton followed by tea. In the early 1920s a member of the Sanford family celebrated his 21st birthday with a party at Chipley Park to which the villagers were invited and travelled by horse and wagon.'

'A founder member of Pilton WI recalls that the lady of the manor used to drive out each afternoon in horse and carriage with a liveried attendant. She would ask a village child to curtsey each time she passed – in return for a ride in the carriage. Much to her mother's delight, our member refused!'

THE GAMEKEEPER

'The estate gamekeeper in our village a few miles from Bishopswood between the wars was a terrifying figure to us children – a huge gruff man wearing a Norfolk jacket and knickerbockers. His capacious pockets held ferrets, rabbits or trapping nets and naughty children were threatened that they too would be put in his pockets. He had been a prisoner of war in Russian hands which added to our terror.'

THE VILLAGE CHARITY

'When I was a schoolgirl at Ashcott in the 1930s, my mother, who had a large family, used to ask us to look on the list which was put up on the reading room door. This list showed the names of village people who were to receive the "poor money" that year, money given by benefactors to the poor of the parish. This came from the John

Hurman Trust, which produced money from 20 acres of land for the upkeep of the church.

In 1730 Richard Miles left £300 to the churchwardens and overseers to purchase land, the produce from which would pay for the upkeep of his own tomb and also give bread or money to the poor. Another benefactor was Miss Sarah Miles who gave £100 to the church-wardens and the interest from that would make an annuity to the poor.

From all this my mother received the sum of five shillings each year, which was a generous amount in those days. The fund is still in existence and the amount paid out nowadays is £5 to eligible persons.'

'In Christmas 1859 at Weare a retired farmer presented twelve poor men each with a new long gown – a most valuable garment to a poor man in the winter, on condition they all attended divine service, twice on Christmas Day and twice the following Sunday. These conditions were cheerfully accepted by the men.'

'My father, a parish councillor at Penselwood in the early years of the century, collected coal from the station with a horse and wagon for distribution to the poor of the parish. I think he purchased it from the Radstock mines, presumably paid for by the parish.'

THE VILLAGE CLUB

'The Club Day at Barrington was the chief village holiday of the year. It was on the last Tuesday in May. The members assembled about 9 am, elected the Committee and Stewards for the year, received the printed statement of accounts, transacted any other business and then went in procession to the farm houses and other chief houses, where cider was supplied freely. At eleven o'clock they went to church for morning prayer and a sermon. After church, they continued the procession to the houses not previously visited. First went the flag man, then the President and Clerk bearing white wands, then came the bandsmen (the band being rather older than the Club itself) four abreast, then the two senior Stewards with ten foot red brass-mounted poles, then the members two by two wearing Oxford Blue club knots (rosettes with nine inch streamers) on their hats and carrying thin blue brass-mounted poles. Meanwhile, the "Standings" (booths for the sale of sweets and toys) had been set up near the Club field, and in the Club field were swings, roundabouts, etc. At two o'clock the members sat down to dinner at tallyboards and the invited guests at a cross table. The dinner consisted of beef, bread and cider,

24

with cheese in addition at the guests' table. The cider was handed round in pitchers marked "B.C. of Crock Street" (Donyatt), said to be as old as the club. The last feast was on the last Tuesday in May (28th) 1912 and was held in Ellen's Close, Court Road.'

'The village of Westbury-sub-Mendip nestles quietly in the Cheddar Valley close to the city of Wells. It is proud of its Friendly Society which has been in existence since 1770, the present one being established in 1875. Around that time many Somerset villages had a Friendly Society but only three have survived. Quarterly meetings are still held in the same public house. An annual Club Day is held on Spring Bank Holiday Monday (formerly on Trinity Monday). The members walk in procession to the parish church headed by a fine old banner borne for many generations by a member of the Lovell family. A dinner follows and there is fun for adults and children alike throughout the day. In its early days contributions were made to help the sick and support widows. Today the Society gives generously to the village but still remembers its original purpose. Until 1975 it was a "men only" society but during that year ladies were admitted.'

THE VILLAGE HALL

'In 1952, a group of people living in Moorland and Fordgate, held a meeting in the village school and decided to buy two RAF huts – used to house civilians – which were for sale in Bridgwater, at a cost of £100 each. Five of these people each guaranteed £50 and were very grateful to a local farmer Mr Richards who kindly offered a piece of land on which to build the new village hall.

Many folk came forward with tractors, trailers and cars, journeying to and fro into Bridgwater to dismantle the old, to rebuild the new. The ladies (some with babes in prams) used to spend many hours on the site – sawing up the trees which had been felled, painting the downpipes and gutterings etc, in preparation for the men to start the building work, and all this was done with a wonderful pioneering spirit.'

THE COMMON

'There is a large common at Ash Priors and various houses had rights of grazing which they used for cows and horses, but with the advent of TT herds this had to be stopped because of the risk of infection. Eventually, the grazing of horses stopped too, because of the danger to both car drivers and stock, and the common has now mostly reverted to scrub.'

THE VILLAGE 1930–1945

This humorous look at village life will strike a chord with many people who lived in just such a community some 50 years ago.

The church was the centre point of the village although it was tucked away at the end of the single street, with the rectory at the other end and along the road to Taunton. When the much-loved rector retired the new man had rather "high" ideas, but he learned to curb these on the day he suggested the choir should sing the Creed. My father, a quiet man, announced it was a dreadful noise and he would never go to church again. The rector and his family stayed for many years and were our friends, but no-one ever sang the Creed again, and there were always good congregations for each of the three Sunday services.

Two small boys in an adjoining pew to ours behaved so badly on one occasion, my mother folded her large prayer book and spanked them both with it. They, however, won the day by retreating under the pew, from where they could "cock-a-snook" knowing the pew was their protection.

At the service for the Silver Jubilee of George V we all stood in the blazing sun in the churchyard while a silver birch tree was planted and dedicated. It was a long, dull service but livened up considerably when an elderly man fainted at our feet. We were fascinated! He was in his best double-breasted thick tweed suit with waistcoat and flannel shirt, bowler hat and very heavy lace up leather boots. He must have boiled.

The social side of the village was confined to celebrations for the Silver Jubilee, the Coronation of George VI, and the wedding of the Duke of Kent to Princess Marina. On these occasions there would be a church service in the morning, and children's sports in the afternoon, followed by a huge tea of buns, jam sandwiches and lemonade, served on long trestle tables in a barn, field or farm yard. In the evening there would be a barn dance, and our morning (after church) was spent sliding up and down the barn floor so that the french chalk would be well worked in and the Palais Glide and the Lambeth Walk would go smoothly.

There was the Girls' Friendly Society, known as the GFS, which was run for young girls in service to have a well-chaperoned night out once a week.

The school was half a mile from the village, and all children from

This photograph, taken in the 1940s, harks back to an earlier era when Somerset countrymen wore their distinctive smocks to go about their ordinary business.

four years old walked there every morning, walked home for lunch, and returned again in the afternoon. There was one school mistress and a young assistant, and every child learnt the three Rs and good manners. Our house was opposite the school, and we could hear the tables being chanted, but not until after morning prayers, with hymns and the Venite being sung.

There was a school concert every year. One year a very solid small boy and a pretty little girl walked onto the stage and climbed into bed. The rest of the pupils acted a dream, and when this was over the two woke up and announced they had had a great adventure. What a pity small children no longer play with such innocence.

In 1945 a plan for meals to be delivered to the schools was put into practice, to be run by volunteers. The first day was not a great success when the volunteer tipped the whole container of stew down his front, and had to borrow a suit from my brother while his was sponged off by the schoolmistress.

There were few cars, and most people went by horse, bicycle or bus. The bus was run by a local man who would always wait for Mrs So-and-So if she was delayed. The journey to Taunton was like a family outing.

My grandfather drove an enormous Humber saloon, making a

drive through the narrow lanes a hazardous journey. He disapproved strongly of the newly formed Co-op delivery service and thought it would put small village shopkeepers out of business. One day he met the van in the narrowest part of the lane and refused to draw to one side, saying there was no room. The perky young driver leant out of his window and shouted; "Room Sir? Room! Why there's room for another!" For all his threats Grandfather did not stir and the young man had to reverse his van.

A young man came to live near the village, and drove a flashy green sports car. One day he missed Mother by a few inches, and she reported this to our local PC Garland, who was the epitome of everyone's idea of a local bobby. He arrived, notebook in hand and asked; "And what, Madam, would have been your position should the vehicle in question have struck you?" "Well," came the reply, "I had always hoped it would be Heaven's gates, but one can never be quite sure." He closed his notebook and bicycled home.

Most of the farmers used horses, and when the first combine harvester was used in 1945 the whole village turned out to see it working. A smallholder kept two cows in the field by our house, and he would walk from the village twice a day to milk them where they stood in the field. Usually he would hitch the two open buckets onto the yoke across his shoulders and walk home, but one day he came to us because one of the buckets was leaking. He borrowed some good green scrubbing soap to plug the hole, which he chose to do from the inside of the bucketful of milk.

The health of everyone was looked after by the dedicated village nurse, with the help of the "panel" doctor from Taunton. He only came in real emergencies, and one Sunday afternoon a distraught young mother arrived with her baby to ask us to ring the doctor because baby had swallowed a nail. We were not his patients, and he was not pleased to be disturbed and suggested giving the baby some cotton wool porridge. Mother was not pleased either, so he relented enough to ask how they knew baby had swallowed a nail. "Oh, I don't really know," the girl replied, "but he does rattle so when I shake him." The doctor replaced his receiver.

The men ran their own cricket team, looking after the pitch in the evenings, and driving the cows to the far end of the field. Girls were not encouraged until about 1938 when they joined forces and made a grass tennis court. What a lot of fun they had, and all made by themselves and some hard work for each of them.

Milk came in a can and was poured into our own jug and covered with the "milk book".

An ice cream man came round every Thursday afternoon after closing his shop in Taunton. His van was horse drawn and his ice cream out of this world! Later a Stop-me-and-buy-one came round from time to time, but we waited for Mr Coles and his pony and cart on Thursdays.

An old man riding a tricycle and wearing a bowler hat and smart grey knicker-bocker suit delivered a local paper once a week. We called him Bungy, but never spoke to him.

The post office was run for many years by a little old lady with no head for figures. When my mother wanted six insurance stamps at sevenpence halfpenny each neither of them could work out the price, and would line up six piles of seven pennies and seven halfpennies along the counter.

There was a tiny shop with a half door between the church and the fields. It sold three kinds of sweets, boiled, aniseed balls or toffee, and tobacco.

Once, when the verger was very ill, the rector called a PCC meeting at which he asked; "We have to decide what we should do when the verger is sick." There was silence until Mother suggested they should fetch a basin. There being no other suggestions, the meeting closed and the verger recovered.

Of course there are changes. The lane to the village is now a road with no stream; more cars and buses run daily. Barns are now houses and Taunton grows nearer, but the village street still bears some resemblance to the one I knew between the wars.'

TRADES AND SERVICES

In any town or village, you would be likely to come across the same kind of trades and services, provided for the immediate community in the days when travel was not something undertaken lightly or often.

THE INN

'My childhood was spent during the 1940s and early 1950s in a village inn. No great changes had taken place for years; the flagstone floors, heavy doors, low ceilings, open fires and brown nicotine-stained walls and curtains and overall a smell of stale beer.

29

The cellar housed large wooden beer and cider barrels lying side by side on a frame, each tapped with a drip-tray and a bung in the side from which frothy bubbles would ooze. Hooks from the low ceiling held strings of onions, a rabbit or hare and a basket of medlars, Russets, Tom Putts or Morgan Sweets shared the window ledge with a rabbit-gin or rat trap.

At midday the locals would arrive with their bread and cheese, for a pint or two of cider, the road-men, farm labourers and the station-master on his bike, and on Sundays the local undertaker. In the evenings they would play crib, dominoes, darts or shove ha'penny.

During the war years the front door stayed shut but the locals found their way in around the back. Not many women were seen in pubs in those days. After the war things gradually changed. My father took over from my grandfather and in 1952 television came to Somerset. We were packed out on Coronation Day, being the only ones in the neighbourhood with a set. Unfortunately that square box was the demise of the village pub.'

'Three miles from North Curry was the nearest train station and to get there you either walked or hired a brougham, kept by the publican, as a taxi service. There was a carrier cart to Taunton via Knapp and Ham, twice a week. The public house also kept a beautiful and elaborate hearse, with engraved and shining glass and horses with black plumes.'

THE POST OFFICE AND THE POSTMAN

'My home was Stoke St Michael village post office and stores, where I was born and brought up with four sisters and three brothers. My father, Edward Perkins, opened the post office in 1896. He was the first postmaster and served 65 years, a record in the Bath area. The opening stock of postal orders and stamps was £5. We all had to take our share in the work, cleaning floors, helping in the shop and delivering bread etc. We baked bread in the old-fashioned faggot oven. The faggots were put in the oven overnight to dry and next morning were lit to heat the oven. After the wood had all burnt, the ashes were cleared out with a mop at the end of a long rod – commonly called a "Macking". After the bread came out, the village people brought their cakes, pies and meats for my mother to cook for them. The bread was delivered to neighbouring villages in a horse and trap.

Like the rest of the houses in the village, we had oil lamps and candles for lighting and coal fires for heating and cooking. All white washing was boiled in a copper over a coal fire. Starching and blueing were a must. The hand-turned mangle was used for wringing the washing. Furnishings were mostly iron bedsteads, chests of drawers, armchairs and sofas. Floor coverings were linoleum and mats. Carpets were a rare luxury.'

'Most Christmas mail was delivered in Castle Cary on Christmas Day on large handcarts hired from local tradesmen.'

'My old aunt, Father's sister, was the postmistress. She had a post office which was in the front room of her cottage at Sampford Arundel. She sold only stamps and postal orders and the pensions, which was ten shillings then.

She had the first telephone in that parish, and we used to have to run to her if we wanted to use the telephone or wanted a car to come and fetch us to take us shopping or whatever.

At Christmas-time she couldn't have a day off or Saturday afternoon off so she used to do her Christmas shopping early. She used to fill up bags and bags and bags of parcels for a special mail-van to come and pick them up; you couldn't get into her house for parcels that had to go. Everybody used to work Christmas morning until about half-past two, so we didn't have our Christmas dinner very early.'

'Pear Tree Cottage, Wick Lane, Brent Knoll has a stone outbuilding with a stable and a small side room with fireplace. The cottager was paid five shillings a week by the GPO to provide hay for the horse and kindling for a fire for the postman when he took his break before returning to Weston super Mare.'

'Dad was a rural postman in the 1920s and did his round on a pushbike. I can remember him rolling the puttees round his legs when I was very small. It was a great day when the motorbike and

31

side-box was introduced for the rounds, and even greater when Wincanton had its first Morris mail van.'

'The village shop at Babcary was also the post office, where a postman came to collect and deliver letters. Sometimes we met him and he would give us our letters to take home. Searching in his bag one day he said "I did have something for yer Mum, but I don't know what I've done with it." After more frantic searching he said "Well, 'twere only a card from Mrs Atwell to say she can't come to do the washin' nex' Monday; 'er got company." The card never turned up!'

'My first recollection of Goathurst was as a boy messenger in 1933 working from Bridgwater with a bicycle. Lord Wharton at Halswell Park either didn't have a telephone or he didn't use it much, because he certainly used telegrams a lot. Telegrams were regularly delivered from North Petherton, except on Wednesday when any delivery was carried out from Bridgwater. Inevitably it was raining and in the dark when I would arrive at Halswell on my bike (in those days we worked until 7.30 pm) with an oil-lit bicycle lamp, and after delivering at the back door we then had to cycle back down that steep drive. I always hoped I did not meet the herd of deer which wandered everywhere in the parkland; quite exciting, especially when one only had a dim bicycle light of about one candlepower.

In 1937 the Royal Mail decided to introduce a new system of motor vans delivering to the Quantock villages of Spaxton, Enmore, Goathurst and Broomfield. In order to get the system started, they introduced the future motor drivers to delivering to the area on bicycles before the motor scheme actually got going. I was given the Goathurst and Enmore round. I used to get to Goathurst fairly early in the morning. I remember the area had been delivered to by old Mr Locke and Alf Betty. I was young and energetic, consequently I used to arrive in Goathurst by 8 am. This meant I used to spend an hour or more every morning at the smithy which belonged to Mr Brown. This was a good place for a chat and exchange of views.'

'At Mark, Miss Annie Webber was the postmistress before and during the Second World War and remained so until she died well into her eighties. She was a very formidable lady, feared, but respected, by all. She had been the local dressmaker, although this was not very evident as her ankle-length skirt was held together with safety pins. When a customer walked up the steps and through the door, the bell dangling from the top of the door announced you would like a little attention – nothing happened, so you would give the door another opening, only to hear a voice from the kitchen

32

calling out "Alright, alright, don't 'ee know I'm busy? I'm just putting on the cabbage!"

Very few people owned telephones in those days so messages, good news or bad, were sent through the post office as telegrams or "wires" as they were called in those days. When a telegram had to be received and the difficulties of H for Harry and O for Olly had been overcome, because the messages often came from places with difficult Welsh names, Miss Webber would stand on her doorstep and blow a whistle three times to call the sexton, who lived nearby, to deliver the telegram by bicycle. Later my mother had the job of delivering the wires. When mother heard the whistle she left whatever she was doing, got on her bike and pedalled off on her journey; needless to say, this sometimes happened several times a day. Mark is a very large village with a radius of six miles, so no wonder mother was glad of a rest on Sundays!

Later some telephones were installed on two party lines, X and Y. The bells rang one to six and you answered when your number rang; but you could also listen in to the other conversations!'

THE GENERAL STORES

'With the advent of supermarkets and the increase in car ownership, the villages have lost one of their most valuable social assets in the closure of the village General Stores. These were the places where the local women met and exchanged family views and shared their worries, ideas and advice. The news soon spread if anyone needed help and it was always forthcoming, the villages then were like large families.

My father-in-law bought our shop in Dunster in 1901 and sold every possible commodity for daily use; food, clothes, shirting, boots and shoes, leather, nails of all kinds for the cobbler and rakes and hay forks for the farmers. The bacon was fat salted bellies, the sugar and all fruit, rice, flour and oats had to be weighed and packed by hand. The lard came in 28 lb wooden boxes and the butter from New Zealand in 56 lb wooden boxes. Oranges were seasonal and came in orange crates which were eagerly sought after for use as hen coups. Wheat, corn and mash were sold loose for the backyard poultry and isinglass for pickling the eggs for use in the off laying season. Deliveries were made around the countryside by horse and wagon, and butter, cream, rabbits and eggs were bought from the farmers for sale in the shop.

In the 1920s customers bought their treacle from a large barrel. One Saturday evening, Bessie was the last customer, and while he collected up her groceries, my father-in-law put her jam pot under the barrel tap to slowly fill. The treacle came out very slowly, one plop every few seconds or so. It was late, and the other workers went home. John finished serving Bessie and turned out the oil lamps and put up the shutters for the week-end. As you can guess, the treacle jar had been forgotten. Monday morning came and oh dear! the barrel was empty and the treacle covered the shop floor. Luckily the right person was responsible, but what a mess. They fetched sawdust from the saw mill and covered the treacle. Then they shovelled it into buckets and baths and took it out to the field. It was piled in a corner and covered with earth. That year they grew marrows on the treacle heap and had a wonderful crop. These marrows were sold in the shop.'

'I was born in 1912 in Hardington Mandeville, the youngest of eleven children, ten girls and one boy. My mother kept the small village shop and my father was self employed as a carpenter and small farmer. There was not much assortment to sell in the shop, mostly farm butter, cheese, rice and bread. There were no tinned goods and no butcher or fish van called. We also sold salt fish at about fourpence a pound and boxes of bloaters at a penny or a penny ha'penny each.

The hub of daily life in any Somerset village was its general store. Here at Hatch Beauchamp it had a garage for petrol too.

34

In those days nearly everyone kept a pig or two in the back yard, as well as chickens to supply the family with eggs and meat. It was at our place a pig was killed about every six months. It was then divided or sold amongst the neighbours and Mother would make faggots, black pudding, chitterlings etc and salt the rest of the meat and bacon.'

' "Hullo, missy; back to visit grandma and grandpa are we?" The cheery greeting from the local taxi driver at Old Cleeve station meant a ride in his gleaming black limousine, a treat in itself. But my mind was on a lovely feather bed, the smell of bacon, a big hug, and helping in the shop.

My greatest pleasure was my grandparents' village shop, housed in the dining room of the cottage. A mixture of bacon (whole sides), butter in huge mounds, sacks of sugar, candles, shopping baskets, vinegar barrels and sharp knives; oh, the excitement of it all.

The shop was an Aladdin's cave for a small girl. We knew everyone in every house. The big brass seals and weights gleaming. Half a pound of sugar in a blue bag. "Mind the scale goes down for the customer," Gran smiled, "Always favour the customer, I want to keep them."

Down the bottom of the long garden Grandad would be mending and making boots and shoes. He was a handsewn bootmaker – there they all were, displayed in his workshop, brown leather, black snakeskin – I longed to own a pair. Repairs a shilling to two shillings, new ones three shillings and sixpence to seven shillings and elevenpence.

"Now, my love," said Grandma, "I've a charabanc coming this afternoon, bringing people for tea. Be a good girl and lay the tables on the lawn." Meaning Grandad's two-tiered, immaculate lawns, surrounded by a bay hedge, where there was also a very grand iron seat, lovely for a photograph. Put the jam (several kinds) into glass dishes, then the cream, fresh from Mr Clatworthy's farm down at the bottom of Rectory Hill, along with the milk, "dipped" into jugs from the churn, which came with pony and cart, and, of course, Mr Clatworthy. Buttered triangles of brown and white bread, cucumber sandwiches, home-made cakes and big pots of tea two shillings and sixpence. St Andrew's church opposite to spend a quiet few minutes in after tea.'

'It was in the early 1940s I first came to Blackford, a small hamlet near Wedmore. There was a small corner shop run by an elderly lady and her daughter. It was really an old galvanised iron lean-to against the house with a passageway between. Threaded from the kitchen through a hole in the doorpost was a wire with a loop on it which one pulled to ring the bell, which was attached to the kitchen ceiling.

The old lady would shuffle out, in her slippers, wearing an old cross-over overall and often a sack apron. She was quite small with little wisps of hair. She'd probably be wiping her hands on her apron and say she was just "picking a fowl".

She would find the key and shuffle around behind the counter and say, 'What do'ee want?" So, maybe, you'd ask for some tea and, as she was quite deaf, she would put her hand behind her ear and say, "What do'ee want, 'alf a pound of sugar?". This would happen several times until she got it right. When it was dark there was a candle burning on the counter – it was never light.

The locals used to pick blackberries. She would pay a few coppers for these and tip them into open barrels back in a dingy corner. The blackberries were collected once a week and taken to a jam factory. Suspended over these barrels of blackberries were lines of binder twine where secondhand clothing was thrown.'

'In the 1950s my great-aunt Em kept house and shop for her widowed brother-in-law in Wells. The shop was in the front room of the house; small, dark and lit by gaslight. It smelled of candles, soap, paraffin, oil and vinegar. The latter were stored in large drums at one side of the room. Tin measuring jugs were kept by each drum, customers bringing their own containers to be filled, and great care had to be taken not to mix the measures up.

The place was crammed with brooms, crockery, pie dishes, door mats and other ironmongery. Once I bought for my Mum a tin tray with a crinoline lady depicted on it. It cost a shilling and I paid for it over three weeks.

A large wooden desk stood in the furthest corner. In it was kept the money and other papers. If the bell went when Aunt was busy I would be sent along the shadowy passage to say "Miss Bishop would be there soon".

The shop also stocked feather dusters, beautiful bright, fluffy things. When the circuses came to town their folk would purchase fuel and other goods from my aunt and would often ask specifically for the most colourful feather dusters. When we asked why, they said they would take them apart and use the feathers to refurbish the harnesses of the performing horses.

Situated in a small street full of tiny cottages, mostly set in "courts", Miss Bishop's oil shop served the community well until the early 1960s, when age, ill health and area improvements caught up with her.'

'The cornerstone of the shopping centre in Minehead, on the site of that destroyed by the Great Fire in 1791, Floyds Stores developed from Floyds Ready Money Draper's to Minehead's largest departmental store, extending into two streets. I remember knitting wool there at fivepence an ounce, and dress material at one shilling and elevenpence ha'penny a yard, with personal service.'

THE BAKER

'I was born in Wincanton in 1920. My father was a baker, who trained in Bristol, and he bought the business when he got married. Life was long hours of hard work, for the dough was mixed by hand in wooden troughs six evenings a week, left to rise until four am, then sealed off and moulded into cottage loaves which sold at threepence threefarthings each. These were delivered by horse and cart, later by petrol vans and during the Second World War by electric vans. As the business flourished, a dough machine was worked by an engine and later by electricity. I shall always remember when the electric street lights were first lit in 1933 – people thronged the streets to see them. During the war the WI organised a meat pie scheme and my father was allowed extra fat to make the pastry and meat which he cooked with onions in the bakehouse oven. The pies were sent to the Parish Room on Tuesdays and sold for sevenpence, a nourishing and cheap dinner.'

'Dora's father was the baker – the bakehouse was at the back of the house with a ceiling, part of which stretched up to the roof, and three lofts for storing bags of flour, which were reached by a ladder. Two faggots of wood were put in the cleaned oven overnight to dry, and set alight early in the morning. "Fat cakes", made from dough with fat and sugar, were popular, as were the buns made on Saturdays. Two grades of fruitcake were made each Friday: one, "Shop cake", was fourpence per pound and the other sold at sixpence. Until 1925 the bread was delivered by pony and trap, with a "tilt" (hood) attached in wet weather. This was replaced by a car, with a sheet placed on the back seat for the loaves, golden brown and crusty at threepence ha'penny (two pound size). Making hot cross buns for Good Friday meant the family working all night in the bakehouse. On Good Friday the buns were put in baskets and taken around the village to be sold at a ha'penny each, large ones at a penny. The baker closed in 1937.

Freddie, the mason, came to refloor and reroof the oven. It was a good thing he was a little man, as he had to crawl in through the oven doorway and lie flat on his back to reroof and on his stomach to refloor. Freddie's great joy was bellringing (for 66 years). His daughter, Emily, was the village dressmaker.'

'I grew up at Curland post office and before the Second World War I can remember my father baking bread. The bakehouse was attached to the shop and house and father used a huge wooden trough. It was all done by hand; he would get up at about 3 am and you could see the dough rising in this great wooden trough and he would then put it in the ovens in the corner of the bakehouse and what lovely smells used to come out from there.

He delivered bread with a horse and cart and he would go right over to Buckland as well as the local area. Cottage, coburg and tin loaves he made.

As well as making bread my father made gingerbread, rock and sugared almonds, all those types of things, which he took to many fairs around the area, sometimes going as far as Weymouth with a horse and cart. It would take them three days, one day to get there, one day there and one day to come back again.

I remember seeing father making the rock on a great big hook in the kitchen, swinging it around and pulling it out, and somehow or another, making it two different colours, a sort of beige colour and brown, twisting it around. It was great fun on those days when father was doing his baking.'

'I was born at Fieldhouse Farm, Stone Allerton, where my father Edward Champeny was a farmer. I remember him growing wheat in the field opposite the house, reaping and sheaving by hand, then taking it to the barn at the Wheatsheaf Inn where I used to watch him whack out the wheat and put it in sacks. I went with him to the windmill and Mr Stevens ground it down to flour for us. My father would take the flour to a little shop at Stoughton and Mr Sparks made our bread which he delivered each Wednesday evening with groceries in his pony and cart.'

THE BUTCHER

'To ensure that your mince was perfectly fresh in the days before efficient refrigeration, you asked your butcher, after selecting your meat, that whilst mincing it he would put your onion through the mincer at the same time!

Early in December the butcher walked his prize purchase home from the Yeovil Fat Stock Show and Sale. The village turned out to see their Christmas dinner walk in "on the hoof".'

THE MILKMAN

'I started school at Pylle aged five in 1928 and was lucky to get a lift home in a milk-float. There being no refrigeration then, the milk was collected twice daily, and there were two deliveries. Housewives had no bottles, they brought out their jugs or put them out ready to be filled from a large milk churn with a measured can.

My milkman lived near the school and would harness his pony to the milk-float just after school finished, to get the evening milk from the farm, so I got a ride home. He was very punctual, so I couldn't visit the sweet shop, or watch the blacksmith at the forge with the other children. Instead, I was lifted in beside the milk churn and the measuring cans. The black pony trotted off with his shining brasses jingling. The brightly painted cart had the milkman's name on the side and he always wore a clean white coat. As we drove along he sang the old songs, *Tipperary* and *Goodbye-ee*, and later on a new popular one called *Amy Wonderful Amy*, about Amy Johnson. I got rather sleepy and once fell off my seat backwards onto the road, but at our speed of six miles an hour, I was not much hurt and soon learned to hold on.'

'Before 1935 milk from one family farm in the village was either delivered on foot, in tin cans, or collected from the farm. In 1923 one pint cost threepence. Cows were hand milked and, straight from the cow, milk was cooled over a surface cooler. The milk then went into a bucket and bottles were filled with a jug and capped with cardboard discs. Waxed cartons had been tried before glass bottles, but abandoned due to cost.

From 1935 to 1940 bottles were delivered in a large crate on the front of a shop bicycle; half pint, one pint, one and a half pint and one quart capacity. Delivery was twice daily, including Sundays, a household requiring its second half pint of the day by 4.30 pm in time for afternoon tea. Customers' requirements seldom varied.

During and after the Second World War, bottles were delivered by pony and trap, the intelligent pony becoming very cooperative, waiting whilst the milk was delivered (including an appropriate length of time at the tea and biscuit stops) or continuing to the next stop if milk was being left by the roundsman at a row of houses. The tread of the driver on the back step was enough to set the pony off again, without command.

After 1948 milk and cream were delivered by motorised transport. This particular round of unpasteurised products ceased in 1981, although people still remember their rich quality and regret its passing.

THE BLACKSMITH

'Grandfather was the village blacksmith at Puriton for nearly 50 years, a craftsman whose skills were well known in the community. Farmers brought horses to be shod, agricultural machinery for repair and heavy chains to have new links forged, while other people brought metal household utensils to be mended and kettles, pots and pans to be soldered, also wrought-iron gates and railings were made and fitted. The glowing forge fire and showers of sparks attracted children of all ages to the ever-open door to watch as he struck with his heavy hammer to bend the red-hot metal to the required shape. Sometimes he would allow one or two children to assist pumping the huge bellows which would blow the fire into a white-hot glow into which he would plunge a length of iron to heat.

One of my earliest recollections of school-days was sitting at a desk in the infants class and hearing the sound of Grandfather's hammer striking the steel anvil ringing across the village from the smithy on the hillside. The quiet of village life in those days was broken only by the hoof-beats of heavy horses, the creaking of wagon wheels along the roadway, the sounds of many farm animals, the cawing of rooks in the tall old elm-trees, and song of the birds.'

'At Winsham, the blacksmith's was a lovely place on a winter's day. We could get tallow candles there for our chests when we had colds. His wife was the village dressmaker. She made coats and dresses from other folks' cast offs for just a few pence. We never had jumble sales.'

THE CARPENTER AND UNDERTAKER

'Father was the village carpenter at Sampford Arundel and his father before that. We had to down the tools when there was a coffin to be made and then we weren't allowed in the work shop at all – father used to be busy until the coffin was made. If he was working at a farm, he'd be fetched away, and he'd just stop whatever work he was doing there to make a coffin.

On the funeral day he used to go up to the vicarage and pull out the bier and us children had to take out the tin of Brasso and polish, polish, polish all the brass on the bier for them to use it – every time there was a funeral that was our job.

Father used to turn out his top hat and get the clothes brush out, and brush all the bits off his black suit, he always had to have a clean white shirt. Not horses, 'twas always push – they had to push the bier. Jimmy Withers had the hearse, lived in Mantel Street and he used to come out if we wanted to go a long way. But Father didn't do coffins that had to go a long way – it was all local, just the village.'

THE LIBRARY

'Miss Florence Blake started the first "library service" in South Petherton in the 1920s. An avid reader with a large collection of books received from relatives as presents, she carefully covered them in brown paper and took them, on foot, to loan to her circle of friends so that they could share her pleasure of reading. Mr Frank Turner started the first county library service in South Petherton in the 1930s in a tin hut in St James Street near where the present library stands. When the hut became too small the library moved across the road (the present car park) to the first floor of a farmhouse. Eventually the books were moved to the local village hall until the Working Men's Club took over the room. The present day library was built in the 1980s and is very well used.'

REFUSE COLLECTION

'Unlike the town with its ashcart collection each week, we in the villages had no one to gather up our rubbish. So each household had to make its own arrangements for garbage disposal. All our rubbish was taken to the bottom of the orchard and thrown on a heap. As children we loved to poke about amongst the rubbish to see what we could find.

During the Second World War a salvage collection was organised and anything which could be of use for the war effort was put outside the gate to await the arrival of the salvage cart. This was the beginning of the modern day refuse collection for country areas.'

'The first refuse scheme in East Coker was organised by the WI in 1928. Householders who joined the scheme paid twopence to fivepence a month to contractors who dumped the refuse in designated areas provided by farmers – old pits, quarries etc. The WI was responsible for fencing off those areas. Electricity did not reach the village until 1937. Coal and wood fires, candles and oil lamps and "toilet up the garden" until 1939 when water and sewerage were laid on to some houses, but not all.'

'Rubbish collection at Hatch Beauchamp was by private arrangement once a fortnight, cost pennies, and was tipped into a pond behind Willcocks Farm.'

41

MARKET DAY

'Market day was the busiest day of the week for shopkeepers. Farmers attended the market and their wives did the family shopping. Most villages ran a private bus service which also served as a parcel carrier service. Shopkeepers could deliver goods to a pick up point, usually the stable yard at one of the many public houses, and the bus driver would deliver parcels to the villagers. The National bus company also ran a service of this kind.'

'My childhood was spent in the market town of Bridgwater and I can remember when cattle were driven through the streets from the surrounding farms on market days, causing quite a stir. On one occasion my husband was driving some fat bullocks home when one decided it had had enough and lay down in the middle of town. After various frantic efforts of persuasion, my husband remembered an old trick and, putting his mouth to the cow's ear, he shouted as loud as he could. This had the desired effect and it had to be chased home quickly while another herdsman took care of the rest.'

'On market days in Wiveliscombe the sheep and cattle arrived by lorry, or they were walked between the railway station and the market through the town by drovers who, with shouts and sticks and much arm waving, managed to steer the beasts away from the shop fronts and alley ways. The cattle were put into pens in the station yard awaiting herding into cattle trucks. The town was always busy on market days when farmers and their wives were able to shop, riding in a pony and trap.'

'In the 1920s and 1930s great numbers of cattle and sheep were herded many miles to markets and fairs. Some villages had a pound, which was a field where they rested overnight. When they were herded through the villages the most important job for the inhabitants was to make sure all doors and garden gates were firmly secured against invasion by the animals.'

THE LAMPLIGHTER

'As a child I can recall the only street lighting was the main street of Langport, connecting Bow Street to Langport West station. It was gaslight and each evening a man employed by the gas company would walk round with a long pole with a hood and put the lights on.'

'In the 19th and early 20th centuries Galmington was lit by two oil lamps maintained at the expense of the Parish. One stood on the corner of what is now the video shop, the other on the north corner of Comeytrowe Lane.

In the 1930s the oil lamps were replaced by ornately wrought gas-lamps. At dusk the lamplighter came round on his bike carrying a long pole with a hook and some sort of lighter at the end. The gas was turned on by the hook being inserted into one of two rings at either end of the balance arm. In the morning it was turned off by a tug on the other ring. The effort hardly seemed worthwhile as the gas light was so feeble it was all but useless. Then in the 1950s electric lamps were installed and some smart fellow from Taunton bought up the old gas standards and fittings from the Council. He paid a pittance for them but after a few years' storage he re-sold them for £100 apiece. The new electric lamps didn't come on automatically. The gas-lighter was replaced by a man from the electricity board who rode his bike to the top of the road round where the Belmont Estate begins and used some sort of gadget to switch on the four village lights at a sub-station.'

THE WORKHOUSE

'As a young woman about the year 1950, I visited an old neighbour from Dunster who had been taken to the Old People's Hospital, or the Workhouse, as it was still called by the locals. The memory has always haunted me. The smell of ammonia was overpowering, the corridors were dark and the ward windows high. The old ladies were all stretched out in bed with white counterpanes tightly tucked in – just waiting to die. I was told that my old lady was having a bath. She was indeed, in a long tin bath in a wide corridor in full view of everyone.

There was also a typical "Darby and Joan" couple who could no longer look after themselves in their cottage; they were 90 years old but still in control of their faculties. They had to be placed in the Old People's Hospital. The old gentleman even took his concertina with him on which he would play all the old tunes. He was more able than his wife, but they were only allowed to see each other at visiting hours. Men and women in those days were kept strictly apart. This couple had been married for nearly 70 years.

Thank God those "good old days" have gone.'

CHURCH AND SUNDAY SCHOOL

Once every village had its own clergyman, who advised, comforted and generally took the lead in village affairs. The church, or the chapel, was at the heart of community life and Sunday was a special day, set apart from the working week. Most children attended Sunday school, often taught by the rector's wife or daughter, and the Sunday school outing, often a child's only trip to the seaside, was a day anticipated with delight and looked back on with nostalgia.

THE TIN CHURCH

'The little village church at Edithmead was made of wood inside and tin clad on the outside. It was painted grey. It had once been an adult school at the neighbouring village of East Brent and had been brought to the village on farm carts. This little church superseded the old railway carriage which had stood in a garden of a house a few yards up the road. Here services were held regularly until the arrival of the new church. In the "tin church", Holy Communion was taken on the first Sunday in the month. This was a morning service and was usually attended by the vicar of Burnham on Sea. St Andrew's church at Burnham was the parent church.

Sunday school for the village children was held every Sunday afternoon and ladies from Burnham cycled out to teach. Evensong was held every Sunday evening. Sunday school outings were eagerly looked forward to. Joining in with the children from St Andrew's, we caught the train at Burnham railway station and visited seaside resorts such as Paignton, Clevedon, Seaton and Sidmouth. Another eagerly looked forward to treat was the strawberry and cream tea given for the Sunday school children and held each year in the church hall at Burnham.

Our Sunday school annual prizegiving was held in St Andrew's church and our little group from Edithmead awaited in anticipation along with the Burnham children to hear our name called to walk up and collect our prize from the vicar and his helpers. This prize could be a prayer book, bible or story book. Children who had attended every Sunday school class through the whole year were given medals. These were highly prized. We were also given bright stamps each Sunday. These we stuck into a stamp book which we kept at home.'

Edithmead's tin church, which superseded its previous church – a railway carriage.

THE BELLS

'Each church had its own team of bellringers. Usually they rang call changes and each ringer had his own special bell to ring, whereas now, with the introduction of scientific change ringing, we ring any bell and travel to various other churches to ring with each other. On Easter, Whitsun and Christmas there was usually an early Communion service at six or seven o'clock in the morning – the bells would be rung for that service.'

'Our village church of Stoke St Michael was dedicated to "The Glory of God and St Michael and All Angels" by the monks of Glastonbury in AD 926. We had three services on Sundays – 8 am Holy Communion, Matins at 11 am, and Evensong at 6.30 pm. There was a strong choir and I remember singing solos in the Harvest anthems. The last day all the church bells were tolled was Jubilee Day 1935 – a Monday – at my wedding. One bell is now unsafe and the treble bell is tolled for services and the bass bell for funerals.'

BUILDING THE CHAPEL

'For about three consecutive years in the late 1920s an Evangelist, Mr Thompson, visited the village of West Hatch and erected a portable wooden building in which to hold services in a field belonging to my uncle. Such was the interest shown that eventually a wooden chapel was built nearby, which served the village for over 50 years. A service was held every Sunday and there was a thriving Sunday school held together by the Misses Wren and their family from Hatch Beauchamp. This continued until the end of the 1960s when it remained empty until, in recent years, it was demolished and replaced by a dwelling.'

'At Staple Fitzpaine visiting preachers came by pony and trap or on horseback. The horses were stabled in a shed by the chapel. A member of the congregation would take the preacher to their home for lunch.'

'In 1846 negotiations commenced with the Society of Friends to purchase or lease a strip of land in Combeland Road, Alcombe, which was the Quakers' disused burial ground. This was agreed at two shillings and sixpence a year. Prior to this a group of Methodists had worshipped at the Dunster church for over 40 years. On this basis the Methodists built a chapel there in 1847. After the opening of the Minehead church in 1857, worshippers decreased and pewholders dropped to four, with only one service. Then, with the advent of mission bands, and the special attention given to children, the cause flourished again and by 1920 the premises were inadequate, so it was decided that a new chapel should be built. Tea was held in the village hall at the opening, on 14th October 1931, of the new building in Lower Meadow Road. Many remember combining with the church groups to sing carols with an organ on a trailer at Christmas, and to share Christmas parties. Methodist religious evenings were always followed by a sixpenny Coffee Supper.'

'At Lympsham, the Methodist chapel was very active, with a Girls and Boys Life Brigade. Every June they held a wonderful "Sale" and visitors used to come by coach from Weston super Mare and Burnham on Sea. They would enjoy the most delicious teas I have ever tasted, and the weather was always good. Sadly, the chapel is now closed.'

SUNDAY WAS A SPECIAL DAY

'Sunday was a special day. We always went to Sunday school and church at Misterton and, being farmers, we had the "White" family box. It seated about twelve, which we shared with my grandparents while Mum played the organ. Trying to keep my little brother quiet so as not to worry or distract Mum was very difficult. We always had a typical Sunday roast lunch at one pm, after which our parents rested and we were allowed to sit quietly and read the treasured encyclopaedias or go for a walk. The radio, or wireless as it was called (as it was run on accumulators) mainly went on for the six o'clock news or a few special programmes in the dark evenings.'

'As a family in the early 1900s at Babcary, we all went to church on Sunday. Dad went in the morning taking the younger children, and Mother went to Evensong with the older ones. The church had a peal of five bells and as we trooped up the long tree lined path to the church entrance I used to think the bells sang "The Barringtons have come" (Barrington was our surname).

We sat in a pew in front of Dad, presumably so that he could keep an eye on our behaviour. Should one of us dare to whisper to our "next door" neighbour, a gentle prod in the back would remind us where we were. Kneeling on the floor was rather painful – no hassocks – and "kneel up straight" – no sitting back on our heels!

How long and puzzling the prayers were (this was before I could read). It took me a long time to find out what one part of a prayer meant. In it the rector beseeched God to give us a "happy issue out of all our afflictions": I thought he said "the happiest shoe out of all the collection." "Our Father we charge in Heaven" – why should we charge God anything? "Have mercy upon us miserable sinners". Even at that early age I realized I was a sinner, doing sneaky little things occasionally, but I hated being called a "miserable sinner".

There was a lot of rustling as the final hymn was announced while we searched in our pockets for the pennies to put in the collection bag – a lovely moment but a crime if a penny was dropped on the floor. Our older sister, Ann, accompanied the singing on an American organ, and I used to think she had to work very hard to pump the wind in by foot pedals, use her fingers to play the notes and sing as well. I always hoped I would be able to play an organ for church services one day.'

'Though not a regular churchgoer my father would never do unnecessary work on a Sunday. He considered the horses should have a rest as well as the men.'

'My parents considered Sunday a day of rest. We children were sent to Sunday school every week, rain or shine, a walk of about two miles across Exmoor. We left the bikes at home and walked across the fields, calling for our neighbours en route. While we were away, from about two to five o'clock, our parents rested. I realise now, having brought up a family on a farm, how my parents must have looked forward to Sunday afternoons.'

'No church bells were rung during the Second World War; they were to be used only as a sign of invasion. As there was British Summer Time all winter, with Double in the summer, it was dark on winter mornings. Holy Communion services were held with just the light from the altar candles. Evensong was held at half past three so that no lights were required in the hours of blackout.'

SUNDAY SCHOOL

'The afternoon Sunday school was very well attended by most of the Babcary children and the older ones were expected to have learned the Collect for that particular Sunday, and each had to repeat it as their turn came. Pretty text cards were given out, and at the end of the year there were prizes for those who had attended regularly.'

'For Sunday school in the 1950s at Meare, we all wore our best clothes, but changed out of them on returning home in case we dirtied the good ones. Prizes for Good Attendance at Sunday school were treasured and when we went to the Christmas party we all took our own mug marked with a piece of brightly coloured wool tied around the handle. In the summer we looked forward to the Sunday school outings, mainly to the seaside.'

'There was a Sunday school in Allerton church each Sunday at 2.30 pm. Children of the same age would go to one part with their teacher and another age group would go to another part of the church. When you attended you were given a stamp to put in your book. Each stamp was a picture of a certain Sunday in the church calendar. In 1932 two Sunday school teachers were married during June and Allerton school children went to see the wedding. Each summer the Sunday school went on an outing to Bristol Zoo or somewhere and the parish treat was replaced with a Sunday school party at Christmas.
In the early 1930s, the Sunday morning Sunday school was revived in the Methodist chapel in Stone Allerton (where the cross is now). They had a party at Christmas in the old schoolroom and an outing in

summer, Weston one year, Burnham another, for a few years then the chapel turned over to Sunday afternoons but we and quite a few others still went to the church Sunday school. It was not long before the Sunday school finished but the ordinary chapel services went on for a long time. Also in the 1930s there were lantern slides for a whole week every evening at the Baptist chapel. They were not all religious subjects.

In 1938 Allerton Sunday school went to Weymouth. It was an excursion laid on by the railway. We went from Axbridge with other Sunday schools. It was a lovely outing and it was the last. The next year, 1939, they were talking of going in July then all of a sudden war was in the air and the outing was postponed for ever. There were no more Sunday school outings.'

'Sunday in the late 1920s and early 1930s: we were a family of six and our neighbours had five children. We all walked one mile to the local Methodist chapel's Sunday school at 10.15 am in the schoolroom, followed by 11 am service in the main chapel which lasted until 12.25, or even later. It was then home to roast Sunday dinner and afterwards back to Sunday school at 2.30 pm. I then very often went to the parish church with my best friend for the 6.30 pm service. We chatted and put the world to rights as we walked backwards and forwards.

From the Sunday school we received a very large orange at Christmas, and a large hot cross bun on Good Friday. On Whit Sunday there would be a special service with the Sunday school taking part. Each child received a prize which was a book of their choice. There were two parties a year: one after Christmas, and one after Whitsun, when there were races and games in a field. In August there was an outing to the seaside. I think all these activities were funded from money left by the builder of the chapel.'

'Galmington social life revolved around the Sunday school in Comey-trowe Lane. That was the scene of Band of Hope concerts, jumble sales, Christmas parties etc. There was an urn for making tea but those attending functions had to take their own crockery. At Christmas parties they served particular cakes which seem to have disappeared. They were called chudleighs – big sweet buns that were cut in half and spread with cream and blackcurrant jam. The Sunday school also ran a sort of youth club – it had a billiard table! For a time a man from the Church Army was assigned to Galmington. He did a great deal to organise youth activities, getting football and cricket teams together. We played the other villages around but before General Hamilton-Gaunt gave the land for the recreation ground in 1935 there was a problem in finding a ground. Sometimes the farmers permitted the use of a field, hardly ideal and not to be relied on.'

THE SUNDAY SCHOOL OUTING

'The annual Sunday school outing was a most exciting event before the First World War. The local farmers lent their men and horses and wagons to take the members of the Sunday school and teachers to a local beauty spot where there was a monument to the memory of a sea-faring man, Sir Acland Hood. It was only three to four miles from Babcary but the children looked forward to the outing with great excitement.

They all ran about gathering sticks to make a fire on which to boil a kettle. Tea was made and buns and currant cake were handed round as the children sat on the grass. After tea there were races for sweets and nuts and various games were played until it was time to be lifted up into the wagons for the journey home, when happy children sang songs all the way.'

'I remember the Congregational church outings in the early 1920s, the children were taken from South Petherton to Crewkerne station by horse and waggon to catch a train to Lyme Regis. As it was illegal for children to ride in waggons at that time they were told to lie flat on the floor while driving through the streets of Crewkerne so that the eagle-eyed bobbie couldn't see them. They were never caught and always had a lovely day out.'

'At 8 am in the morning, during mid-summer once a year during the 1930s, there was a great deal of excitement in South Petherton as nine or ten charabancs pulled up in Roundwell Street for the annual Congregational Sunday school outing. About 350 people including parents, grandparents, aunts and uncles carrying their picnic baskets filed up the steps of the coaches laughing and chattering. Mr Frank Harding and Mr Masters were in charge of the proceedings and the usual destination was Weymouth, Burnham on Sea or Weston super Mare.

As there was no motorway travel in those days the journey took about four hours. On arrival the beach was invaded with the masses, blankets were spread on the ground, picnics unpacked and eaten with relish. After lunch, mother and father settled down for an afternoon nap, he wearing a knotted handkerchief on his head to protect him from the sun and she her old straw hat that she kept for summer gardening. Little girls would tuck their frocks into their knickers, remove their shoes and socks and spend the afternoon with their brothers and friends building sand castles or paddling in the

50

sea. Usually, the local Congregational church would provide everyone with afternoon tea in the church hall before the journey home. They arrived home about eight in the evening, pink, sandy, very tired but gloriously happy after the best day of the year.'

'The Sunday school outing to Burnham from Burrowbridge was made by horses and waggons – the first stop being at Marchants Tea Rooms, where bread and jam and seedy cake was the order of the day. On the return journey there was always a sing song.'

'I was born in 1925 at Winsham. In my day Sunday school was attended as regularly as day school. On special Sundays, which were known as Anniversaries, we recited poems, sang duets and read to our teachers and parents. The teachers were very strict. We didn't dare forget our lines. We always prayed for good weather for our outing to Weymouth. We had two buses and took buckets of all sizes, spades and bathing costumes if you were lucky. If you weren't, you tucked everything in your pants. Then to Woolworths – the wonder shop – to spend a few pennies.

The Buckland Dinham chapel Sunday school always had an annual trip to Weston super Mare by coach (charabanc), while the church Sunday school went to Weymouth by train from Frome station. The Sunday school children had little books to collect the weekly attendance stamp.'

'There was a Sunday school at Stoke St Michael and before motor transport our outings were in farm waggons decorated with flags. We often went to Cranmore Tower and had tea in the rooms underneath the tower, and swings under the trees. Sometimes we went to Weston or Burnham on Sea, riding to Cranmore station in the waggons. Wouldn't the children of today enjoy it! Both the Primitive Chapel and the Wesleyan Chapel were well supported, and the yearly church fete on the vicarage lawn was very popular.'

THE VICAR, THE VERGER, THE GRAVEDIGGER . . .

'The Rev Portman of Thurlbear in the 1920s was a very nice gentleman with a white beard. He was good to us children and not "uppish", and as it was a church school he would come into the school. I remember when he died. I was about eight years old and it seemed so sad. In those days the bell in the church was tolled for the age of the person and the bell went on and on . . . it was an awful mournful day. I think he was 85.'

'My father was rector of a parish in Somerset. Mother helped Dad visiting, running the Girls Friendly Society, Mother's Union and numerous meetings and socials in the village hall. We were a large family and expected to help around the house, feeding the chickens, egg collecting and feeding the cats on the left-overs.

I was sent on errands to the village with cough medicines, syrup Farnel and Mum's special concoctions for coughs, mauve, very sweet and sticky. The miners were ill due to coal dust and not able to work, so with no health service it was a must to help as much as possible. We were always greeted with a smile from the wife or mother, usually wearing a bright pinny over her dress. Although I was very young I knew how little some families had to spend.'

'The gentleman who became verger and sexton at St Andrew's church in Wiveliscombe in 1946 has many memories of his working days there. One of his first jobs was to cut down the grass which had been neglected during the war years, and then to level down the graves, all of which were raised up. This was accomplished with the help of German prisoners of war. An additional duty, which brought him an extra three shillings a week, was to wind up the church clock every other day. As the clock would sometimes go for three days on a two-day wind, it was easy to forget which was the winding day!

He clearly remembers two of his neighbours in Church Street. One was very tidy, the other was the reverse, and was subjected to scrutiny by the tidy friend before she went shopping. If, as invariably happened, she had holes in her black stockings, these would be disguised by a good brushing over with the black lead brush.

His trips into Taunton cost him one shilling and fivepence by bus, but the Saturday train journey became the favourite mode of travel, at a return fare of two shillings and sixpence.

He decided to change his occupation after ten years at St Andrew's, by which time he had dug 270 graves.'

'Father was a decorator and painter and he used to make cider at Sampford Farm, with the cider press. He used to dig the graves and afterwards he had to fill them in – not flat, he used to make the mound. He'd make the turves just as they were before, a very tidy job. There was no such thing as putting the corpse in the church in them days, they were left from people's home.

Father also used to wind the village clock, every Saturday night; we used to go down with him and used to wind the clock. He'd climb up the steps to the belfry.'

... AND OTHERS

'Spaxton is a straggling village on the north side of the Quantock Hills. In the late 19th century the Agapenome or "Abode of Love" was started here by the Rev Henry John Prince (who claimed he was the Messiah). He encouraged good looking, rich young ladies to reside with him and follow his teaching. The Agapenome was entirely enclosed with its own chapel, and it drew people from all over the countryside to stand outside its big heavy gates just to catch a glimpse of its inhabitants. The Agapenome was sold in 1962 and bungalows now stand in the grounds.'

'At Poole, Nynehead, there was a Pentecostal chapel run by Pastor Buttle who baptised his congregation in the river Tone near Wharf Cottage. I found this amusing as a child, as did the people who flocked from Wellington to see the spectacle and listen to the screams of those who were completely immersed in the cold water.'

'Sometimes Evangelist "missionaries" would set up a tent in Pilton and would ask for local volunteers to play for services. One volunteer remembers being asked "Are you saved?" Not understanding, the young girl replied "No". "Your music will not then be acceptable to the Lord."'

CAROL SINGING

'Carol singing was great, it gave everyone in Montacute the benefit of our voices long before Christmas Eve. From candles in jam jars, a tuning fork and unaccompanied singing we progressed to torches and two violins and a recorder, then the use of a station trolley to transport the church harmonium and the organist (me). Once nearly a catastrophe; the two senior choirboys pulling the trolley let go at the same time – result trolley and contents careering down the slope of Middle Street until rescued by the best sprinter in the party. Always at midnight on Christmas Eve Mr Cannon from Abbey Farm transported us by truck and trailer to Batemoor to sing *While shepherds watched* where old Shep Bradley was coping with lambing.

We were allowed to use the church harmonium by the vicar Rev Beechey providing we returned it in the same condition as it was borrowed. Horror of horrors, one year a pedal webbing broke but all ended happily. Old Mr Fred Rogers, then in his late nineties, the village undertaker, was woken after midnight and did a successful repair.

We often wondered at the hospitality provided – large hams (we

53

helped ourselves), new bread, pickle, steaming cocoa and home made wine in cottage and farmhouse alike, and a favourite carol sung as a thank you. Eventually we discovered one of the choir boys who was also the paper boy made sure the residents knew we were coming.'

GETTING ABOUT

Until well into the 1920s, the pony and trap remained the favourite, and often the only, form of transport. Most people walked wherever they had to go, sometimes miles to school or work or to the market. But the bicycle was bringing a new freedom of movement, and the first cars had appeared on Somerset's roads, their peculiarities fondly recalled by their owners.

WALKING TO WORK

'In about 1900, Sarah, who lived in a farm cottage in East Mere, a farm in the middle of Minehead North Hill, was twelve years old. A job had been obtained for her at Cloutsome Farm, a distance of six to seven miles. The journey there was up hill and down dale along narrow paths and lanes. Her mother packed her clothes in a tin trunk and put it in a wheelbarrow. She pushed it all the way to Cloutsome and then brought the wheelbarrow back again to East Mere, a total distance of about twelve miles.'

PONY AND TRAP

'Stephen Brownjohn was the carpenter at Buckland Dinham in the 1920s. Each Sunday morning and evening he could be seen wearing his frock coat and top hat to church. Stephen's high pony trap had one passenger by the driver and two sitting behind, back to back with those in front. He provided a service to the stations at Mells Road and Frome. On one occasion the two passengers at the back were found to be missing, having slipped off when going uphill!'

'I remember a cold winter's night towards the end of 1921. We were met at the station by an uncle driving a pony and trap. It was already dark, and snugly wrapped up in the swaying vehicle, I was only dimly aware of the one or two villages we passed through. At one point my uncle stopped the trap and called my attention, pointing with his whip, saying "There lies the chapel, you will go there tomorrow." That road, 70 years later, is no safe place for a pony and trap. Today thousands of cars pass the chapel on their way to and from the South West.'

'My transport when I started school at five years old was in a pony and trap driven by an elderly neighbour who took several of us from Yarrow. As I was the smallest and the trap was full, I had the privilege of standing between the driver's knees. That was all right, having a front view, but the driver always sang hymns heartily all the way, only interrupted by wishing someone "Good morning" and, after another verse, "Come on Jimmy, you little Jebusite!" – this to the pony. But it was better than walking, particularly on a Monday which was a difficult day for walking.

Monday was market day at Highbridge so all the cattle for sale were driven by several drovers along the road over a distance of about ten miles. Drovers, dogs and animals getting tired and difficult meant the comments we had to hear were not very educational!'

'When I was a child living in Churchstanton, some 60 years ago, my brother and I would be taken to Taunton market by our parents. My father would take us in his governor's cart. The journey from Churchstanton, over Blagdon Hill, about six or seven miles, would take about an hour. When we arrived in Taunton, the pony would be left at the Crown in the High Street, where it would be looked after until we were ready to go home.'

'Between the wars if my in-laws wanted to travel anywhere, daytime or evening, they went by pony and trap. A licence to keep one carriage with less than four wheels to be drawn by a horse or mule cost 15 shillings in 1925!'

'We drove from Othery to Bridgwater, and the market, by horse and cart every Wednesday. We could tie our horse up anywhere along the river while we did the shopping. There were no wardens then, or thieves!'

'As a child, the highlight of the year was our annual visit to my grandparents at Doniford. My father would hire a pony and trap from the Malt Shovel Hotel at Bridgwater to convey us to our destination on Easter Monday. At 6 am he would collect the trap, and then

LICENCE N° 394287

FOR

ONE CARRIAGE (drawn by Horses or Mules) at 15s. 0d.

* *Mr Alfred John Quattly* of *Powden* in the

Civil Parish or Township of *Stogumber* within the

Administrative County † *of Somerset*

is hereby authorized to keep ONE CARRIAGE with *less than four wheels* to be drawn by a Horse or Mule or Horses or Mules, from the date hereof until the **31st** *day of December* in this year; the sum of FIFTEEN SHILLINGS having been paid for this Licence.

Granted at *Stogumber*

this *9th* day of *Jan* 192 **5**.

by *Hwatts*.

* NOTE—Name to be inserted in full.
† If the residence is within a County Borough strike out "Administrative" and insert "Borough" after "County."

1181

The best means of transport in the country was a pony and trap. But Shanks's pony was the cheapest.

returned home to collect my mother, my sister and myself. Our route was via Wembdon Hill (before Quantock Road was cut) and through the leafy lanes to Holford, where we stopped for breakfast and to give the pony a rest, and so to Doniford. My grandfather had the farmer's permission for the pony to graze in the adjoining field until it was time for the return journey.

On one occasion a rabbit ran from the hedge and startled the pony, which promptly bolted. The traces broke, but Father was able to make a temporary repair with the aid of the drawstring from Mother's handbag. This lasted until we reached West Quantoxhead school where a more satisfactory repair could be made.'

'The busy and sometimes dangerous road which now runs through

56

Galmington village didn't exist until the late 1950s. The old route from Trull Road over the ancient packhorse (Rampshorn) bridge and up Hoveland Lane once formed part of the turnpike highway to Exeter. When the Electricity Board or the Gas Company go digging they occasionally reveal a gruesome legacy at the junction of the eastern end as this was the spot where suicides were buried with a stake through the heart. At that end also is the steep descent into Galmington where cyclists can free-wheel. In the days before cars – and bikes – the incline was a strain for horses pulling carts or carriages. The latter were fitted with shoe-brakes but many of the former were less sophisticated and the braking was effected by tying the back wheels together with strong leather straps. For really heavy vehicles the ascent could be accomplished only with the help of an extra team of horses. In earlier centuries it would have been oxen. When the highway was a mere lane pot-holes and ruts were dealt with by a man from the Poor House whose job it was to sit by the roadside breaking up piles of stones to fill in the holes as required.

From the northern, or Wellington Road end, Galmington Road has another deep descent as it passes down the bend between the post office and the fish and chip shop. Here the speed limit is exceeded so often that public meetings are being held to try to resolve the problem. Nothing's new. In the first half of the century, when the road turned abruptly into Galmington Lane, carters were wont to take the corner too fast and collide with the corner of what is now the garden of 107. Today we install sleeping policemen to slow down the traffic. Formerly, a huge boulder was placed at the turning point which may have protected the property of the then-owner of No 107 but probably concussed a number of horses.'

'Two miles from Bridgwater meant a ride in a waggon just large enough to hold eight people a side – knees touching – no standing room. Busy times meant an extra plank or two being placed across the aisle to squeeze the extra bodies, who boarded up a step at the rear door. No tyres or padding or windows. The driver sat up front, complete with whip, dressed warmly to confront the wind, rain and clouds of dust that rose up from the stoned and rutted (A38) road. The horse was usually temperamental and needed much encourage-ment from the whip. One wonderful night he bolted from the shaft and vanished into the darkness.

What a wondrous sight it was to arrive at the Star coaching inn and crunch over the cobblestoned yard and see dozens of lights (three or four lanterns I expect) ablaze with welcome. Our waggon was allowed to remain in the yard – other drivers had to leave theirs out-side in the street. The yard was alive with people shouting, horses

57

clattering over the cobblestones to be fed and watered and those wonderful lights.

The return journey was different – the non-cooperative horse knew he was homeward bound and would gallop along as fast as he could – no whip needed, and the weary passengers being jostled around. The journey home always seemed quiet – I think the travellers were saying their prayers.

After one such dark and uncomfortable journey, my mother was shocked to hear my sister remark "I think Mr Young's carrier cart must be just like Heaven"! "Whatever makes you think that," said mother (knowing that she had told us that Heaven was a most delightful place: "Because he says – there's always room for more" said Marjorie.'

CYCLING

'The unique "Ordinary Club" based in Brent Knoll was for those interested in penny-farthing bicycles. Mr Smith owned several, which could be seen propped up outside his house. What a picturesque sight it was to see half a dozen expert devotees bowling majestically through the village on a calm day.'

'At one time the doctor travelled to Mark on horseback, but later on he came from Highbridge on a bicycle. The postman brought the mail from Highbridge on a bicycle, delivering all the way and collecting again at half past five in the evening.'

'In the early years of this century I always cycled to Curland Methodist Sunday school, never walked. Right at the beginning I couldn't reach the pedals, so I had to have little blocks of wood joined on so that I could sit on the seat. I would cycle with Miss Nancy Matravers and she would give me a push to get me started.'

'I can vaguely remember going once on the carrier's cart to Taunton. A Mr Kerton who lived at Higher West Hatch drove a horse-drawn vehicle on a Saturday, taking would-be shoppers to the town.

Later on the only way to get to Taunton was to walk one and three quarter miles to get the bus, unless of course one cycled. I can remember being taken when I was very young in a wicker seat attached to the carrier of my mother's bicycle. When I was eleven I had my own bicycle so I could cycle to the bus to go to school in Taunton. Before the Second World War I think there were only about three or four car owners in the village. At that time a train also ran from Chard to Taunton, stopping at Hatch Beauchamp, but this line was closed by Dr Beeching.'

'PUFFING BILLY'

'Out walking from Nether Stowey in the 1920s, our one fear was meeting the Puffing Billy. This was a huge monster carrying flour, and the men with it were covered in flour and to us children looked like ghosts. It chugged up steep hills, black smoke coming out of the round chimney. Our one aim if we saw this monster approaching was a quick jump over a gate into a field. The monster took up most of the road.'

THE CANAL

'The canal runs through Durston and was a great source of entertainment. Whilst swimming, one lad dived into a clump of weed and came out minus his trunks. An annual event was the "money boat", from which money was thrown onto the towpath for children to collect. Eel fishing was popular, a method called clatting required a ball of worms for bait. The coming of the railway was the commercial death of the canal.'

BUSES AND TRAINS

'Witham Friary is a remote village lying in the Witham Vale and prior to 1954 it was owned by the Duke of Somerset's estate. It had an important railway station with the main GWR running through (Frome to Weymouth). This was also a junction to Shepton Mallet and Wells. The station was a great asset to the village, bringing in coal, cattle feeds and the Royal Mail, and taking out milk (brought to the station in churns) to London, timber for pit props etc.'

'The railway was once a very important part of Highbridge life, being on the main Great Western Railway line and also a branch line of the Somerset & Dorset Railway (locally affectionately known as the Slow & Dirty), which ran from Burnham on Sea to Bournemouth. This line crossed the main road at Highbridge and the sign that the line-gates were closing was a signal to any children around to run to the top of the bridge over the line while the train passed underneath them, not caring that they were enveloped in steam and smoke at the time. The demise of the S & D and the rise of the car in post-war days meant that every Saturday during summer was a nightmare for local people, as holiday traffic crawled through the town from morning to night, making it virtually impossible to cross the road. This state of affairs continued for some years until the coming of the motorway.'

'The railway was very important to Watchet, taking the bales of paper from the paper mill and coal to various parts of the country. As a passenger service it was very popular. Not many people owned a car so the cheap day return to Taunton for one shilling, known locally as the "Bacon Train", proved a great success.'

'The railway was the focal point in the business life of Hatch Beauchamp, bringing in all supplies and taking away all produce, such as sugar beet from Ilminster, teasels for the woollen mills of Yorkshire, and goods to market as well as passengers for the main lines. There are still many relics of those days around the village treasured by railway enthusiasts when the line closed, the most notable of which may be a table for flowers in St John's church between pulpit and pews, which was made from a redundant signal arm.'

'An entry from a Martock pupil's school book dated 1930 shows that there were six trains a day from Taunton to Yeovil and eight in the opposite direction, the journey taking a little over an hour. Fares from Martock were one shilling return to Yeovil and two shillings and threepence return to Taunton. There were eight stations on the line all serving the surrounding villages. The line is now closed and there is no longer any direct public transport between Martock and Taunton except via Yeovil.'

'In 1928 the GWR opened a halt at Creech St Michael, later closed under the Beeching axe. The halt was famous for its wonderful floral displays, the work of the employees who worked on the Creech section of the railway. They won many prizes and it was a landmark for passengers who regularly passed through on the trains on the Exeter to London line.

Prior to this, in 1915 a bus service to Taunton was started costing tenpence return from Creech Heathfield. This service ended when the proprietor sold out to what is now the Southern National in 1946.'

'Between the world wars there was no bus route through the village of Coxley, only on the main road which ran along the top of the village street. Here bone-shaking buses with solid tyres ran to Bristol, Bridgwater or Weston super Mare. Each bus had a wood and glass partition halfway along inside. The back half was for smokers.'

'A Mr Smith from Taunton owned a charabanc called "The Rambler", which went every week from Taunton to Sidmouth, stopping at all the villages along the way to collect passengers. There was also another charabanc, known as "Lady Betty", which ran a weekly service from Churchstanton to Taunton.'

'In the 1920s a conveyance called "The Toast Rack" ran from Alcombe to Minehead for a penny. It was an open-sided bus and got its name from its appearance, which resembled a toast rack.'

'During the war in the early 1940s I well remember coming home from school at Taunton on the "gas" buses, with the boiler outside at the back. They often broke down on the hill at Preston Bowyer, or the hill rising out of Milverton. This necessitated a long walk home to Wiveliscombe, complete with books, cookery items, and gas mask on string around the neck. Sometimes if everyone left the bus it managed to splutter to the top of the hill at a walking pace without the weight of passengers, and we all piled on again.'

'Everyone walked everywhere until the 1930s when an old-type charabanc christened the "Red Robin" came into use at Marston Bigot and a few cars appeared on the roads. By 1940 a bus service ran three times a day on Wednesdays and Saturdays.'

'The Radstock area was well served by buses which ran fairly frequently to Bath and Bristol (tenpence return). And, of course, we had then the good old Somerset and Dorset, with the Pine Express roaring through at four-thirfy each day. From Radstock's two stations there were holiday excursions to Weston (two shillings and sixpence), Bournemouth (three shillings and sixpence) and other exciting places. When I left home for London I could still get to Bath from Paddington on a Sunday excursion for five shillings.'

ACCIDENT ON THE PEAT FIELDS

'Every year the moors lay under water during the winter, until eventually pumping stations were built at Tealham and Huntspill. The Huntspill pumps controlled the water supplied to the ammunition factory at Puriton throughout the Second World War. In Sharpham a family lived in a house which was always marooned in the winter and the lady of the house was boated across the floods to higher ground, where she picked up her bike and cycled into Street to do her shopping.

From 1930 to 1940 peat was loaded onto flat bottomed boats which

61

were pulled by men to the station. Small "locos" were also used to transport the peat from the fields and these were driven across the main railway line from field to field. On a frosty foggy morning in 1949 one of the locos got stuck as it was crossing the railway line and the driver had no detonators with him to raise the alarm. Thus when the 9 am passenger train from Ashcott came along it hit the loco full smack. The engine and tender fell off the line and into the canal. The carriages were also derailed but miraculously no one was injured. Naturally, the derailed engine and tender presented a major removal problem and could not be lifted out of the softbedded canal until the waters of the canal had been diverted. Only then could the engine and tender be cut up and lifted out in pieces. The weight of engine and tender was 110 tons.'

THE LAST TRAIN

'I lived in Burnham on Sea in the late 1950s when the town was the terminus for the old S & D railway or the "Old Slow & Dirty" as it was affectionately known, although it was probably no slower or dirtier than any other small local railway! The train used to bring the "bucket and spade" brigade for their annual two weeks by the sea, running out from the main line station at Highbridge along the back of the houses, across the main road by a level crossing, then on to Burnham on a single track line.

I saw the last train run from Highbridge to Burnham in 1958, although the rest of the line didn't close until 1966. The train came into the station decked with flags and bunting, and all the passengers were leaning out of the window waving flags, banners and balloons, making a festive occasion out of what seemed to a lot of us a very sad end to an era. We were now cut off from the railway altogether. Anyone wishing to travel by train had to first catch a bus to Highbridge, so losing our railway line was quite a hardship for many people.

The only reminder of the railway in Burnham today is the pub which stands on the opposite side of the road to where the station once stood, "The Somerset & Dorset".'

'The Taunton–Chard railway line ran through our farm, and we would say "There goes the 8.30 (or twelve o'clock)" as it chugged up the steep incline. We had always intended to catch the train at Thornfalcon, and travel through the farm to Chard, but it never happened – until the last day and the last train.

My daughter, god-daughter and myself cycled to the station, and squeezed onto the already crowded train. There was much hooting, and people waving along the line – all very good until we arrived at Chard and asked the guard (who was heavily under the influence) the time of the next train back, to be told there was no train. So we set off from the station on foot although it was getting dimpsey! There was no chance of a lift for three, so the girls went ahead, and when a car stopped I rushed up to vet the occupants – father, mother and two youngsters, all quite respectable – so off went the girls and I continued alone. A commercial traveller gave me a lift, and after a while he said "I hope you don't mind, but I have some shoes to deliver". Around Beercrocombe and Isle Brewers we went, and finally arrived at Thornfalcon station, where the girls were patiently waiting to retrieve the bicycles. How we ever got three bikes out over the five-foot locked gate I'll never know, but we did and cycled home with tales to tell!'

OUR FIRST CAR

'Before the First World War the first car in Bradford on Tone was owned by Mr Langworthy, who ran the post office. Children and adults would come out of their houses to watch it go by. Sometimes people were given a lift in it to nearby Wellington or Taunton.'

'When my brother was born before the First World War at Penselwood, the doctor arrived in a De Dion Bouton car. The radiator had to be drained and refilled with boiling water to assist the car to start.'

'My father claimed to be the first man to drive a motor car up the dreaded Porlock Hill. The gear ratio being what it was he had to go up backwards. When he arrived at the top, in a cloud of steam, and a great deal of noise, he found there was a meet of the hounds. This extraordinary machine caused total chaos, and horses and hounds scattered in panic. Some days later, my grandmother received a letter, I'm not sure from whom, but the writer asked her "How could you possibly allow your son to drive such 'stinking diabolical machines' about the county?" My father, at that time I think must have been well over 30. Times change.'

'John Stevens had the first car in Allerton, a Ford with a canvas top, and Herbert Ham, licensee of The Wheatsheaf, the first taxi. We had our first car in about 1926, a Morris Oxford. I was taught to drive by Mr Burnell from Cheddar who gave me three or four lessons, which cost £2. I had no idea how the engine worked, how to change down gears or even change a tyre, but I drove my parents to Frome. We would only see two or three other cars.'

'After the First World War, my father had the first car in Brompton Ralph, a "Tin Lizzie". We went for family outings and had to wear motoring veils. At the hill up Tolland Rocks the family had to get out and walk while Father drove the car to the top, then we could all climb in again.

Mr Shattock was the first to own a wireless. That was in 1924 and he invited the members of the church choir to come and listen with headphones to a service from St Martin-in-the-Fields.'

'We came to the farm in Mells in 1928. Our car was a bull-nosed Morris Cowley. A handle was to be turned vigorously to start the engine. On market days my father would remove the back seat, and the yellowy celluloid windows, put down some sacks and straw, and load up with calves which would be tied to iron uprights between the windows.

When cars became more commonly used, we bought an old Essex two-seater, to sweep in hay to the rick. We children used to love riding in the dickey-seat.'

'In the late 1920s my father bought his first car, a grey Argyle with a dickey-seat, which was eventually converted to a truck when he bought a blue Daimler from one of the Clark family in Street. We had a regular Sunday outing in it to Burnham, but the car was a bad starter and was replaced by a new yellow and black Morris Oxford.'

'There was only one doctor and a one nurse in the 1930s in South Petherton. Dr Gomez was of Spanish origin and had a rather quick temper. Miss Gillard, the nurse, bicycled around the village delivering babies and tending the sick. When motoring became more popular, Dr Gomez decided to teach Nurse Gillard to drive, to save precious time and a good soaking in inclement weather.

Poor Nurse Gillard, after suffering an hour or more of abuse from Dr Gomez and being called a "stupid woman" in no uncertain terms, she got out of the car, slammed the door and walked home. She vowed never to get behind a steering wheel again and kept her word.'

'In the middle 1930s Dad bought a second hand Citroen car for £10. An old fashioned car in appearance, but it was "coach built", well sprung and very comfortable. Dad spent all his spare time under the bonnet doing repairs to improve the car's performance. We children were under strict instructions on behaviour in the car – no jumping about, nor anything to hang from the windows. From Taunton we visited the seaside, Bristol Zoo, Longleat, and relations in Bristol.

Food for the day was always a well stocked hamper prepared by Mother – home made sandwiches and cake, fresh fruit, cold roast chicken, flasks of tea and lemonade. None of us had ever been in a cafe or restaurant until we were "grown up".'

LOCAL CHARACTERS

THE MAN WHO STARTED THE CATTLE MARKET

'My grandfather, from Brent Knoll, was a great character. As a boy he was a bit of a rebel, but as he grew up his great interests were wild life, the farming community and the church. His wife had died in childbirth, leaving him to bring up eight children. I remember riding in his pony and trap, when he taught me the names of many trees and wild birds.

It was he who started the Highbridge Cattle Market. The local made Cheddar cheese sold here used to take six months to mature, so Grandfather encouraged some cheese-makers from South Wales to come over and show us how to make Caerphilly, which matured in a few weeks. As a surveyor, he was partly instrumental in bringing mains running water to the village. He was interested in the betterment of cattle breeding and he lent pedigree bulls to local farmers to improve their stock – a most generous undertaking. I proudly own the handsome silver cup the farmers presented to him in appreciation.

He once took a cutting of the Holy Thorn at Glastonbury and planted it near Brent Knoll church porch, where it flourished and is now a fine tree.

Although Master of the Weston Harriers, he had no kennels and so persuaded villagers to keep a hound. On the morning of the Meet he would ride through the village blowing his horn, and answering his call, the hounds would leap over the garden walls to follow him.'

AN INDIAN INTERLUDE

'In the summer of 1937 and 1938, my father was doing a locum for the doctor at Long Ashton. We lived in a house called St Martin's, which had once been a school.

Just up the road lived Lady Dyer, widow of General Dyer, well known for the part he played in the suppression of rebellion at Amritzar.

To step into her house was to enter another world as she had brought India to Somerset. Dark wood furniture, vast cushions on which we reclined and the all pervading scent of sandalwood. Shawls and drapings of Indian fabric and the gleam of brass ornaments, added to the feeling of unreality.

One afternoon Lady Dyer and her friend took me on a drive through Cheddar Gorge. I well remember the stately drive in the chauffeur driven car, stopping every so often to admire the view, and ending at the foot of the Gorge with afternoon tea.'

THE TWIN SISTERS

'Two of South Petherton's great characters in the 1940s were twin sisters, Gwen and Cis Gayleard. Cis was a conductress on Safeways Services and the smarter of the two in her uniform, while Gwen used her pony and trap to deliver the Royal Mail to the Lambrooks and other outlying districts of the village, also to collect the local papers from Crewkerne on Friday afternoons. This trip involved crossing the busy A303, for which she had no regard except to say "I'm working and they are on holiday," whereupon she would drive the pony straight across the road with no hesitation whatsoever; they both must have had charmed lives.

She cared nothing for her looks. Her weatherbeaten face was topped with unkempt strawlike hair and she invariably kept her false teeth "out to dry". One tale says they fell out into a load of manure in the trap but she calmly wiped them in her old tweed jacket and put them back. We also thought that she had been born with two left feet and Cis two right ones, as they seemed to shuffle along at odd angles.

A kinder, more caring couple would have been impossible to meet, every stray animal was given a home and looked after and there wasn't a child in the village who didn't have a ride in that very special pony and trap.'

A GENTLEMAN OF THE ROAD AND OTHER STORIES

'A special tramp ("gentleman of the road") came regularly to Buckland Dinham and spent a while sleeping in cattle sheds. He was nicknamed "The Professor' as he was obviously well educated (having purchased a secondhand book of Greek poems for twopence). One year he was taken ill, so the vicar let him stay in some outbuildings with an oil stove and a lamp. He did odd jobs gardening, lighting the church fire, and could even play the organ. He wrote several plays and also composed a piece of music. This was during the Second World War, and at the village "mock auction" he gave a silver ring set with a "cat's eye" and said it had belonged to his father, having been purchased in India. His name was discovered to be George Drummond when the vicar succeeded in getting him an old age pension, but he would say nothing else about his family.

Another character was Jane Brownjohn, nearly as big round as she was tall, and often ailing. She once said, "I be that bad, I be zure I shall wake up one o' these marnins and find me-self dead!"

One Silas Grant was known to drink more than was good for him, and on one occasion was found asleep in the churchyard. When someone roused him with "Wake up, Silas!" he sleepily replied "Let I bide! Wake some o' they 'tother-em up, they bin 'ere longer than I!"

Marshall Willis, another familiar figure, drove a farmer's milk float to take the milk churns to Frome station, to be sent off to London by train. He stood in the float with reins and whip in his hands, and a pipe often upside down in his mouth. Having deposited the full churns and collected some empty ones, before leaving the station he would find the bundle of London daily papers for Buckland and bring them back, leaving them at the baker's shop for their readers to fetch.'

OLD JIMMIE

'As a boy in the 1930s my husband lived at No 3 Whitehall, Wincanton, and his grandfather lived at No 9. Old Jimmie Rumbold, as he was fondly known, was quite a character in the town. He was a dealer in scrap metal, copper, brass and furs, i.e. rabbit skins. He also did a little bit of poaching. The amusing part of this story is that Grandfather Jim was stopped by Mr Billy Loud outside his butcher's shop, who told him that Mr Angerstein who owned the Holbrook estate, had just been in and bought two of his own rabbits, which of course Old Jimmie had just poached and sold to Mr Loud.

The pair of them were tickled pink about this and fell about laughing. My husband told this story to Mr Angerstein's grandson, Mr John Smithies who farms at Holbrook, not long ago and he said, "Well I don't blame Old Jimmie, times were hard, and it made him laugh too."

If the lads raised their caps and wished Mr Loud "Good morning", he would give them sixpence, which was great wealth to them in those days.'

THE GIPSY WEDDING

'We saw many gipsies around Bickenhall. They camped by the

roadside and they always had dogs, mostly lurchers – good rabbit catchers? Once there was a gipsy wedding and a great gathering of vans. I think the bride was about 17 years old. Part of the ritual was that the bridal couple jumped over a bonfire together, a test of how they would tackle life's problems together.'

ELECTION FEVER

'A strong Liberal supporter went to vote, but his wife refused to go with him. Later in the evening she decided to go, and reached the polling station just at eight o'clock. When home again, she told her husband? "I never gid yer old Liberal a vote, but I gid both o't'other 'em one!".'

'My mother, who was born at Walton Farm in 1886, went to a small private school in Glastonbury and she was driven every day in a governess cart. One general election day the pony was decorated with blue Tory ribbons and when she went past Clark's factory, some men outside who were supporting a different party shouted abuse and tried to stop the pony, which was frightened and bolted.'

'Pilton had a few laughs at other people's expense. Keeping up with the downfall of others was a serious business at one time. There was the farmer who hired the Shepton Town Band to play *See the conquering hero* after a Parish Council election when he was a candidate. Unfortunately, the peasants didn't know the band was coming and hadn't voted for him.

Elections were always good for a bit of fun. A barn door belonging to a red-hot Tory carried the message "Vote for H . . ." who was the local Liberal, and a Liberal farmer had his horse, tethered outside the Crown, painted blue. And nobody saw it happen.'

NICKNAMES

'A notable feature of Wookey was the almost universal use of nick-names among the men. Some were based on appearance or trade etc – "Chucky" collected chucked out food for his father's pigs, "Bantam" was small and fierce, "Rasher" long and lean. More strangely, many men were known by Christian names other than their own – Ivan, Harold and Cyril were all called "Joe" and Frank became "Jack". These adopted names were often passed from father to son.'

DANGERS AND DISASTERS

From fire and flood, there were dangers to be met from time to time, particularly out on the moors or on the low Somerset Levels.

SNOW AS HIGH AS THE HEDGES

'One winter at Curland the snow was as high as the hedges and one could walk from field to field and across the road on the snow. Children had great difficulty getting to school but I and the caretaker had to get there in order to get the school warm and cook the lunch as some children always managed to arrive. We had no delivery of bread or milk for weeks.'

THE THAW AND THE FLOODS

'We were living at Northover Manor, Ilchester during 1963 when the winter was the worst for many years. The frost which followed the snow froze all the pipes in the village. A friend with three small children had to gather bowls of snow to enable her to do their daily washing. Eventually fresh water was delivered by tanks; we filled everything possible – washing machines, boilers, baths and a twelve gallon borrowed milk churn. Deliveries continued until 6th February, when the thaw began.

That evening we heard a peculiar rumbling noise which was coming from the river Yeo. Wrapping up well, we sped through the orchard to the river bank. There we beheld the sight of huge lumps of ice, resembling small icebergs, rushing, swirling and crushing into one another as the swollen river swept around the bend. The noise was deafening. Amazed by the sight, we watched by the light of torches until we realised that flooding would be our next experience!

Thankfully the flooding only reached the garden, not the house. Afterwards, there were burst pipes to be repaired. Upstairs ceilings which had been so heavy with frozen snow, which had got under the eaves, collapsed, as thawing progressed. When the lath and plaster had been removed, we discovered that the roof had been insulated with thick layers of pine needles. We were told that they must have been there for at least 150–200 years, by a Somerset builder who worked mainly on old houses and churches.'

'In the winter Dad did casual labouring for the land owners at Henton, clearing the ditches of weed etc. In very wet winters we would watch the water levels rise. My mother would be getting ready to pack our belongings upstairs. Sometimes the water would rise twelve to 18 inches high in the house. Mum and Dad would place wooden boxes around the sides of the room and lay planks of wood across them for our furniture to rest on. The floods did not last long, perhaps a week or so, but it made it hard work for my parents, who carried on with the daily chores as usual. Their grandparents' farm animals had to be fed. There was just one field that didn't flood which we called the high ground. That's where the animals went, and to get the hay to them was great fun because we went in a flat bottomed peat boat.'

'The village on the Somerset Levels where I was born in 1920 was a busy little place with a school, church, three pubs, village stores, railway station and a brass band. Looking back, to me it was a contrast of two things, long hot summers and very wet cold winters.

Summer meant early morning milking out in the fields, long sunny days in the hayfield following the hay-waggon, and swinging on the back of it on the way home; the "Harvest Home" with procession, large lunch, sports etc, and our once a year trip to the sea-side.

Winter brought flooding to all the fields around. Cattle were brought in to sheds, the punt was got ready for emergencies, gloves, socks and boots would be drying on the black kitchen range, and there was hot cider and ginger before bed; then it was Christmas, and the band going round to all the houses playing carols.'

'Peter was two years old (now 77) when his parents moved to Curry Rivel from Bere Regis. They and all their goods came in a farm cart – 40 miles – and the horse and cart must be returned on the same day! They lived under the hill on the north side, so he went to school (via Wick) to Langport. When the floods were out the men walked along the forbidden railway track to get to work in or near Langport, but the children were not allowed to do this. In a wet winter they could not get to school for weeks at a time. He tells of setting off to take a girl to a dance. Walking in wellies, shoes under his arm, he tripped on a brick and fell into the flood in Water Street. No dance! He could change his shoes – but not alas his only suit.

George born in the village in 1915, tells of Water Street. The water drained from the springs into the runnel (which followed the road from Redhill) just below the sharp turn of the road. The stream then ran on towards the village diagonally across the field behind the school and then across to Bell corner, where it joined the main drain.

70

By the time George went to school it had been piped, but the pipes were not big enough for the volume of water. The springs – yes. Heavy rain – no. After a storm or prolonged rainfall it came down to the Cottage-of-Content, and then flooded. Bliss for boys with bikes, a natural playground. But when "the floods were out" the children from Redhill must come across the field paths behind the Manor Farm; much longer but safer than through knee high water. They brought their sandwiches and stayed in the school for the dinner hour. The lucky ones who lived in the village went home for dinner. George grew up, served during the war, and became the village butcher.'

'In July 1949, after a very sultry day, a heavy thunderstorm broke over Lydeard St Lawrence. Water rushed off the fields, through the bakehouse and flooded across the village street, burst open the doors of the chapel and up to the organ stops. The coconut matting was floating hip high and hymn books and bibles were floating in the village street. The damage took months to dry out and the organ was ruined. However, in 1950 a generous local family presented a new organ to the chapel and eventually all was well.'

THE PRANK THAT BACKFIRED

'When I was a child in the early years of the century, my father often told the tale about the lad who lived at Maiden Newton, and who was always boasting how he was afraid of nothing. One night when he was walking home in the dark alone, the other village lads planned to play a joke and catch him out. One of them dressed in a white sheet, lay in wait, and popped up behind a hedge making a screeching noise. The lad, who really wasn't afraid of anything, beat him over the head with the hames from the horse harness he was carrying, and killed him. My father would use this as a cautionary tale to warn me, and the other children, not to play foolish pranks.'

THE WILL O' THE WISP

'My grandfather, who was a herdsman at Greinton near Street before the First World War, told of the dangers of walking over the moors on dark nights. It was easy to walk towards a welcoming light only to find oneself floundering in the icy waters of a rhine. It was commonly believed that when men were found drowned in a rhine, they had been fooled into following the "will o' the wisp". This phenomenon is real enough and is probably the glow of phosphorus on the water.'

FIRE

'One never to be forgotten day at Combe Florey we had a chimney fire in our big open fireplace. The flames shot out of the chimney like a blow lamp with an enormous roar and large lumps of burning soot came down into the room. The local fire brigade was summoned. They were mostly volunteers and one of the firemen was at a wedding at the time! Whilst waiting for them to arrive we sent my brother on to the roof with a stirrup pump, which kept him busy but did nothing to diminish the blaze.

The firemen decided to pump the water from our pond; they put the hose through the window and prepared to squirt the water up the chimney but unfortunately the nozzle flew off and the dirty water flooded the room! My sister and I worked like slaves sweeping the water out of the house and when we had finished we found all the men, having put out the fire, outside the cider house refreshing themselves and having a jolly time. We decided to have a cup of tea.'

'Martock Fire Brigade was formed on the 22nd October 1874, as a result of a meeting convened by the Parish Vestry under the Poor Law Amendment Act which authorised the purchase of fire equipment from the Poor Rate. On 30th October 1874 the first alarm occurred and the engine turned out with a crew of four to a hayrick fire at Cartgate for which a claim for expenses of £1 was made and paid by the Royal Farmers' Insurance Co. During the Second World War under the NFS, constant turn-outs covered bomb incidents, plane crashes, 'blitz' calls from as far afield as Bristol, Reading, Bath, Exeter, Plymouth, etc. The Auxiliary Fire Service has now been disbanded and the station is on a part-time retained basis in the Somerset Fire Brigade and serves as a back-up to Yeovil as well as dealing with local calls. It is interesting to see from the records that members of the same families have given continuous service to the Martock Brigade since its inception, the surnames of a number of the original members still appearing in the roll today.'

OUTDOOR DELIGHTS

LONG SUMMER DAYS

'Spring and summertime in Meare was a delight. Small herds of red or roan shorthorn cattle grazed in fields carpeted with golden butter-cups and cowslips. In the blossoming apple orchards, long grass and wild flowers were hiding places for frogs, toads and mice. Every farm had a pond with frog spawn, newts and water plants.

Elm trees made shade for the multitudes of small birds and night-ingales sang in the area near Ashcott station. Along the river banks the trees and reeds gave cover for moorhens and kingfishers.

Out on the moors the wet conditions made farming a problem but provided the habitat that suited the waterloving birds, and the singing skylarks. The heron has always enjoyed this profitable hunt-ing ground.

The sounds were the sounds of nature, everywhere the droning of bees punctuated occasionally by the clip clop of horses' hooves on the tarmac road. There were no tractors and few cars or lorries, mostly bikes, horses and carts, though there was a regular bus service and a rail service of sorts.

To the group of children who swam and played among the lily pads in the river on the long summer days, the adults' talk and concern about Berlin and Poland seemed to be of remote and cold places too far away to affect us. But eventually they were to bring changes which altered the countryside we loved.'

SWIMMING

'The vogue for public bathing and swimming began in the mid Victorian period and by the end of the century had spread to the villages. Pitminster parish boasted two locations where villagers took part in this pastime; the dammed stream at Peggy Leggy steps and the mill pond near the church.

My father used to tell me how he, his friends and relatives used to swim there. His uncles, members of the Bermondsey Boy's Cycling Club, would cycle from London at weekends to join them. I have a postcard written to my grandfather showing the boys at the mill pond and naming them.

My mother also remembers swimming at Peggy Leggy steps and when at school in Taunton learned to swim at French Weir on the river Tone. They changed in wooden huts which were still there in the 1930s.

As a child I remember swimming in the sea and changing under a voluminous tent affair which was tied around my neck. I wore a prickly woollen costume with a skirt which sagged when wet, on my head a tight frilled cap with two rubber daisies on the side and matching paddling shoes, complete with daisies. I have 'The Zouave Marine Swimming Costume'; this, with body and trousers cut in one,

73

has a sailor collar, is of dark-blue serge and is dated 1865. My father's costume was a shapeless black stockinette affair, sleeveless and with knee-length legs.'

HOUSE & HOME

THE HOUSES WE LIVED IN

The idyllic cottage set in Somerset's glorious countryside certainly existed, but it often had cold stone-flagged floors, ill-fitting doors and leaded lights which would not open. Many people lived in cramped conditions in those days of larger families, whole families sharing one or two bedrooms. Water was drawn from the well or pump, a practice which continued in some villages until quite recently, and a candle lit generations of children to bed, their eyes darting from shadow to ghostly shadow. Yet despite the discomforts of life, many look back on their old homes with affection. At the heart of the house was the fireplace, around which the household routine went on, games were played and the new invention, the wireless, was listened to.

OUR HOUSE

'Constructed of mellow, hand-made bricks, my home at Edithmead was a typical Somerset farmhouse with the usual long passage from front door to the back. The building appeared to be of various ages and over the years parts had been built on or demolished.

All the downstair floors were paved with blue-grey flagstones. Some very smooth and others quite rough.

Although the walls of the house were more than two feet thick in places, the wooden doors were ill fitting and let in terrible draughts.

During my early childhood I recall the windows at the back of the house – a much older part – had leaded panes which did not open. These were later replaced with modern wooden casements. Wallpaper was used to decorate the living rooms and bedrooms, but the landings and stairways were colour washed. The only two colours used, probably the only two available, were a dark blue, reminiscent of woad, and a deep, rusty red.

Other places such as larders and pantries, wash houses, outhouses and, of course, the ceilings, were whitewashed each spring with a wash made of lime and water. This mix had to be handled with great care especially if the lime was "new". It could burn the skin quite severely.

My parents' garden and grandmother's together amounted to a good half acre. In this large garden we grew all our vegetables in season and potatoes which lasted us all through winter and spring until we were able to dig the new earlies the following Whitsuntide.

The long row of runner beans was staked with withy sticks cut from the withies growing around the orchard ditches. The smaller and more brashy withies were used to stick the peas.

We had gooseberries, raspberries, red and blackcurrants, loganberries and strawberries. The orchard abounded with cider and eating apples, plums, greengages and pears and boasted two magnificent walnut trees.'

'My home in Coxley was made of Mendip stone. We had stone flagstones downstairs for floors: A bread oven was set into the chimney piece and we made our own bread. The dairy had mud walls (daub and wattle). Away from the house stood an open shed. This too was made of interwoven wattle or withy.

Attached to the house there was an upstairs storage loft which we called a tallet. A cider press was in the room below.

Father would take the horse and cart and make the journey over the Mendips to Radstock to collect coal. All coalmines in this area of Somerset are now closed.'

'My great-grandparents' small farm on the Somerset Levels was a two up, two down small house. My parents had half the house in return for Mum looking after her grandparents and helping on the farm. My father was by this time away fighting in the Second World War in Burma. After the war my father returned home and my brother was born, so the four of us shared the one bedroom. We had no electricity or mains water. We collected our water on a bicycle with two large buckets on the handlebars. In about 1948 my parents progressed to a horse and cart, when we could get ten gallons in a milk churn.

Our lighting was oil lamps and candles. The cooking was over an open fire, a range or a primus stove. The washing was boiled in a big iron urn over a fire built outside. The water for washing clothes, our weekly bath and hair wash was rain water collected in various water butts around the house – bath time was a tin bath by the fire.'

'Our farmhouse home at Huish Champflower had kitchens with stone slab floors, with perhaps a mat in front of a large open fireplace. A large iron kettle hanging on a chimney crook would provide some hot water. The baking was done in an oven in the chimney, heated by wood. Everything was put into the oven at the same time, bread, cakes and meat. Sitting by the fire at night, you would be very hot in front and very draughty behind because of the size of the room, and perhaps with some doors left open to prevent smoking from the fire. In most farmhouses there was a large settle and a high backed wooden chair, usually sat in by the man of the house. Washday

Monday usually started on Saturday by getting the wood ready to light the fire under the furnace which boiled the clothes.'

'I was born at Portsmouth in 1921, and it wasn't until I was seven years old that I was taken to visit my grandparents in Somerset. We were met at the station in Wells by a horsedrawn vehicle called a governess cart: we jogged along for two miles to the village (West Horrington) and the farmhouse – which to me seemed cold and dark. The thing that frightened me the most was going to the toilet, which was around the back of the house under archways of roses and honeysuckle. It was filled with spiders and all sorts of creepy crawlies. The wooden toilets reminded me of the three bears – large, medium and small, each with a wooden lid. I hated the place and did my best not to use it: consequently, I suffered acute constipation! Then, my grandmother made me drink a concoction she made by soaking seed pods. Even a bullseye sweet wouldn't take the taste away.

In the evening there was a gathering of the clan when lots of relatives had supper in the kitchen which was lit by a large brass hanging lamp. I was put to bed in the room above, which had a wide chimney ledge where my Gran stored all her jams and preserves. I chose a pot of blackcurrant jam and licked it from the pot until I felt sick. Then, as I sat on the floor, I saw a large bolt under the bed. I proceeded to spend quite a while turning the bolt, until there was a terrific crash from down below and lots of shouting and yelling. My mother dashed upstairs and told me that the hanging lamp had crashed onto the supper table – it was blamed on rotten floorboards and not on me!'

'During the 1920s I remember holidays spent with my grandparents who had a small-holding in a little village on the Polden Hills. My grandfather was a postman and kept ten cows, some hens, a horse, cart and a trap. There was no public transport for me, so a neighbour took me in his side-car which was attached to his motor cycle.

I enjoyed getting the cows into the shed for milking. My gran usually did the milking by hand. She sat on a stool with three legs and collected the milk from the cows' udders into a bucket. Customers came to the house with their jugs for milk. My gran made cream and butter. I well remember the cool dairy with shallow bowls of thick cream, just right for finger dipping when no one was looking. The half-pound pats of butter had a cow imprinted on the top.

Crystal cool water came from the pump outside the front door. My grandfather and my father had dug the well under the pump – no other water was available. We washed in this cold water in a bowl which stood on a stool in a back room known as the back-house. I did not think much of this; neither did I like the lavatory at the top of the garden. There were two wooden seats, one lower than the other for us children. There was no flush and no toilet rolls, instead squares of newspaper tied up with string and hung from a nail. These had to be torn from the daily newspaper – hands as black as soot from the print – how did we keep so healthy? I remember carrying the lantern to the loo and being afraid – someone having to wait at the door for me.

I slept in a feather bed which in winter was heated with a fire-brick which had been in the oven of the black range. It was wrapped in a piece of blanket and warmed the bed, but was not much to cuddle! When my cousin stayed with me we unscrewed the brass knobs or balls on the bedstead and rolled them across the linoleum – no carpets to cover the floor, just one at the bedside.

It was fun to gather eggs straight from the hens' nests for breakfast. We always had a fried breakfast of bacon, egg, potatoes and bread – it tasted so different from what we have today. Trips to the market at Bridgwater on Wednesdays were great. We took butter, cream and eggs, and my grandmother did her weekly shopping. We went in the horse and trap. The horse was stabled at a hotel or inn until my grandparents were ready to go home.'

'Before 1927 when the first council houses were built in Barrington, the villagers lived in very small cottages which, if they survived, were eventually converted, two or three making one house. The council houses cost £500 to £550 for a pair.'

'When I was about eight years old I went to stay with my grand-parents on a farm at Norton Fitzwarren. I can still recall the open fireplace where Grandmother made the porridge and fried the break-fast. In the spring, lambs' tails were a delicacy and I remember being horrified to find them being served with some of the wool (uninten-tionally) still left on!

The loo was a privy at the bottom of the garden, riddled with woodworm, a two seater with a stack of newspaper handy and complete with running water – that was the stream running beneath. In the farmyard a large water wheel provided power to grind the corn which fed Grandfather's many prize pigs and cattle and a veritable army of rats in the barns. A large cat population never seemed to have any effect on these rodents but were always to be found in the kitchen waiting for Grandmother to forget to shut the larder door after a busy cream-making session.

Grandfather was a talented fruit grower, his forte being the grafting of many different varieties in his orchards. In the evenings we played

RECEIPT.

No...........

Wyatt Stuckey, Manufacturing Stationer, Triangle, Clevedon.

August 8ᵗʰ 189 6

Received of *Mr Sidney Perry*

the sum of *£130* Pounds ———— Shillings and

———— Pence, *One Hundred and thirty*

Pounds for House & Garden at North Curry.

£130; - : - *Job Perry*

£130 is the cost of a house at North Curry in 1896. But every generation has to view the cost of a home in relation to their income.

draughts by the light of an Aladdin lamp, the company fortified by the local cider. At bedtime I was warm and snug in a double bed complete with a deep feather mattress – then it was "blow out the light", not turn off the switch, as now!'

'"Zoggs" cottage at Stogursey has a rectangular hole in the corner – not for the boiler or the oven, but for the grandfather clock which was too tall for the room.'

'Two brothers who were born in Stocklinch lived in the oldest house in the village. It was thatched and the floors of the upstairs rooms sloped towards the walls. A "mud" wall faced north and corrugated iron sheds were propped against it in the winter and the space between served as a dairy.

Inside, the inglenook fireplace had a curing, or smoking, chamber beside it. Fuel for this was culled from the hedges and local trees. The kitchen had an ancient stone trough and the water came from a well and a pump outside. A stone privy was up the stream side of the house and was ditched on both sides (the most hated job was to empty the bucket).

A great deal of cider was made to drink at meal times and about 100 lbs of jam and large quantities of pickles were made.'

'Our farmhouse at Staple Fitzpaine had a stone floor, and a black-leaded range with a bread oven. There were two bucket loos, one at the front of the house for ladies, one at the back for men and workers. There was also a wash house with a copper boiler. Electricity came to Staple Farm in 1939, and to the rest of the village in 1953. In some cottages the loos were at the bottom of the garden (in one case a three-seater directly over a running stream). The farm cottages at Staple Farm had water from a pump in the back yard until 1953, at which time water was brought to the house.

There was a farm at Ludney where about five women would do their washing in a tub about five feet in diameter – all washing by hand.'

'From 1934 until 1953 I lived in a two bedroomed stone cottage at Knapps Lane Huish Episcopi which was without toilet and bathroom. We had no back entrance and everything had to be taken through the house. My mother stripped withies and the bundles were taken from the brook in front of the house and dragged, dripping wet, through to the back garden to be stripped and laid out to dry.

Our toilet was halfway down the garden, a small brick building and no light. It was very scary especially on a dark winter's night. My father had the awesome task of digging a large hole at the bottom of the garden to bury the excrement!

Bliss came when we moved to a modern home with bathroom and running hot water.'

'As a child at Compton Dundon in the early 1940s, we had a flush toilet, but I don't know how the drains worked because we didn't have a cesspit put in until 1950.

At my friends' houses and at school they had dry closets, with either two or three holes and of course the newspaper, cut up into neat squares and strung on a nail close at hand. It was pure bliss at Christmas to be able to use the orange wrapping paper.'

'Accommodation was scarce just after the Second World War, so many young couples started married life living with their parents. In 1948 we moved in with my mother-in-law in a small terraced cottage in Church Lane, Brent Knoll. We had no electricity, refrigerator, hot water supply or washing machine. There was one cold tap and a clay sink; a large tin bath hung on a hook outside the back door. Water for washing and baths was heated on a gas cooker. We had a wire mesh safe where meat and perishables were kept. In our living room was a black range with an open fire and an oven each side. Rent was three shillings and sixpence a week.'

'The word electricity was not in my vocabulary when I was young and living in Badgworth. How, I wonder, now, could one survive without it? I remember the oil lamps which were filled on the kitchen table each day – the chimney cleaned and the brass polished. I also remember the dark passages and corners which I always ran past thinking a ghost would spring out.

The cooking stove had a large glass bottle of oil which was turned upside down within its cage and all the bubbles gurgled to the top.

Outside in the wash house was a large boiler and hot water for the house had to be pumped upstairs into the bath. No telephone, no radio, no vacuum cleaner, only a dustpan and brush and wet tea leaves, but we did have a sewing machine and sometimes I was allowed to turn the handle.

I never went to the shops, the tradespeople all came to us and I would swing on the garden gate waiting for them.

I lived a quiet, peaceful existence and was unaware of a different kind of life only a few miles away.'

'Our stone built cottage at Henton in the 1940s had the luxury of one cold water tap in the kitchen, where the cooking was done on the black-leaded range. The fire in the backhouse was lit on Mondays and the washing was boiled in the copper and put through the mangle situated in the outhouse which also served us as the "stickhouse". This was next to the "outside inconvenience" which consisted of a scrubbed bench with a round hole and a large metal bucket placed under the hole. The contents were emptied once a week into a hole three feet deep in the garden; the garden crops were prolific. The house furnishings were very plain – one settee, farmhouse and kitchen chairs, one farmhouse table, a few rugs, no bath, three feather beds and candle and oil lamps.'

'I had heard of the green hills of Somerset. In 1956 I moved from Surrey to one of the green hills, the north slope of the Blackdowns, to a very isolated cottage. It was a beautiful place, a profusion of ferns and primroses and musical running streams, with glorious views of the Quantocks and Brendon Hills. The cottage had no services and was so far from the beaten track that a WI member who had lived there during the Second World War was one day late hearing it had started and one day late hearing it had ended!'

WATER

'I was born in 1912 and when I was quite young my family moved out in the country to a small cottage – two up and two down and a back kitchen. We had no electric, no water, we relied on oil lamps and my mother cooked on a fire, a coal fire that had an oven at the side.

We had quite a way to go to fetch our water. There was a well at the side of the road called Brookwell and it was real hard work going backwards and forwards with buckets and watering cans, especially in the summer when we couldn't catch any rainwater. The seasons then seemed to be different from what they are now and it seemed one long summer and one long winter.

In our home at Yarley, my siser and I slept in the one bed in one room and the rooms went from one to the other, they weren't separate. Downstairs was mostly stone floors, with just a mat by the fire. We lived there a few years and then we moved to the bottom of the hill to a place called Hembury and that still only had two bedrooms and you went from one to the other. It was bigger downstairs but we still didn't have any electric or water. We had to walk up the road and there was a pump in the bank of the garden to get our water. In the winter my father used to wrap it up in sacks but it still froze and you couldn't move it or try to get it working or else you would break it. So very often we had to manage with soft rainwater which my father caught a lot of, and it was always boiled. But I'm still alive to tell the tale. Then sometimes I've known my father scrape the clean snow and melt it to have some water.'

'I was born in a tiny cottage in Templecombe in 1920. Our drinking water was handed through the kitchen window by my brother who worked on the farm nearby, and it came from the spring. Water for other purposes was taken from the standpipe several yards down the road.'

'My home at Coxley got its water from a deep well which also served three other houses. My brother was taken ill with typhoid fever. Well water was blamed as the cause of this, so they decided to drain the well and investigate. This was a complete waste of time for as soon as they tried to empty it of water, it kept filling up again as fast as they dipped.

My parents never believed this to be the cause of my brother's illness, and were inclined to blame it on a trip to Bristol which he had recently undertaken.

Until piped water came to Coxley village, most villagers had access to a well. Some inhabitants were still using their wells as late as the 1980s.'

'Water to the houses at Farthings Close, Nynehead was provided by a windmill pumping water up to a large tank from a well at the bottom of the gardens. The wind pump was replaced by an electric one housed in a small shed when electricity came to the village, and the vanes were then removed. This continued until mains water was received from Clatworthy Reservoir.

Often the well went dry in the summer months. This meant carrying water quite a distance across an orchard from the next house. Consequently rainwater was collected in a butt and used whenever possible. My mother recalls how she boiled the water in a small tin bath which she put outside to cool so that she could safely bath me as a baby. It was some time before my father discovered what was causing the brown patches on the lawn!'

'Hot water for our remote farmhouse was provided from a coal and log-fired copper about two and a half feet across. This hot water was also used for washing the milking pails and other dairy utensils. It was the morning's first job to light the fire so that there was ample hot water by breakfast time.'

'Water for the house at Horsington was collected in butts. If this ran out, then water had to be drawn from a well in the village. One day, a lady of 90 recalls, her small brother fell into the well. Her father was "winkled down" in the bucket to rescue the child. Everyone had to help "winkle him up again 'cos he was heavy".'

'It was the turn of the century before running water was supplied to Barrington by Langport Rural District Council and then only from six standpipes. The installation, with additional fire hydrants, cost £600. The estimated cost for households was twopence per week for houses rated at £8 or less, provided that the water was not used for a bath or the horse. Children were bathed twice a week in a tin bath in front of the fire. Some down Water Street used to wash in the pond.'

THE FIREPLACE

'Our living room fireplace was the heart of our home at Dunster in the 1920s. We had an open fire with bars in the front to hold in the coals – a very dusty place. There were ovens, one on each side. All was black and cleaned and shone with blacklead "Zebra" polish every day. Two flat-irons stood on the grid in front of the hot coals, ready when needed. Often a wooden clothes horse full of wet clothes stood in front of the fire and a line of wet clothes hung above and from the mantle shelf, which was quite high. In front of this fire we toasted bread, dried our hair and bathed in a long tin bath, often called a "bungalow bath", on Saturday nights. We burned discarded wrappings, and at Christmas time roasted chestnuts. At the fireplace we all gathered to keep warm, but most of all it was the place where we all sat and talked or listened.

We had a gramophone, "His Masters' Voice" with a large trumpet. On Sunday evenings, Mother played the piano and we sang – chiefly hymns. I remember in 1926 my uncle came and fixed up a crystal radio set which he had made. We had to share the ear phones – often one each. Of course there were requests to be quiet to the rest of the household. Later on he produced a loud speaker. This was great. The radio opened a new world to us. We loved to listen to the Children's Hour with Uncle Mac. This radio had batteries and an accumulator which was recharged overnight at the local garage for fourpence.

We had rugs scattered over our red and yellow tiled floor and one in front of the fender which was on the floor in front of the fire, and prevented hot ash from reaching the rug. We played games here such as Ludo, Snakes and Ladders and with cards, Snap, Donkey, Old Maid and Sevens. Our room was lit by an oil lamp which sat on the table until gas came, and then we had light suspended from the ceiling – no more problems with knocking the lamp over.'

THE KITCHEN RANGE

'The kitchen range was the hub of our house at Pylle. It was polished with blacklead every morning and provided everything hot required by everyone, from bath water to food. It blazed merrily all morning, but after mid-day dinner it was banked with small coal, the oven door opened, and a large clothes horse holding everything that needed drying was put in front to benefit from the warm air.

The cats, who had dined off the scraps, lay on the mat asleep until evening, when the clothes and the horse were folded away, and the fire revived with logs for the return of the family. One morning when Mother went to put the joint in the oven, she was shocked to find a cat inside. It looked quite normal, but as she lifted it out, it fell into ashes, quite cremated!'

'My first memory of my mother and grandmother who lived with us is that cooking was carried out on an open hearth with large black iron pots and a kettle which hung on long crooks, suspended from a bar built into the chimney. She also used an oil stove for some of the cooking ie frying and baking of cakes and pastries. The oil stove was at times temperamental and would burn up and smoke, particularly when her back was turned for a moment. This would result in greasy black smuts forming on items of laundry, cups and saucers etc that were exposed to the smoke. Of course this meant Mother was none too pleased as she had to turn to and wash all the items again.

After a time a modern stove of the era was installed – a Triplex, which consisted of an open grate with a back boiler to heat the water and three ovens, a roasting, simmering and warming ovens. Some years later a solid fuel Aga was invested in. The Aga at that time was very economical to run and needed only to be stoked and filled with anthracite, a slow burning smokeless fuel, twice a day, morning and night and the ash removed once a day. This was sheer luxury after the other cooker, plus the added comfort of a warm kitchen whatever the time of day or night. Some farmers' wives have saved many a lamb from dying by putting it into the bottom oven to keep warm when the conditions out in the farm shed were too cold for them.'

'In Brean regular callers at our farm by horse and cart included the oil man bringing vital paraffin for our lamps and the Valor oil stove which was our standby when the black coal-fired range had to be let out for its weekly cleaning and blackleading; this was usually Fridays and how we missed that fire on winter mornings. Oil lamps were trimmed and filled daily; there was a lovely Aladdin lamp which gave a better light, but if placed in a draught its mantle would blacken and it had to be turned down to clean it.'

BUYING THE FURNITURE

'When my parents were married in 1911, my father stocked the farm and my mother was responsible for furnishing the house. Her oak dining room suite was specially made for her in Park Street, Bristol. There was a dining table, six chairs, two carvers, a large sideboard and a writing desk. The main item of furniture in the drawing room was a walnut Erard concert grand piano, which my grandfather had bought from the Abbey House in Glastonbury, and on which stood a bust of an early rector of Walton, Lord John Thynne, under a glass dome.'

A CANDLE TO BED

'Until the early 1940s our house at Wiveliscombe was not wired for electricity upstairs and so we took candles to light our way to bed. As a child it seemed a long way to my bedroom, and if I walked quickly, or the slightest draught blew, I was soon in darkness, and scared when the floorboards creaked.'

'Lighting in our farmhouse at Sampford Arundel was by oil lamps and candles – quite dangerous when one looks back. As a child it was the only means of light to see myself to bed, and as the farmhouse was old and draughty the flame flickered making weird shadows on the walls and ceiling.

I can remember it was quite a ritual for my mother to trim the lamps every morning, particularly during the winter months as the men required Tilley lanterns to see the way to do the work outside, ie milking the cows and feeding the animals. It was also her job to see the lamps were lit for them as soon as it became dimpsey (dusk). When calor gas came on the market we had that installed for the lighting of the main rooms, also to heat the room when it was very cold and a calor gas iron – great after flat irons that needed heating on the oil stove or range.

Although we lived quite near the town we did not have electricity connected until 1958, as the supply in the area was insufficient to maintain a power supply to us and our neighbours.'

'Mains electricity came to Weare in 1928 but in 1965 when we were connected we had to pay the expense of getting it to the farmhouse. In 1942 we had a Lister diesel generator installed to give us lights and limited power to run the milking machine and some indoor appliances. The engine ran even for one light. It was started by switching on a light or appliance to which it was connected. Before that a small generator provided lights for the farmhouse.'

THE DAILY ROUTINE

With no modern labour saving devices, the women of the family shouldered a never ending round of drudgery and sheer hard work. Nothing epitomises this so much as washday, which came around every Monday, come rain or shine, and swallowed a whole day in soaking, scrubbing, washing, blueing, wringing, mangling and drying. And then there was Tuesday, when the clothes and the linen had to be ironed with flat irons heated on the fire, and there were no easy-care fabrics to help you through. Bathnight has also stayed in the memory, as families dipped one by one into the galvanized bath in front of the fire.

A WELL FURNISHED HOME

'Our home in Sutton Mallet was well furnished, the only heat being from a range in the kitchen or open fire in the front room (used only on Sundays). Mum mainly cooked on a paraffin stove with three burners, one of which heated the oven on top. Everything was washed by hand or boiled in the copper, which was lighted on Saturday for a bath in front of the range and on Mondays for washing. Our lavatory was some way down the garden path, a large, long wooden seat with two places to sit, which my father had to periodically empty. One of the first early morning chores was to empty the chambers under all the beds.

Our only lighting was oil lamps which Mum had to trim and fill most days. We used candles to go to bed. Mum made a lot of our clothes as well as her own and she did a lot of cooking, we always had enough to eat even in rationing. Mum also had to help with the milking. Farm life was very happy, especially at haymaking, harvesting and threshing times. I can remember only once in my childhood going to the cinema in Bridgwater and it sticks very firmly in my mind to this day, it was Shirley Temple in *Grandfather*.'

WASHING AND IRONING

'My husband's grandmother, in about 1916 at Westbury-sub-Mendip, used to take in washing. She washed all day Monday and Tuesday and ironed all day Thursday, and was paid a shilling a day. On Monday mornings a fire was lit under the copper boiler, water was pumped up and the copper filled. They used block Sunlight soap, rubbing it on the clothes and then rubbing the clothes on a board. It was then boiled, rinsed and put through a mangle, rinsed again (using Reckitts Blue), mangled again, then hung out to dry. If it was to be starched this was made by mixing starch powder into a paste with cold water, then adding boiling water, stirring until it was clear. The clothes were ironed with flat irons which were heated on the fire, then wiped clean before they could be used.'

'Mother and Father and seven children lived in a two-bedroomed cottage at Dunster, with no bathroom or indoor toilet (there was a toilet in the yard shared by three cottages). On washday in the 1920s we children had to fetch sticks from the wood to light the fire under the copper for boiling the clothes. The copper was in an outside shed and filled with buckets of water. Mother lit the fire before we went to school. The cleaning agents were hard soap and washing soda. After boiling, the clothes were rinsed in a separate bath and put through blue water before being starched, mangled by hand and hung out to dry. The coloured things were then washed in the same water. This took all day, and Mother was often still working at ten o'clock by candlelight. Everything had to be ironed by flat irons heated in front of the open fire. There were no drip-dry non-iron materials then, everything was cotton, wool or silk.'

'On the rising bend at West Porlock is a cottage, today named "Laundry Cottage". After West Porlock House was built in 1920, a very large room was built onto this cottage in which the laundry was done for the House. There was a large coal burning copper in the corner to do all the boiling. Two large stone sinks for the washing, which was done with hard soap on wash boards, a long wooden table for all the ironing and a black Larbut range with six flat irons upended on it, which ranged in size from three to eight inches. There was also a gophering iron like a tiny fluted mangle for all the frills, as well as a large iron mangle with big wooden rollers.

As in those days, apart from towels and sheets, the pillow cases, table-cloths, napkins and aprons were all blued and starched. The washing, drying and ironing took nearly all week.

A few years ago the cottage was modernised and then got its name, but the present owner now has her own automatic washer and dryer.'

'Monday was washday. A lady came from the village , Nether Stowey, to the rectory, arriving very early. The copper was lit and water boiling. To me she was an amazing person, tall, always wore a hat rather flat looking, around her waist a sack apron, and my memory of her was of steam around for most of the day. We were allowed to turn the handle of the wringer that clanked and the rollers banged as the sheets dropped into the basket. Dinner on Mondays was always cold meat, chutney and spuds.

Tuesday was carpet cleaning. Tea leaves had been saved and were thrown over the carpet, the chairs were put together in a corner, then down on the knees using a dustpan and brush sweeping all the carpet – hard work. Lamps were filled, coal was brought in from outside – there were so many everyday jobs.'

'Washday was always Monday. The copper in the kitchen was stoked with wood and coal and filled to the brim with household linen and the family's clothes. The washing was stirred around with a round smooth stick and when boiled sufficiently was taken out and then washed out by hand in a tin bath which stood next to the copper. The white sheets and white underclothes were always rinsed in blue water and some of the linen was starched before being put through the mangle. My memories of washday in the 1930s are of coming home from school on Monday lunch times and seeing the washing lines full of billowing, brilliant white washing and the sun always seemed to be shining.'

'My pre-school days were spent living in an old semi-detached cottage at Nailsbourne, a hamlet near Kingston St Mary. Our cottage had no mains water, electricity or a sink. Situated to the side of the cottage was a wash-house – a stone built shed with a stone floor. Inside the main piece of "equipment" was a copper which had to be filled with five buckets of water before the fire could be lit underneath in order to bring the clothes to boiling point. There was a long wooden table (made by my father) which held three baths, a large galvanised one in which the clothes were washed, an enamelled one for rinsing, and one with Reckitt's Blue for the whites to be rinsed. On another table was a bowl of freshly made Robin Starch. There was also a wringer which was quite new – we had progressed from a mangle.

My mother worked very hard, especially on Mondays which were always washdays. We would get up early and she would take two buckets, one half filled with water left from the previous day and I would take my little bucket also. We would walk up the road, about 100 yards to our pump which we shared with two other families. Mum would lift the top off the pump and pour the water in (which she had brought with her) to prime the pump, and then she would pump very quickly to get the water to come up from the well below. She would fill her buckets and I would fill mine. Then we would go back to the wash-house and start to fill the copper. This journey was repeated many times because besides filling the copper, water for rinsing was also needed. Sometimes rain water was used which made life a bit easier. We had a large tank between the two cottages to catch the rainwater. Mum would always try to use this for woollies and delicates even if there wasn't enough to fill the copper. It was very precious because the clothes would feel much softer when washed with it. It was lovely for washing hair too. Sometimes our next door neighbours would "steal" some of the rainwater from the tank when no-one was around (after dark or if we were out).

When the copper was filled with water, the soap powder and white cotton sheets, towels etc would be put in and then the fire would be lit. On windy days sometimes the fire had to be lit two or three times before it would burn properly. Whilst waiting for the copper to boil we would fill the rinsing bath with cold water and Mum would make the starch, the wringer would be uncovered and a bucket placed underneath to catch the water. The woollens and delicates would be washed and rinsed first, put through the wringer and put into the clothes basket and hung on the clothes line to dry.

When the copper reached boiling point it was allowed to boil for a few minutes before the "whites" would be removed by means of a large white stick and put into the big bath for washing. Clouds of steam would be everywhere. Coloured towels etc would be put in next and boiled. No more fuel would be added to the fire because there would be enough left to heat the remainder. Whilst Mum washed the clothes she would stand on a slatted board (a duck board) so that her feet wouldn't get wet. She would rub, scrub, wring, rinse and wring again, starch pillow cases, table cloths, etc. Then put everything through the wringer. It would take practically the whole morning before she would finish. If the weather was fine she would hang the clothes on the line outside to dry, but if it was wet it would be draped on clothes horses and left indoors to dry. In winter sometimes the clothes would freeze on the line and Mum's poor fingers would be white with cold by the time she had removed them.

Washday lunch was always cold meat, home made pickles and beetroot in winter (salad in summer) with mashed potato followed by hot rice pudding. After lunch Mum would empty the copper by means of a galvanised bowl with a wooden handle (a dipper). Some of the water would be used to wash the floors and paths. In summer all the water would be saved, cooled and then used for watering the garden. The cold soapy water would sometimes be used to spray plants to get rid of pests such as greenfly. In the winter the surplus water had to be carried in buckets and emptied down a drain in the garden.

Washdays have improved beyond our wildest dreams. Mum now uses a washer/dryer (she has mastered all the knobs at 84 years of age). I sometimes wonder if she still has that look of pleasure and satisfaction on her face when she has finished which she used to have

91

as she turned in the doorway to look back on the brilliant white and coloured clothes blowing on the line in the wind on a glorious summer's day.'

'When I came to live in Ivy Cottage, Bickenhall on Good Friday 1951, I went into the kitchen and there was a lovely white sink and a tap! How thrilled I was to see that as I'd only had a well before and the bucket closet up the garden path.

What a lot of washing though with five children. I did it in an old bath tub, lighting up the fire under the furnace to boil the clothes. I ironed with an old flat iron. I bathed all five children in front of the fire. One daughter put her foot in the very hot water before I'd cooled it down – she wanted to get in before the boys!'

'For baths and washing at Henton in the 1920s my mother put the water in an old-fashioned copper that was heated with coal or small coal or any rubbish you had, and then there was a galvanized bath put in front of the fire. My sister and I bathed in the same water and then afterwards my mother used to put the clothes soaking in it. She used to scrub all the dirty washing and then boil it, which was hard work and took quite a long time.

The ironing was hard work too, because you had to put the irons on the fire and heat them and then they got sooty and you had to wipe them clean or else you got it on the clothes. I remember my grandmother was a marvellous person with washing and ironing and she used to do it up beautiful. She would starch everything, and she had a pair of tongs she used to push in the fire and get hot. Then she'd wipe them well and pleat the lace on the garments. She also had small flat irons and they were bevelled on the bottom and made of steel – they shone beautifully and she used those to iron the men's cuffs and collars on their shirts.

On Saturdays my sister and I always had to clean the shoes and the knives and forks. We had a board and we scattered what they used to call Bathbrick and rubbed the knives on this till they were clean. For the forks and spoons I think we used to wet the Bathbrick and rub it with a cloth and then use the cloth on the cutlery. The shoes we did with shoe polish and they always had to be done properly and shine.'

'I was the envy of all my friends in the early 1950s as I could really iron my doll's clothes. Although the newly built council house in Wells had given my mother electricity for the first time, the sockets were positioned so that an electric iron flex ran across the door, too dangerous for young children. So she continued to heat her flat irons on the range – my job was to do the hankies using the tiny "collar and cuff" iron, after which I could do my doll's things.'

BATH NIGHT

'Our home at St Audries in the 1920s was a small cottage which consisted of two rooms up and two down, an outside toilet and a large kitchen garden, which catered for the everyday needs of the family. Bath night was Saturday, when the gas boiler was lit to provide hot water for the tin bath which had been erected in a small scullery. Washday was a nightmare, always on Monday, whether wet or dry, and was carried out in a wash-house some 20 yards from the main dwelling. This had to be shared with another tenant who occupied an adjoining cottage and the boiler was heated by a wood fire. The rent for the cottage was three shillings and ninepence simply because my father was employed by the owner.'

'Washday was always Monday and bath night the same evening, in a tin bath in the scullery, with the door of the furnace open for warmth at one side of me, and a draught from under the back door on the other.'

'Saturday night was bath night, in a tub in the warm bakehouse, for we were lucky enough to have hot water from a tank over the ovens at my father's bakery in Wincanton. The WC was in the garden with a wooden seat across, newspaper our toilet paper. Chamber pots were kept under beds for night use, which were emptied into slop pails. Monday was washday, when the copper had to be filled and heated by a fire. Clothes were scrubbed and hung out to dry with pegs which gipsies used to make and sell at doors. Then the flagstones were scrubbed.'

'My mother did the washing in a copper in one of the outbuildings. The water had to be brought from the house or taken from the massive rainwater butt and heated by a fire underneath the copper; this "soft" water was always used for washing one's hair. Saturday night was bath night, taken in a tin bath in front of the kitchen range. The hot water was brought from a gas boiler or from kettles heated on the range. There were only gas lights in three downstairs rooms, candles were used upstairs.'

'In the 1920s at Dunster we bathed every Saturday night in the living room in front of the roaring open fire in the cooking range, on which kettles and saucepans were boiling. The youngest of five of us was

93

bathed first in the long tin bath. Then we all got in in turn. The water was not emptied after each one, but topped up as necessary. After we had all gone to bed, it was Mother's and Father's turn, and then the water had to be dipped out and carried away to the outside drain.'

'Bath night at Kingston St Mary meant the copper was filled with water and heated. Then the buckets of hot water would be carried to fill a galvanised bath. For men, though, it was usually a sluice down under the cold water pump!'

'Saturday night was bath night. Three in a bath together and we all had to wash our own socks! The bath was in the scullery and when not in use, a hinged cover came over and it was then used as a table.'

IN SICKNESS AND IN HEALTH

Before the National Health Service was introduced in 1948, calling the doctor out was done only in extremity. Most people doctored themselves and their families, relying upon old home remedies passed down the generations. Sometimes, though, serious illnesses such as typhoid touched a community, and many a child was taken off to the isolation hospital with scarlet fever. There was usually a woman, or women, in the community who could be called upon at times of birth or death, but later the District Nurse came to take over this role, becoming a familiar figure as she cycled on her rounds.

BIRTH AND DEATH

'My grandmother often attended and helped at births in the Coxley area. She had no specific training, but each village had one or two ladies who could be called upon as an unofficial midwife.

Grandmother was also called to lay out the dead. Father had a black suit and a black tie which he kept for funerals. Village men were often called to act as bearers at a funeral. The bell, tolling out from Brent Knoll church, gave news of a death. There were a set number of tolls, more for a man than a woman. Mother would always count when the bell tolled out and then make her announcement.'

'Births in those days usually took place in the home, watched over by local women who attended most of them and gave word when the District Nurse should call. The prospective father was banished until it was all over. Relatives or neighbours would look after any other children until their mother was able to cope. Baby clothes were usually kept and handed down, and in extreme cases there was a parish layette which was in the care of the vicar's wife and loaned out to needy cases.

Death was heralded by the church bell. The bell would toll three times for a man, twice for a woman, and once for a child, followed by one stroke for each year of the person's age.'

HAVING A BABY

'My grandfather was a gardener at the Big House in Dinder. This was the way in which the village people managed the many births of those days. When my grandmother went into labour, the doctor had to be fetched from Wells, so my grandfather set off in a donkey trap. This entailed stopping twice on the way to entice the donkey with a carrot – always at the same spot. It would go on strike until the carrot appeared, then off he would go again, up Tor Hill and over. My grandfather would have five shillings in his pocket, the doctor's fee for a visit outside the surgery. The fee for a visit at the doctor's house would be about two shillings and sixpence. While the doctor took his pony and trap to Dinder, my grandfather would be making sure he still had two carrots left for his own journey home.

Back at the cottage, a neighbour would be making necessary arrangements for anything the doctor might need. This was my grandmother's first child but normally when there were other small children to look after, the neighbours or a grandmother would see to them for two weeks following the new baby's arrival, since all mothers were expected to stay in bed for a fortnight, closely bound up to keep them in good shape. New clothes and presents would arrive and the village would give a big welcome to the newcomer; life in those days was largely confined to home-made pleasures and local work, so each family event was shared by all.'

'Having a baby in the 1940s meant two weeks in a maternity ward, mostly in bed, because movement was said to cause haemorrhage. It was a very happy place, the new parents, the visitors, the staff, everyone was pleased with life except the babies, who howled a good deal. But they were in the nursery except for feeding times, so the new mother had a complete rest. Breast feeding every four hours was the rule, and with two weeks supervision it was usually going well by

95

the time they went home. Babies were not fed between ten o'clock in the evening and six o'clock in the morning. We were told their digestive systems benefited from a rest, but the babies didn't always agree. If they woke, they were changed and laid down again. If this failed, they got a little warm boiled water. We were told "If you feed once, you will have to do it every night". It was the exact opposite of today's feeding on demand, but much easier to cope with.

All nappies were towelling and there were no washing machines. There was a mountain of washing every morning, and we prayed for fine weather. All the domestic helps were doing war work, and electricity did not reach us in Pylle until the 1950s, so there were no helpful gadgets.'

TYPHOID FEVER

'In the village of West Huntspill we had an epidemic of typhoid fever in 1938. Sadly we lost two teenagers and the mother of one of them. The school was closed for a long time.'

'Other than having an infant sister of six weeks die from whooping cough and later on a younger sister sent to Shute Shelf isolation hospital near Axbridge having contracted scarlet fever, the doctor was rarely called to our house.

Tuberculosis or 'consumption' as it was called then, did carry off a few people from time to time.

Not far from my own village of Edithmead a serious outbreak of typhoid fever broke out in the villages of East and West Huntspill and Basonbridge. Many theories were put forward as to the cause of the outbreak and rumours were rife. There were deaths and many villagers taken ill and sent away into isolation.

In the early stages of the disease, my sister who attended Bridg-water Grammar School, had to pass through West Huntspill each day on the bus which took her to Bridgwater. She brought home heart-rending accounts of ambulances waiting outside homes as stretchers carried out the typhoid victims. She saw bundles of bedding and mattresses taken away to be burned.

Soon all public places were closed and my sister was told to stay away from school, passing as she did each day through the infected area.

It took a long while for the disease to run its course and for many months afterwards there were still a few people in isolation being treated as carriers of the typhoid germ.'

HOME REMEDIES

'We must have been a very healthy family because when Dad died aged 85 after 63 years of marrige, the family was still intact; the oldest member being 62 and the youngest 43. I cannot remember any serious illness affecting the children as we grew up before the First World War in Babcary. Most certainly there were no broken limbs, but Mother had the home-made remedies for the usual ailments. As winter approached small squares of camphor in linen bags were sewn into our vests. These were removed each Saturday and sewn into the clean vests. If colds developed we were given a sugar cube on which a few drops of eucalyptus had been sprinkled. Should a cough become troublesome our chests were rubbed with a mixture of camphor and goose grease (from the Christmas goose). Friar's Balsam was used to heal cuts, and an ointment made from vaseline and eucalyptus for grazes and sprains. For a festering wound, a madonna lily leaf, warmed by the fire, was rubbed gently between the hands to extract the juice, and bound over the wound was a definite cure.

Every Friday night we all lined up for a dose of senna tea (otherwise how did Mother know if our bowels were working correctly?). The senna pods were put into a basin and left to infuse for an hour in hot water. For stomach trouble we were given a drink of hot whisky and sugar.

In the spring we lined up each morning for a dose of Health Salts which Mother had made from five ingredients – Epsom salts, bicarbonate of soda, cream of tartar, citric acid and sugar – a lovely fizzy drink. We also had to take, under duress, a teaspoonful of brimstone and treacle to "condition the blood", to be followed later by sulphur tablets.

Visits from the doctor were very rare. His surgery was five miles distant, so somebody had to cycle to contact him (there were no phones) and he would make a belated arrival by horse and trap, or on horseback in fine weather, so he was never summoned unnecessarily. If one of the children happened to be a bit "off colour" Dad would feel the forehead and with a twinkle in his eye would say "I think you must have Lapsy Larvy, or U-per-zooties." I never knew what that meant, but it reassured Mother that there was nothing to worry about.'

'As recently as 1991 in Crowcombe, Mrs Agnes Pike remarked, when someone complained of having a bad chest cold, that they should go and lie down where the musky sheep had lain . . . and she meant it. On the same occasion another old lady said her mother had always told her to breathe deeply when she passed the gasworks to clear her chest, or inhale the fumes from hot tar being spread on the road.'

'Until the National Health Service was introduced, doctors had to be paid so naturally there was much "DIY" doctoring. TB was prevalent and flourished in many of the ill nourished families. Night air was supposed to be bad for you and open windows were definitely dangerous.

I remember my mother talking of a woman whose husband had pneumonia. She got some sheep's lungs from the butcher, and tied them to his feet and this was supposed to be a remedy. He lived, but whether it was the sheep's lungs or not I wouldn't know!'

'The school doctor visited Ruishton once a year, and also a dentist, who terrified everyone. Scarlet fever was dreaded, and the isolation hospital was at Cheddar Road, Taunton. Other childhood illnesses were impetigo, measles, mumps, chickenpox and whooping cough. For measles the patient stayed in a darkened room, and for mumps a woollen scarf was wrapped around the head. Most births were delivered at home by the local midwife or District Nurse. When someone died the coffin was carried to church on a bier, with the mourners walking behind.'

'If my sister and I had a bad cold or chest cold, my mother would rub our chests with camphorated oil and I remember her hands were always very rough. We used to hate it. For colds we had home-made blackcurrant jam put in a cup, hot water poured on and we drank that. At weekends we always had to have brimstone and treacle, that was horrid, or epsom salts. Also for colds we had honey, brown sugar and vinegar to sip.'

'Goose grease was always used for sore throats. Hot tar fumes were considered good for whooping cough, as was a soup made from snails! The milk from dandelions was supposed to make warts disappear.'

'Goose grease for chests, and an old sock (sweaty) wrapped round the throat for a sore throat. A little ball of tar from the road could be swallowed to cure recurring boils (this was a gipsy remedy). Use a blue bag for wasp or bee stings. Two Shapwick recipes for cough medicine went as follows:

¼ lb alum, carefully powdered
½ lb coarse brown sugar
1 quart water to be poured on boiling

Let it stand until cold – bottle and cork well. Dose for a one year old was one teaspoon, for a two year old, two teaspoons.

2 new laid eggs

3 or 4 lemons
¼ lb brown sugar candy
1 oz salad oil
1 pint rum
Put the eggs in a bowl whole. Squeeze the lemon juice onto them. Let them stay about three days turning each day until the shells dissolve. Beat together well and add sugar candy. When dissolved strain, then add rum and oil. Put into dry bottles well corked. Shake well before taking. Dose a half wine-glassful night and morning.'

'We had all the normal childhood complaints as we grew up in the 1940s in Sutton Mallet, ie measles, chickenpox, mumps (we were all put in one bedroom with a lovely coal fire to keep us warm). I remember Mum bringing us a bowl of snow as we couldn't go out (it melted very quickly). Chilblains were our main concern at wintertime. I had them badly every year on hands and feet. Mum would scorch rags and wrap them up. She used a lot of home remedies – onion broth for colds, a small onion in the ear for earache, a clove on the tooth for toothache. Bricks were heated in the oven and then wrapped in blankets when we went to bed and we were given a teaspoonful of syrup of figs at night and a dessertspoonful of cod liver oil and malt in the morning.'

'Clove and whisky was used for toothache. Salt for cleaning teeth. Paraffin for chilblains. Rub on raw beef for warts.'

'We were always a healthy family, living up high in the fresh air on Exmoor, but I can remember my sisters and I suffering from "leg ache" as we called it. We were told it was growing pains, but maybe it was to do with all the cycling we did to and from school. We took it in turns to rub each other's legs with embrocation oil, otherwise known as "horse liniment" – it did the trick.'

SAWDUST ON THE ROAD

'Occasionally at Wiveliscombe in the 1930s, when a person was very ill in a bedroom in the front of the house, sawdust was scattered on the road and pavement outside to deaden the noise of the cart wheels.'

'In my childhood village at the foot of the Blackdown Hills, the older people used to tell how straw or bean haulm was laid along the road in the early 1900s outside the house of someone very ill or dying, to deaden the sound of the passing cartwheels and horses' hooves.'

'Most deaths took place at home and there was a local woman who could "lay them out". Coffins were left in the house, but someone always stayed in the house with it and people were expected to pay their respects to the body. One girl, on visiting her boyfriend of two months, was invited to "see his father". She was not prepared to be shown into the front room where his father was lying in a coffin! Traffic and pedestrians came to a halt when a hearse approached and men doffed their hats as a sign of respect and curtains were drawn in the windows of houses along the route.'

'There was no shop or school in the little village of Ash Priors, but there was an inn, whose landlord sold vegetables and honey from his hives. When his father, who lived with him, died, he went and told the bees. If someone died, the church bell tolled the years of their age, and a small part of the churchyard was reserved for suicides and unbaptised babies.'

THE DISTRICT NURSE

'In my memory of West Hatch there was always a District Nurse resident in the area to help in maternity cases and keep an eye on elderly or ill residents. The local hospital at that time was supported by free contributions and helped a lot by the local gentry. Anyone could, however, belong to a Hospital Scheme for which a family paid twopence a week. There was a local collector and the contributions were recorded on a card. These payments entitled any member of the family to free hospital treatment.'

'Nurse Lloyd was the District Nurse at Sampford Arundel. She was a familiar figure in the area. She used to cycle around the district on an old upright bicycle with her black bag to see her patients. She called on all the mothers-to-be to make sure they had all the necessary items that a new baby would need and would be in attendance at the birth (no maternity home in Wellington until 1926). She was a very strict and stern person but a very efficient nurse and was held in high esteem by all her patients.'

'As a District Nurse I covered an area from Horton Cross to Henlade, from Staple Fitzpaine to Curry Mallet. This covered midwifery (about six babies per year), lots of blanket baths, general nursing, and health visiting. Nursing was often carried out on feather beds!
There were many TB hospitals with open balconies. There was also a fever hospital in Taunton for infectious diseases. A person with a fractured femur was nursed on a Balcon Beam (traction) for about six

months. Hernia patients were kept flat for a week and were in hospital for three weeks. Probationer nurses had to sluice the dirty linen and sort it (on night duty a horrible smelly job). Patients were often woken at three-thirty am to start washing the very sick ones. Ward lights went on at five-thirty am to start washing all the patients. All beds and breakfasts and treatments had to be completed before the day staff came on duty at seven am.'

'There was a District Nurse living in Nynehead, who for years refused to have the telephone installed for fear of too many call-outs to attend a confinement, the majority of babies being delivered at home. Consequently my mother received many requests to deliver a message, often to be grumbled at by the nurse for involving her in a home visit after the completion of her morning rounds. Such visits were made on bicycle as she did not drive.'

'The District Nurse would come round on her bicycle and she attended me in 1949 when my daughter was born at Brent Knoll. We had a marble topped washstand upstairs, with a jug and basin on top, and this basin was used to bath the baby.'

'An urgent call from Doctor in 1933 asked me as District Nurse to meet him next day at a certain farmhouse near Brent Knoll, where he was to amputate a leg as the old chap refused to go to hospital. I arrived early to disinfect the iron bedstead and floor with lysol.

The operation had scarcely begun when the anaesthetist was called to another case. He put the ether bottle in my hand, saying "Keep him under and don't let him swallow his tongue". The doctor was sawing away when he felt his braces slipping – a button had come off – "Help, nurse, I'm losing my trousers" he said. I produced a safety pin and some tape and secured them. While the doctor applied a tourniquet to the patient, I went to the kitchen for hot water, taking a paper parcel which I asked the wife to burn or bury. When the patient's condition had improved the doctor left; I remained on duty until I felt it safe to leave.

When I arrived next morning, the wife said "I've a bone to pick with you. When you gave me that parcel I said to Daisy, for God's sake take this, it's thee granfer's leg; then I went down in a dead faint". On hearing this the old chap said "You ain't burnt 'e or buried 'e? I ain't going to be buried a limb short. Leave it out there and I'll get the undertaker to make I a box for 'e." Well, that's just what happened. A box was made and the limb duly put somewhere in the churchyard.'

DOCTORS AND HOSPITALS

'Seward Payne of Litton Ford recalls a visit to the doctor during the winter of 1904 when he was five years old. His father was ill in bed with a gastric ulcer and was a patient of Dr White of Temple Cloud, who came to visit him on horseback. One particular afternoon, however, his father needed more medicine and so after leaving school in Litton at 4 pm Seward and his sister Mabel, who was a couple of years older, set out to walk to Temple Cloud to collect the medicine for him. It was almost dark as they walked through Hinton Blewett and on through Cameley, finally reaching the doctor's at about 6 pm. It had rained a lot and in one place there was water right across the road, so on reaching the doctor's they sat by the stove in the waiting room to dry out, perched on a trestle stool with their legs dangling above the ground. Their mother, who was to wait for their return at Ford corner in the village, did not see them back until 9 pm.'

'In the early 1900s most General Practitioners were exactly what their title suggested. Our local GP at Castle Cary would set broken bones, do minor operations in the home, deliver the babies and even remove teeth. The anaesthetic was administered by drops of chloroform being dripped onto a pad of cotton wool and held over the patient's nose. My husband recalls having his adenoids removed under these conditions when he was about five years old. He was told to start counting and reckons he counted to nine before he "went under". In 1941 my first child was delivered by the same GP in my own home with the anaesthetic administered in the same way.

There was an isolation hospital at Wincanton and patients suffering from infectious diseases were conveyed there by horse-drawn ambulance. If they stayed at home, a sheet soaked daily in carbolic acid had to be hung over the bedroom door.'

'During the Second World War I lived in Somerset and was a patient in Ham Green Hospital which was then a Sanitorium, and treatment for most patients was fresh air and rest. During the time I was there, several air raids took place. I remember the sky was ablaze like millions of fireworks. In the morning we heard Bristol had been bombed and the city razed to the ground.

My first breakfast was a lump of something brown looking which I was informed was a fish cake. I had never before had one and was a bit wary but it turned out to be quite nice. We did nothing all day except read, embroider or sleep. Sometimes we were allowed out for a walk. Considering the circumstances the food was quite good, we had rabbit stew once a week, shot or trapped by the orderlies. We had to drink a pint of milk a day plus milk puddings.'

One night we had an air raid when a bomb was dropped which didn't go off and we were moved in the middle of the night to a vacant ward. Looking back I suppose I was not concerned about the war. It was going on but I was not involved.'

'One of the evacuees who came to us in the 1940s was a carrier of diptheria and we all three had to go to the isolation hospital at Cheddon Road in Taunton. When we were well enough part of the treatment was to walk around the grounds. It was midwinter and I well remember the TB patients waving to us as we went by, looking out from their chalets with the stable doors open to the elements in the belief that the fresh air could cure them.'

'My mother used to pay sixpence a week to the hospital in case any of us needed treatment. The hospital at East Reach, Taunton carried the legend "Supported by free contributions", which is still carved in the stonework although it is now an office block.'

FOOD AND DRINK

Most people were fairly self sufficient in their way of life until after the Second World War. Vegetables and fruit came from the garden or allotment, many women made butter, cream and cheese from the milk from their own cows, hens provided fresh eggs, and a pig was often kept for the future provision of bacon and pork. Home made wines and, especially, cider made a welcome addition to the diet.

SELF SUFFICIENCY

'Looking back, I suppose our family (like most village families) was quite self sufficient. We lived at North Cadbury, in a house with a large garden and orchard. Our grandparents living nearby had an equally large garden and rented two fields. We kept poultry and one year a couple of very unfriendly geese. Grandad also kept hens and ducks and it was usually my job after school to feed the poultry and collect the eggs. There were sheep in the orchard and we helped at lambing. At one time a pig was kept in the back garden, fed on kitchen waste. During the Second World War each family was only allowed to keep half the pig, which was slaughtered at Wincanton. The other half went to the war effort. I have a lasting memory of my Gran cleaning bowls of disgusting-looking pigs intestines – known locally as chidlings.

The orchard provided a good crop of apples; some were made into cider and some were for eating. Camelot and Bramley for cooking and Morgan Sweet and Beauty of Bath for dessert.

The garden was full of vegetables and fruit of all varieties, and we always had a row of potatoes in the fields. All the farmworkers had a row too and all helped each other harvest the crop. It was also common to see marrows growing on the manure heaps all over the farm, and everyone knew whose was whose.

All these crops would be stored and bottled, jams and jellies made, eggs stored in isinglass, and any surplus sold or given to neighbours who would return the compliment. And of course there was the bounty of the hedgerow and field. Blackberries (some of which were sold for dye making), also mushrooms and nuts.'

'Many people in the country in the 1920s were very poor but they managed to live and bring up large families. They had milk, usually because the man worked for a farmer, some poultry scratching around an orchard, and a pig at the bottom of the garden. At Bickenhall we could see the cottagers hoeing round their peas and beans in the evenings; they would salt the beans down for the winter. People cooked on their ranges and there would be milk "scalding" on the top to make cream. Later some new oil stoves came in, "Florence" or "Beatrice" they were called. They were quicker than cooking on the range but they made a mess of the ceiling.

During the war my mother made 300 lbs of blackberry and apple jam on an oil stove.'

FROM THE BAKEHOUSE

'There are nostalgic memories of the appetising aromas which pervaded the length and breadth of Church Street, Wiveliscombe on Sunday mornings. This was the day when the Sunday joint could be cooked at Barrington's the bakers, for the princely sum of fourpence. By all accounts, this was an extremely popular feature with the many housewives who had to rely on a coal-fired oven. Visual images can readily be invoked of the crisply cooked joints being collected, and rapidly rushed home to the eagerly awaiting families.

Equally well remembered is the house in Church Street where superb home-made faggots were cooked and sold. Jugs and basins

104

were taken in which to collect them, and if as many as seven faggots were purchased at a cost of sixpence, the accompanying peas were given free of charge.'

'In what is now the car park of the Walnut Tree Restaurant in West Camel, stood for many years the Old Bakery, where the children used to come with their china basins to collect the steaming faggots and peas which was their speciality over 50 years ago.'

'As we were a large family (13 altogether, twelve survived), Mother usually sent a large bowl of potatoes down to the baker in Bickenhall for baking – I think this was usually twice a week but always on Sundays. She also purchased dough from the baker and made superb and very large dough cakes, these were cooked at the bakehouse and the baker used to charge a penny or tuppence.'

COOKING AT HOME

'Growing up before the First World War we were always well fed, but not by today's standards. Babies fed on their mother's milk as long as possible and then (in our family) progressed to a food made by Dad (who was a baker and confectioner) which was a kind of rusk made from white flour, yeast, sugar and milk and cooked slowly until dry and crisp. One or two beaten up in warm milk made an acceptable meal for a baby.

The older children would have a breakfast of fried bacon (from the home cured pig), fried bread or muffins, which were the uncooked bread dough made into small flat cakes and fried in the bacon fat until brown and crisp (delicious – I can taste one now).

The midday meal would be light as Dad would be out on his bread round. There would be bread, butter, cheese and pickles (pickled onions, walnuts, plums and mixed pickles), cake or bread pudding and cocoa.

The main meal would be a roast joint of meat, or some kind of stew with suet dumplings, tripe and onions cooked in milk, hot boiled ham with parsley sauce, home-made faggots and always lots of vegetables. This would be followed with fruit pie in season, suet pudding with golden syrup, boiled apple dumplings or rice pudding. Later in the evening there would be a supper of cold ham or cheese and salad with home made cider.

We were not encouraged to express likes and dislikes but to eat what was given to us. The meals were served in the large kitchen-cum-dining room, and we all sat quiet and still while Mother and Dad put food on our plates, then the youngest child would say grace and we began our meal. My place was next to Dad, and he used to give me tit-bits from his plate because I was never a good eater. These bits seemed nicer than those on my own plate!'

'We lived in a small rented farm at Clewer, all five of us. Every day Mother cooked over the open fire in the kitchen. The meal was always ready for six o'clock when Father got home. A joint of meat or a chicken was cooked in a dutch oven with roast potatoes, the vegetables in a saucepan beside them. There was a bread oven in the kitchen and every Friday was baking day.

Mother made her dough in a large earthenware pan and put it to rise by the fire. The oven was in the kitchen wall and we used dry sticks and turf (ie burning peat) to fire it. By the time the oven was hot, Mother had made pastry and cakes besides getting the bread ready for the oven. Mother then cleaned out all the sticks, turf and ashes and after that she put in a milk pudding, fruit or apples to be baked.

In the morning we always had a fried breakfast cooked over the fire. Mother was a good cook, and also used to make wine – elderberry, parsnip, blackberry, rhubarb and mangold. Before she was married Mother was cook at the Manor House near the church in Wedmore. My favourite meal was tripe and onions. Delicious.'

'There was no gas or electricity in Coxley, so cooking was done on the kitchen range or on a paraffin cooker. The kitchen range had an oven which would cook milk puddings to perfection. It also baked apples. A large trivet would be slung over the open fire to boil saucepans or kettles. The paraffin cooker was a temperamental piece of equipment. It consisted of a large oven which fitted over two or three burners. The burners themselves needed constant attention and trimming of wicks. Unexpected draughts would cause the flame to burn unevenly and rise high and smoke. The kitchen and house could soon be full of black smuts and soot. This often meant the washing of all curtains and fabrics and complete redecoration. It was most wise to keep an eagle eye on the burners at all times.'

'Father would light the open fire with half a faggot of wood and the cast iron kettle hanging on the handymaid on the backcrook would soon boil to make the morning tea. The backcrooks held a boiler, and a crock, which Mother used to bake cakes in – she would put coals on the lid to brown them. She used the open fire to fry breakfast and boil vegetables. When killing a pig a 27 gallon cauldron was used to heat water. Grandmother had an oven under her open fire and a drawer where coals were put in. As a child I enjoyed her cakes made in this oven in a meat tin.'

'Before the advent of the coal range, all cooking was done on an open fire. The pots and kettles hung on fire dogs over flames, the meat was roasted in front of the fire by means of a "Dutch oven". This contraption had a top and three sides, the meat was skewered and turned frequently, and a tray caught the juices with which it was basted – a very hot job. Cakes were made on a griddle placed on the red hot embers.

These were country practices in lots of villages up to the end of the Second World War. Large towns had gas before the First World War, but many country districts waited until after the Second World War to have electricity brought to them.'

'The first job every morning was to clean out and black the range and then light it. Breakfast was about eight o'clock; eggs and bacon, fried bread and potatoes. There was another cooked meal at half past twelve, meat and vegetables and maybe a pudding. Tea was at four, before milking – bread, butter, cake and tea, and supper at half past seven with bread and cheese or ham and salad.'

BACON, CHEESE AND BUTTER

'We had an orchard at our cottage in Goathurst and Mum used to keep fowls and we had our own eggs and sometimes we had a pig. I remember once we had a pig and we had it killed on the premises. Frightened us to death. We should never have done it, it was too much really. There was no fridges in those days, Mum used to salt it down. But it didn't keep so much in those days so she used to give a lot away. Really a waste of it. We used to keep the bacon up in the attic, salted.'

'With large gardens most villagers at Nynehead were self sufficient, growing their own fruit and vegetables, rearing chickens and a pig or two. The latter would be killed by a local butcher who was usually willing to buy half the animal with the remainder returned for "salting down". It was usually possible to buy a rabbit for about sixpence, recovering twopence for the skin when the rag and bone man called!'

'The meat safe was kept hanging on the coolest outside wall of the house. Half sides of pigs were hung up in an outbuilding, wrapped in butter muslin, rashers and joints being cut as required.'

107

'In the days before the Milk Marketing Board, my grandmother, Mercy Barnes, who was an excellent cheesemaker, made cheese from most of the milk at Walton Farm. This was sold for the princely sum of sixpence a pound. Butter was also made in a lovely old butter churn, which I well remember, and which was also used to make fairly small quantities when I was young. My grandfather used to buy his gin by the gallon in stone jars from the wine vaults in Glastonbury.'

'During our time at the farm at Combe Florey in the 1950s we had our groceries, meat and bread delivered. The grocer would call and sit down and have a cup of tea while he took our order. Two days later the items would be brought. The baker used to come three times a week, generally about eight or nine o'clock in the evening. He would bake the bread early in the morning and then go on his rounds. Even in snow he never failed to get through. When we first went to the farm we kept a pig and had it killed. The wife of the man who worked for us used to come and help me salt it down and put it in the big wooden pig salter. Every Saturday I used to make clotted cream for the man and his wife.'

TEA ON SUNDAYS ONLY

'In the Henton area, many of the older cottagers only drank tea at Sunday teatime. The remainder of the week they relied on the 36 gallon cider barrel "hossed up" in a convenient backhouse or outhouse.'

PARSNIP WINE

'We made our own cider from apples grown in the orchard at Coxley. Gran made parsnip wine. This was very potent and looked and tasted like whisky.'

TRADERS TO THE DOOR

If you could not grow it or make it yourself, there was always a trader who would bring goods direct to your door. The decline in the custom of "calling" is perhaps one of the greatest losses suffered by those in village communities.

THE BUTCHER, THE BAKER . . .

'Rings were provided on the side wall of the pub in South Cadbury for the many visiting tradespeople to tie up their horses, and they included a covered wagon with furniture in it. The coalman sold blocks of salt for twopence a block.'

'The butcher from Burnham on Sea visited us weekly with his high, horse-drawn cart. The baker called every day in his motor van. We also had a "cakeman" call on a bike. He sold all kinds of sticky buns and small cakes which he carried on a large front carrier covered with a cloth. Occasionally we had a boot and shoe-lace seller. He walked.

A family who sold paraffin came each Saturday to replenish our supply. The motor van housed a tank full of paraffin which was drawn at the back by a tap. We put out our two gallon can each week for a refill.

When wirelesses became popular we had a man call each week to replace our rundown accumulator for a recharged one.

Gipsies also called with clothes pegs. They helped themselves to withies to make the pegs.'

'A baker called three times a week to our home in Staple Fitzpaine, and the butcher came twice a week. The man from County Stores called on a Monday to take the order for groceries which were delivered the following Friday. This was quite a social event with a piece of cake and a cup of tea – one wonders how the poor man managed this at every house!'

'At West Hatch between the two world wars, there was a small village shop which sold groceries etc, and bread was delivered by a horse-drawn cart from the bakery at Curland. Messrs Paul and Hooper (later North Stores of Taunton) delivered groceries every Monday, orders having been taken by an "outrider" as he was called, either on

Before the advent of the motor car, tradesmen made their calls by pony and trap along the quiet narrow lanes of Somerset.

a bicycle or later a motor bike, on the previous Thursday.

Coal was delivered but we usually fetched ours with the horse and cart either from Hatch Beauchamp or Thornfalcon station where G. Small & Sons had a coal depot. Paraffin for lamps and heaters was also delivered regularly each week or fortnight according to the time of year. There was no electricity at that time, although a few of the "richer" people made their own with a small petrol engine, the power being stored in batteries.'

THE TAILOR

'Once a year before the First World War, a tailor (Mr Coggin) from Somerton came to our house to measure Dad and the boys for new suits. Mother made most of the girls' clothes, and garments would be handed down from the older members of the family to the younger ones.'

'During the 1930s my father always wore 'britches' (pronounced this way) of a fine beige ribbed material, and polished brown boots and leggings to market. He would go to Farrington Gurney on Mondays and Frome on Wednesdays. He always wore tailor-made clothes and the tailor used to call.'

THE RAG AND BONE MAN

'Sammy Taylor is remembered for the sporadic visits he made from Washford to Wiveliscombe in the 1930s in his horse and cart. He travelled round the houses collecting rags and bones, and also sold items of crockery and ironmongery, which even included patches for saucepans with holes. As he went round children would be waiting at strategic intervals with galvanised buckets and spades, in the hope of collecting horse manure left in his trail.'

SIKHS, BUTTONS AND FRENCH ONION SELLERS

'At Keinton Mandeville a man from the Co-op called on Tuesdays for orders, which were delivered on Friday. In the 1930s several people came, selling articles from suitcases. One such man always came on a Tuesday and we called him the Tuesday Man. Another was a Sikh, wearing a turban. Gipsies came regularly, selling pegs and paper flowers.'

'Milk was delivered to Saltford by pony and cart in the early 1930s – it was in large churns and dipped out into customers' jugs. There was the hardware journeyman, Mr Carter from Keynsham, with his horse and cart and the pots and pans jangling and the smell of paraffin and wax, the scissor grinder on his bicycle, and the Frenchman with his onions strung from the handlebars of his bicycle.'

'During the Second World War two ladies came to the door in the Nynehead area selling buttons etc from a suitcase. They were excused war service because one had poor sight, but I remember people commenting on the fact that she could spot small aircraft in the sky. Obviously she was very long sighted!'

111

POP GEORGE AND THE ICE CREAM MAN

'A weekly treat at Pilton was the appearance of a character known as Pop George, who came from Shepton with a box on wheels to sell sweets in the village – gobstoppers that changed colour and striped humbugs were the favourites.'

'The butcher, baker, greengrocer and coalman always called with their goods in mostly horse-drawn vehicles at Bickenhall in the 1930s. The Walls ice cream man came with his stop-me-and-buy-one bike, and the dairy ice cream man used a pony and trap.'

THE TRAVELLING BAZAAR

'A colourful and useful caller was the travelling bazaar – a lorry which sold paraffin from a central tank with shelves around some eight feet high, stacked with crockery of all types nestling in straw, from a chamberpot to a cup. There were saucepans, tin baths, brushes, mops, cleaning materials, garden tools, rabbit nets, snares, cartridges, small oil stoves and wicks, and all forms of chick feeders and drinkers. The driver would purchase rabbit skins and moleskins from his customers en route.'

CATCHING THE HORSES

'Before the days of supermarkets and public shopping by car, the country traders at Dunster delivered to their customers within about a twelve mile radius, by horse and trap or by wagonette. It was the job of the sons of the baker, butcher and grocer to catch the horses before they went to school so that the animals could be fed and harnessed early. My husband was one of these boys, and one day refused to catch his horse as he had seen it being ill treated by the van driver. No one else could catch it, and it galloped off up the hill. His father had to hire a horse for the rest of the week. The next Saturday he had to climb up the hill to try to find the horse, which came to his call and stood for him to mount. The hunt was out that day and young Jack enjoyed a bareback ride with them.'

USING EVERYTHING

'At Shapwick, soot from sweeping the chimney was kept weathered (kept outside for a few weeks), then dug into the garden. People tried to beat each other with a bucket and spade for horse manure on the road.'

112

PRICES IN 1935

'When mother and father-in-law got married at Kingston St Mary
there was 30 shillings a week for housekeeping –
   Coal was one shilling and elevenpence a hundredweight.
   Turfs for the fire were one shilling for 14.
   Cigarettes (Woodbines) were threepence for ten.
   Players Cigarettes were sixpence for ten.
   Players Digger Tobacco was sevenpence ha'penny an ounce.
   Milk was a penny a pint, but they had it free from the farm.
   Sugar was threepence ha'penny for two pounds.
   Meat was twopence for a pound.
   Beer was threepence a pint.
   New cider was a penny a pint, old cider a penny ha'penny a pint.'

SHOPPING IN THE 1940s

'Although it was wartime we were served very well in our village
three miles from Wells. Mother did not have to struggle home from
the supermarket with plastic bags!

There was a post office which also carried sweets and very limited
supplies of general groceries. Milk and eggs we collected from a
neighbouring farm. Milk was also delivered by two sisters who
carried several jugs in each hand for some considerable distance.
Customers' jugs were charged much as milk bottles today.

At least two bakers from Wells delivered lovely cottage loaves, also
tin loaves which my grandmother called a quartern. Only occasionally did our baker bring cake, which was in a slab. Cakes were almost
always home-made. Cordials, lemonade, stout etc came from Shepton Mallet in tall bottles in a four-section wooden crate. The company
who delivered these became very famous for a product called
Babycham.

A really wonderful hardware dealer came from Glastonbury. He
carried paraffin for cookers and oil lamps, candles, crockery, soap,
soda, saucepans and a thousand and one household items. His van
was quite large and had a flat top with a small rail around, and this
carried the buckets and bins, galvanised of course. The sides had
several roll-blinds made of tarpaulin material which he put down in
bad weather. Smaller items were carried in pigeon holes or hung on
hooks all round two sides. The paraffin was at the rear.'

'The grocery delivery was the most exciting as there was always a
chance of finding a little extra which was not rationed. Every Monday
"the traveller" came and sat in the kitchen, with a cup of tea, and

wrote out Mother's order in his book. Then on Wednesday it was delivered in quite a large old van. The groceries were, of course, the good old-fashioned sort. Loose biscuits weighed up into a thin white bag; sugar in strong blue bags; cheese in grease-proof paper; absolutely super dried fruits; 'Diadem' flour; Oxo cubes in lovely red tins (very handy for our child's treasures). Although, as I say, most of the items were not pre-packed, I cannot remember Mother ever complaining about breakages.'

CHILDHOOD &
SCHOOLDAYS

CHILDHOOD DAYS

Life could be hard, but childhood memories capture the pleasures of country life, the freedom to wander and to play and the easy familiarity children once felt with the natural world around them. Most children were expected to help around the house or on the farm, perhaps milking the cows before school in the morning, or pumping water and collecting firewood. Games were simple and time-honoured – marbles, hopscotch, hoops and spinning tops, and sweets were a real treat, to be savoured and remembered to this day.

COUNTRY LIFE

'Home was a delightful old country house at Babcary, with large rooms and windows overlooking a field through which a stream lazily meandered and was a great source of pleasure. I was the tenth child of eleven (four boys, seven girls), born in 1900. We had kind, loving parents and, although so hard pressed with business, they would always listen and help with understanding. I remember Dad saying "Our family of children is the best investment we have made" and I hope I grew up worthy of his statement.

I realise how very fortunate we were to have lived in the country where there are so many pleasant things to occupy our time. There were pet lambs to be fed, wild flowers to gather, and fishing in the brook as we paddled and picked the lovely golden water lilies and forget-me-nots, and caught fresh water oysters with a pointed stick.

The days always seemed to be warm and sunny and most of the time during the August holiday from school was spent out of doors. In autumn we gathered blackberries from nearby woods where huge ones grew and ripened. From these Mother made jam and pies. We also searched the hedges for sloes, the fruit of the blackthorn, from which sloe gin was made and bottled to mature in readiness for Christmas.

We all had our regular jobs to do after school; cleaning boots ready for the next moring, getting and chopping sticks for firelighting, filling the copper (an iron boiler that provided hot water). The girls lay the table in preparation for tea, and washed the dishes after. Then we could go out to play.

In the summer months we played outside mostly by the river Cary, a tributary of the river Parrett. It was very exciting to fish for minnows and fresh oysters. We sat on the old wooden bridge and sang rhymes to the games we played.

Dad bought us an old bike which we had to share and learn to ride. This we did in the orchard where there was a sloping patch of ground. We got on and careered down this slope until we had learned to balance; if we fell off it it was just too bad, we got up and had another go!

There was a lovely may tree in the garden under which was a long seat and a table. Here many activities took place – knitting, crochet, sewing, reading, writing etc. We learned to knit on wooden meat skewers. What happy hours we spent there.

During the winter evenings we made scrap-books, played card games and sang songs round the piano. Dad got concert parties together for adult entertainment but we were expected to contribute an item. Bessie and Nellie sang duets – Nellie treble, Bessie alto. They had very nice voices and were well appreciated on the night of the concert. They were then about twelve years old. My first contribution was the bass section of a piano duet played with my teacher. I was then seven years old, and so very excited to be in the programme.

We did not get a lot of sweets. Mother used to buy mixed ones which were home-made at a small shop and cost threepence for half a pound. These were put into a tin and we could each choose one before setting out for school, and one at bedtime. If we were lucky enough to have a penny we never spent it all at once. Lovely things could be bought for even a farthing – liquorice "boot-laces", sherbet bags, nutty toffee, acid drops etc.

We did not get regular pocket money (there were too many of us). Sometimes visitors gave us pennies which we were encouraged to save in our money boxes to spend on our annual day's outing to the sea. Dad did not like us to take money from people who asked us to do small jobs – shopping or posting letters etc. He encouraged us to do this as a kindness.

Books were very difficult to obtain in the country districts and those of us who enjoyed reading could never get enough. We usually had some given to us on our birthdays and at Christmas and how jealously we cared for them! They were only lent to our closest friends and even then the following verses would be inscribed:

Steal not this book for fear of shame
For in it lies the owner's name.
If you do, God will say
"Where's that book you stole away?"
If you say "I do not know"
God will cast you down below.

117

We always went to bed early; six o'clock in the winter and seven in the summer because Dad always insisted on Mother having a quiet relaxed evening. What fun we had as we went to bed! Sometimes getting a mattress which was about a foot thick with feathers – so lovely and soft and warm – onto the floor to sleep there for a change. We once took a sheet from a bed and secured it over the four huge mahogany bedknobs with our elastic garters to make a tent. This was fine until someone decided to climb on top, when the sheet split down the middle. Sometimes we decided to sleep four in one bed, two at top and bottom; not very comfortable but nice for a change.'

'In the early 1930s at Saltford I remember fields – no fertilisers other than farmyard manure – full of wildflowers, cowslips, orchids, and under the hedges primroses and violets. Ragged robin and bluebells in the woods. Dewponds which have long since been filled in, containing frogspawn and tadpoles; a child's delight with a jamjar.

Meadows yellow with buttercups being mown for hay using horse-drawn implements, manual turning and raking. The hay being made into ricks, then thatched and in the following winter cut with a large hay knife for feeding to the animals.

Corn being cut in the late summer with a binder that spewed out the sheaves. They were then stuck up manually, collected and ricked. Many a good meal was made from the rabbits which ran out of the corn and were killed by the helpers. Later the sheaves were fed into the threshing machine and a whole gang of men employed to bag the corn and stack the straw. It was a sporting time for the terriers which killed the rats as they ran from the ricks.

There was ice skating on a field which was flooded each winter at Sheppards Boat House on the river Avon, and eating chestnuts round the huge bonfire which was built in the corner of the field. And I remember the flickering of the flames of a real fire in the bedroom of a sick child. No electricity, just gas which at times guttered in the mantle, but plenty of coal from the North Somerset mines. We played with tops which could be started in the grass verge of the road – no need to worry about traffic. One could even mark out hopscotch grids safely and play with hoops. And there were picnics by the river Avon, walking the mile and a half to sit on the river bank, picnic and watch the rowing eights of Clifton College.'

'Growing up in the early 1930s at Merriot was wonderful. We walked through the cornfields in the centre to school. In three places round the village were dumb-bars (two iron posts set apart) to keep cattle and horses either in or out of the fields. Two lots of the dumb-bars are still there, but the centre fields have been filled with housing now.

118

The Pebbles, huge stones I've not seen anywhere else, were also part of life. One outside the school was a landmark for various happenings. One was the day the man would come with gifts to exchange for rags "by the Pebble". We would take our jamjars and rags to school and exchange the rags for a goldfish. My brother got into trouble once when he took Father's two best shirts, but he got a lovely goldfish.

The other Pebble, in a corner of the mill-stream, was where every boy and girl for generations took their jars on string to catch minnows. If you were lucky you caught a "bidde-head". The first Pebble is still beside the school, but the second has sadly been removed. Other Pebbles, not so large, are to be found around the village. They are thought to be old siting stones used by ancient travellers.

I remember playing at the recreation field and being told to "be home by the time of the Motor Mail". We played in summer evenings until the sound of the big Motor Mail at eight o'clock chugging up the hill. Then there would be an exit of children. Going down the hill we would notice the canary cages being brought in for the night. The sound of the Motor Mail would have been the only motor around at that time. Now we hear motors all day and at night.'

'My parents were strict but loving and kind. Money was scarce, but our house near Dunkery Beacon was full of fun and happiness. In winter, homework was done around the table with an Aladdin oil lamp in the middle. As we grew older we were expected to help on the farm or indoors to the best of our ability. I remember leading the cart horse pulling a load of hay when I could barely reach the horse's head. What fun the picnics in the hay field – cakes, cream buns, milk from the cow and always home made butter, brought to the field by my mother or grandmother. There were also picnics by the river which was the boundary of two farms, and riding on branches precariously hanging over the water. My mother fell in one day, when handing over the picnic basket, but not to worry, she just stripped down and hung her clothes on the bushes to dry.

I learned to milk the cow at about eight years old. Sitting on a three-legged stool, I soon learned not to pinch her teats! As I grew older I learned to drive the tractor, and I really enjoyed going off for a day's ploughing or chain harrowing or rolling. The tractors then had iron spiked wheels and iron seats on which to sit. My father looked after sheep mainly and every morning he would mount his pony and with his dog and his shepherd's bag on his back, he would be gone all morning. One of my great pleasures was to ride over the fields and moors, to watch the deer and fox cubs at play.'

119

'Seventy years in the same road at Cheddar brings many changes. Gone the piles of sand, the smell of hot tar and the very big steam roller with friendly driver. We could play top and whip, hopscotch, hoops, tennis and football, there was only the occasional car then. Deliveries of milk, bread, coal and turf for the fire came by horse and cart.

What fun it was to watch the steam waggon from the lime quarry suck up water from the brook on its way to the station; to hear the toot of a train whistle and see the primrose covered banks in spring-time just a field away; and to listen to the owl hooting in the barn next door where Nippy our cat always had her kittens. The orchard was full of blossom and how we loved the apples when they came, not forgetting the tummy aches when green. This was also a home for baby chicks and turkeys. On hot summer days, there was a little round house on top of a nearby hill where we could roam freely and have picnics.

We had three weeks holiday in June for strawberry picking and two weeks in September for blackberries, and there always was snow at Christmas.'

'Dark blue violets nestling in their bed of leaves within the long garden wall surrounding my grandmother's house in Bawdrip. Con-stant cawing of rooks in the tall elms across the road. Pale primroses in Loxley Woods, picked and bunched and tied with wool in neat bows and lodged in moss upon the sills in the little stone church at Easter. Daisy chains, cowslips and milkmaids to pick in the small paddock where her pony grazed. Jack-in-the-pulpits, pale green lilies in their spade-like leaves on the verges as we toiled up the lane to the ruins on the top of the hill for our picnics.

Helping to water the cascading fuchsias and geraniums on the high staging in the conservatory on summer evenings, using water from the well. Brown and gold fist-like calceolarias, pots of lilies and carnations saturating the air with their heady perfume.

August holidays, long days playing croquet with my brother and cousins; pausing only to munch the windfall Beauty of Bath apples – pink and juicy – pouncing before the fat wasps gorged themselves.

Lying in grandmother's great feather bed, afraid to move for fear of kicking her varicose vein, listening to the corncrake calling in the night air, and wishing he would go away as his cries were believed to foretell of a death in the village.

Helping to harness the pony to the governess cart and then clip-clopping off to Bridgwater on market day. How I longed for it to rain so that I could hold up the large umbrella which was normally kept rolled up in the basket-work sleeve on the trap.

Crunchy stockings hanging on the bed posts on Christmas morning. Slipping and sliding down the lane, past the icy duck pond and stopping to throw pebbles, on our way to the tiny 13th century church, with its association with the "Mistletoe Bough" legend. Returning to enjoy Christmas dinner, roast goose or turkey, flaming plum pudding, mince pies and crackers, the table decorated with the first Christmas roses. Waiting patiently for my grandmother to produce the key to the drawing room from her petticoat pocket under her long black skirt. Crowding into the room with gasps of delight at the candle-lit, present-festooned tree which reached to the ceiling. Excitement subdued and all sitting quietly to hear the knock at the door; why, oh why, did it take me so long to realise that this Father Christmas was my Uncle Edward?

Boxing Day away to Pawlett to spend the day with another seven cousins. Hide and seek in the old farmhouse – dark passages and many places to hide; games in the stone-flagged kitchen – Turn the Trencher, Postman's Knock and Charades, whilst the grown ups played cards in the drawing room.

Church on Sundays, nine children sitting on wooden benches in the box pews. Small boots clattered and banged as we wriggled and whispered – "Sh-sh-sh-sh" was the constant admonition.

Occasional visits to the seaside at Burnham, where another cousin lived. Access to the beach was forbidden, as it was not considered to be the place for young ladies, so time was spent in Manor Gardens.'

GAMES, TREATS AND SWEETS

'In the 1920s life was hard and in some respects the hard times have made my recollections of happy times seem more poignant. The simplest of little things were so much enjoyed then.

For instance, the highlight of my week was when my father would stroll across to the village shop at Stratton on the Fosse. There he bought a half ounce of tobacco (Golden Virginia) for his pipe, a quarter pound of pink and white striped sweets called "Shrimps" for mother, two one penny bars of chocolate for my sisters – Joy aged three and Eileen aged five – and for me, a tuppenny Fry's Cream Bar, for I was then a big girl of ten. This lasted me all week, unless Eileen found it – she was the "sweet tooth".

I remember other sweet-treats too. Every year, just before Christmas, Mrs Smith who owned the village shop in South Street, would prepare the window before "trimming-up", taking out all the "goodies" on display. As she worked, she placed in one box bits and pieces of broken sweets. In another box she placed black jacks, chocolate dragees, gob stoppers, sherbert dabs, aniseed balls, tiger nuts, locust beans and liquorice sticks! Can you imagine the picture she had of several woolly hatted faces peering in at her as she worked? Eventually, one of us was beckoned into the shop where Mrs Smith handed over one of the boxes. We lovingly held the box between us until we reached the light of the paraffin lamp, opposite Penny's Pub, properly named The King's Arms. Like pirates with our swag we eagerly shared out between us the sticky broken sweets.

I also remember early Saturday mornings, helping to dust and mop out the bedrooms of our cottage. I had to do the same at my grandmother's cottage too, for her sight was bad. Later in the morning sister Eileen and I were sent off by mother to purchase groceries from the Co-operative Store in Chilcompton. We usually took a short-cut across the fields which shortened the journey by at least a mile. But should there be a bull in the field, we were too terrified to cross and so, reluctantly, we had to walk the alterntive lane-ways route instead. If all was correct with the groceries when we arrived home, I would sometimes be rewarded. A halfpenny piece was appreciatively pressed into my day-work-worn hand. This, more often than not, I spent on aniseed balls which, of course, I generously shared with my sister.'

'When I was a child at Templecombe in the 1920s, my mother would sometimes give me a halfpenny to fetch from the grocery shop a bag of broken biscuits. The friendly grocer would fill the bag right to the top, always remarking that if I ate a few on the way home then I could close the bag as he did.'

'In the winter we used to have our hoops and because there wasn't the traffic in the 1920s, we used to play them to school. And we played horses – made the reins, one was the horse and then the other one used to drive them with a whip and we would run on to school like that.

In the spring we picked flowers (because we were allowed to then) along the grass verges and took them home to Mother; violets and

122

primroses – they were beautiful!'

'I was born and brought up at Bayford alongside the then main road London to Cornwall, later the A303 and now bypassed.

The road was our playground – a car was a curiosity being a rarity, horse and cart was the usual mode of transport. We played hopscotch in the road, chalking out our squares and circles, then perhaps a ball or skipping rope craze would take over. Wooden tops brightly coloured with chalks were set spinning from one end of the village to the other with a piece of fine string tied to a stick. Then we had our hoops, wooden or iron, bowled along with a stick or crook.

On a moonlit night we played hide and seek, chanting "Moonlight, starlight, bogey won't be out tonight".

We played in the fields and copses without fear of being molested and we built dens with fallen branches and twigs. In the summer it was hay houses – no bales then.

Then gradually came the cars and we lost our playground. But we did enjoy our Sunday school trips to the seaside in a charabanc, perching on our seat behind the perspex and when it rained over came the hood to much merriment.'

'In and out of school, the council infants school at Burnham-on-Sea, our games consisted of marbles, hoops, spinning tops and skipping (singly or in groups). We played Creepmouse, Stealing Apples, What's The Time Mr Wolf, and hopscotch.

An enterprising parent, perhaps with problems of torn or pulled out-of-shape skirts and jerseys, had knitted many pairs of reins for the children's playtime. Kept in a large cardboard box, they came in all colours and had two holes for arms across the breast piece. We selected our colours and harnessed up teams of horses to parade and prance around the playground.'

'Games used to go in fads when I was a child in Wells in the 1950s. Skipping would be popular for weeks on end, then suddenly it would be replaced by hopscotch or marbles. Hopscotch was usually chalked on the road and a flat stone (a chipper) was used to throw. Skipping was usually accompanied by a rhyme sung aloud, eg "All in together girls, this fine weather girls, when is your birthday please run in (or out), January, February, March . . ." Dolls and prams were very popular. "Mothers and Fathers" was the "in" thing and we used to take the dolls for long walks. Endless hours would be spent with a magazine, a scrapbook, a pair of scissors and some flour paste. I remember once playing "hairdressers" with my friend. Luckily she cut my hair and not her own lovely long hair in ringlets. I had to wear a hat for weeks afterwards to cover the results. In the autumn games with conkers were extremely popular. Holes for string were made with a meat skewer. In later years bicycles, home-made carts and roller skates became fashionable.'

'Parties were always held for birthdays and the food was nearly always the same – pink blancmange, red jelly, egg sandwiches, fancy cakes and a chocolate birthday cake with icing and candles.'

'Before the age of sophisticated games, a ball and a wall were all we needed. The routine for South Petherton children involved a complicated ritual of groups of ten ever more difficult sequences.

As I remember it from the 1940s, "plainsy" came first, throwing the ball against the wall and catching it, chanting "onesy", "twosy" up to "tensy". "Leftsy" was the same with the left hand. In "backsy" you threw round the back and the left hand variant followed. In one set the ball was bounced under the lifted leg, in another the ball was patted against the wall before catching, first once then on up to "tensy" and repeated with the left hand. "Clapsy" sandwiched one or more claps between the catching.

Of course, if you dropped it, the next had a turn, and when it came back to you, you started from the beginning again. It must have been a fidgety noise for Mother indoors!

The spin-off was that we all achieved a degree of ambidexterity and

Coxley school pupils perform the Rose Dance in 1920.

considerable co-ordination of hand and eye. Could it be that we were better fitted for an active life than our descendants playing their computer games?'

'When I was growing up at Sutton Mallet in the 1930s pocket money was non-existent but we did pick many pounds of blackberries, which were collected, and the money we earned from them we spent at Bridgwater Fair every September, a real red letter day. We didn't have family holidays but we did spend two weeks of our summer holiday with various aunts. My mother put us in the care of the guard at Burtle station and we sat together in the guard's van and were met at Salisbury by a great-aunt.'

'In winter we slid on one of the two ponds in Poolhayes, we were not allowed on one as it was very deep. Chinese geese lived on the ponds and chased us as we went past to school.
    As small children we played "Sheep, sheep come home – what are you afraid of?" – "The wolf"; In and out of the windows; Here we come gathering nuts in may; also Mothers and Fathers – we made houses from stones and used moss in the door.
    Later on we cycled to Weston after tea, and there were whist drives and dances, particularly at Harvest Home. There was hare coursing and hare hunting on the moor – no fox hunting as foxes were not a problem until, it was said, they were driven down to the moor by the hunting on Mendip.
    The boys used to play Tip button on old Mr Norris. They tied string to his knocker, then tapped on the window and ran away. Gerald always got caught.'

'I remember Tom Putt apples – the yellow and red striped variety that were infested with maggots which we used to flick at each other!'

'A highlight of my schooldays in a village on the Somerset Levels were the boys' fist fights under the "Conker Tree" where the combatants settled their differences after school.'

HELPING OUT

'Children at Mark made their own play with simple games – hop-scotch, hoops, marbles along the way. I never remember feeling bored at home although we did not have even a crystal wireless set until about 1925. With only two sets of headphones to share among the family you laughed when those wearing them laughed and rather impatiently waited for your turn.

There were plenty of little jobs found for the children to do – bring in the logs and coal for the range fire, pump the rain water for the cows to drink at milking time, collect the eggs which the hens laid just everywhere – they were not kept in houses as there were no foxes around this area then. Quite a number of children were expected to help with milking the cows, even on school days.

When I was twelve I was allowed to make a day's cheese from start to finish. It was the hard way then, as you had to carry the milk to the furnace to warm, and all the water to keep it hot, as well as carry the whey to the pig sties.'

'Children's holidays were spent picking whortleberries, selling them for dye for sixpence a pint. Another chore was to take a bottle of cold tea to the men working in the allotments, probably over a mile away.

Children loved to ride on the milk carts delivering milk straight from the churn. It was also great fun hunting tadpoles with jamjars. Then there was always the carnival to look forward to, especially the year an application for a path to the sea from Alcombe was turned down and men dressed in black carried a coffin in the procession. For many years the manor house was the home of Lord and Lady Cromer, and there are happy memories of guide and scout meetings at Aldersmead, especially of picking primroses to send to a London hospital.'

'Mother and Father rented Moor View Farm, Clewer. In the 1930s, when I was about 13, Father bought a shorthorn cow called Dumpling for £5. In the summer holidays I used to take her to graze by the side of the road. I always had a heap of socks to darn while sitting on the milking stool watching her. We were a happy family.'

'We always had to help in the hay field by turning hay by hand with a long-handled rake, but much more exciting was horse raking. Picking up potatoes was a chore for after school or weekends. Our favourite pastime was whipping a spinning top up and down the road and trundling a hoop, usually an old bicycle tyre, or playing hopscotch on the pavement – not much traffic to worry about.'

'We had a lovely orchard at Goathurst and further up again there was another orchard, there was two, and when we used to go up and pick sticks for mother's fire we used to have a pair of trucks or a sack bag. Me and my sisters we used to go up there and have a bit of fun and that, pick the nuts and eat the apples. If we couldn't pick up any sticks we used to pull 'em off the trees and sometimes we got a really big one, you know, a long one we used to call that a dragger. No, not a dragon, a dragger. We used to drag it 'ome you see.'

'My sister and I used to take the cows out to the fields before going to school, and then fetch them in again after lessons in the afternoon. We later delivered milk in Buckland Dinham, pushing a little four-wheeled trolley containing two five gallon cans. The householders would come out with their jugs and we measured with half-pint and one-pint measures.'

WHAT WE WORE

'Children's clothing was very different to today. Next to the skin was a vest, over this was a pair of combinations, a bodice and knickers with a petticoat. In the winter these were made of wool, flannel, or fleecy-lined material, and in summer they were cotton. Stockings and socks were wool or cotton according to the seasons. No wonder they didn't complain of the cold!'

'As a five year old, one of my earliest recollections is of my boots having to be fastened with a button hook, before walking three miles to school.'

'Some children would be absent from school for a day as their only pair of boots was being "tapped" (soled).'

'The children at Burrowbridge school wore boots with "tips and clamps", which they were measured for by a gentleman from High Ham. One schoolmaster used to do a bit of apple dealing on the side, so when the children were taken for nature rambles it was always to the orchards which were being auctioned and the children were able to enjoy themselves while the schoolmaster did his bidding.'

'I remember my first pair of welly boots. I was six. The first time wearing them I went to the shop, opposite the Wheatsheaf in Stone Allerton. On my way back I met two schoolfriends. They were quite envious and said get in the ditch and see how deep it is. We had just had a lot of rain and the ditch was almost full. I filled the boots up to my knees. Getting home I was soon up the stairs to escape a good spanking. The boots were a birthday present. My father said "Better send them back as they are obviously not long enough in the leg!"'

'New outfits were bought each year at Easter; navy blue skirts and blazers, white blouses, white ankle socks, black patent ankle strap shoes and creamy white panama hats.'

'In the 1950s clothing coupons were a regular affair and used at the local Co-op in Wells. I remember a biscuit-coloured coat with a matching hat (shaped like a beret) which was trimmed with brown velvet. "Daps" or sandals were worn in the summer with white ankle socks, cotton dresses or sunsuits and cardigans.'

TROUBLE WITH BERRIES

'One day, in about 1915, my mother had picked a lot of raspberries out of the garden and had promised some to old Mrs Woodland, who lived on the coach road (until recently the A303) near the turning to Overstratton. My sister and I were told to take them one hot after-noon.
There were three or four of us in the party and we all took our bikes. I was dared to ride with the basket across the bars near the pedals the last 100 yards (little or no traffic in those days). Off I went, but not for long, the basket fell to the ground upside down and left all the contents all over the road. We scraped up as many berries as we could and Mrs Woodland and mother were none the wiser.'

'My home as a child in the 1930s was between Highbridge and Burnham on Sea. In those days fields and hedges were predominant; behind us we could see the Quantocks and to the north Brent Knoll and the Mendips. There were miles of blackberry-covered hedges between, which we garnered on walks with Mother, armed with a walking stick and little baskets.
Mother escorted me to school for the first year, and for the next three I sauntered along with the other children, and between the old brick terraces and the school there were uninterrupted banks of blackberries. For each of the three years, at blackberry time, I was diagnosed as having scarlet fever, and Father had to stay home

from work for fear of cross-infection. After a couple of berryless days I recovered and doctor, shamefacedly, said it was an allergy to over-indulgence in blackberries! The next years he was again sure it was scarlet fever – but no. My next school involved a walk along the beach so no further temptation was placed in my path.

In wartime Father led family expeditions out to droves on the levels and we picked in earnest. How was it that we children selected all the best and biggest berries, whereas the adults seemed to stand still and filled their baskets in no time at all, with all our rejects? In my childhood, family groups picking and picnicking at a week-end were a customary sight – today they would be considered a "rare species".'

SCHOOLDAYS

Village schools changed remarkably little up to the 1950s, except that where their mothers and fathers wrote on slates, a newer generation used pencils and exercise books. Later on, school meals might be provided, but in the early years of the century children spent all day at school with only sandwiches and perhaps a drink of milk or cocoa for comfort. Most walked to school, sometimes several miles, and the majority left for good at 14, needed at home to bring in another wage or to help on the farm.

THE VILLAGE SCHOOL BEFORE THE FIRST WORLD WAR

'We all really loved going to school. The headmaster was a kindly man who taught with patience and understanding; encouraging those who were anxious to learn. My two eldest sisters who began attending school at Babcary in 1889 had to take twopence per week school fees, but soon after all tuition became free. The teachers gave a good grounding in the "3 Rs" and history and geography, but not many other interesting subjects. When pupils in the lower classes, how much we enjoyed repetition, and being able to say the multipli-cation tables and alphabet forwards and back, the dates of English monarchs, geographical definitions etc. I remember my first day at school when I was three years old (1903), I learned to count coloured beads on a frame, and to read from a wall chart (Is he to go in? No, he is to go on. On, on we go.). I learned to read easily. Mother had been a teacher prior to getting married and she helped a lot. I remember being scolded by my father when I was quite little for reading a daily paper. "There is nothing there fit for little girls to read," he said. Are the papers any better today?

My father was a school manager and it was his duty to visit the school periodically to check the registers. I felt so proud when my name was called to answer "Present Sir" to my father and he would smile at me.'

'Uniforms were never worn at our school at Stoke St Michael, but we had to be tidy, and I remember the white pinafores we wore. The boys had a football team and we played netball and various games in the schoolyard. A weekly gardening lesson was held in the local allotments for boys, and sewing lessons for girls.

Every school day started with a scripture lesson and the vicar often attended. Any late-comer was made to stand in the corner for some time and had to give a good reason for being late. A slap on the hand with a cane was punishment for talking in class or eating a sweet. On Empire Day we all lined up in the schoolyard to salute the Union Jack

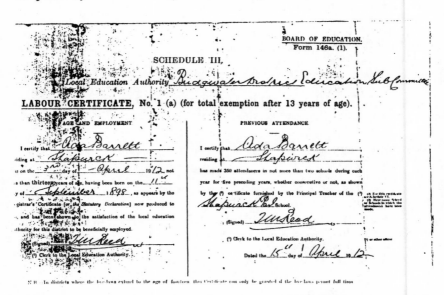

In the early 1900s children could leave school at the age of thirteen, provided they had a job, by means of a Labour Certificate. This one was for Ada Barrett of Shapwick in 1912.

and sing the National Anthem. There was a school choir and we gave concerts at Christmas. I remember very well the last one I joined in before leaving. It was the musical *The Golden Apple* and I sang the solo part.'

'My nearest school in 1916 was at Dunster, one and a half miles away. At five years old we wore our button-up boots, as walking all that way on a rough country road was hard on our feet. We had to be at school by 8.45 am. Our satchels contained not books or homework but sandwiches and a cup with cocoa; during the lunch break our teacher gave us hot water and milk to make the cocoa.

We started in the infants class and progressed from Standard One to Seven. Reaching Standard Seven was quite an achievement, and you then left school at 14. Scripture, reading, writing and sums were the order of the day, with needlework for the girls and woodwork for the boys. Each day a class would have drill in the playground. To get higher education, exams would be taken at 13. The Headmaster would choose who would possibly pass and if so they would have to go to Taunton. It was 24 miles to school, and money and transport was the difficulty there.

Children at the lower end of the village had to go to school on North Hill, where they had two hours for dinner and had to walk home for it. We had fun and games on our way to and from school, with hoops and skipping ropes along the road, no cars to worry us. If we had a penny to spend, it would either be sweets or at lunchtime a penny buster (a huge currant bun as big as a plate). At Hallowe'en the boys would dig a swede from a field, cut the middle out, make a face, put a candle in and put it in the hedge to frighten us.'

'Girls had to look after the younger children in their family, with the older girl keeping house while mother worked. The eldest child would leave school and begin work, and the next child in line would then take her place.'

'I started school in 1913, age five. There were two teachers, one taught the infants, the other the older ones. We began by lining up in the yard, smallest first and marching into school. First we had prayers and a hymn. The infants began with slates for writing, but as we improved we were given exercise books and pencils until we could write properly, then we were allowed to use pen and ink. The ink came in powdered form and was mixed with water and poured into inkwells on each desk by the ink monitor.

The first lesson was scripture; we were read bible stories and taught to recite psalms, the catechism and prayers. Children were tested on their scripture by inspectors. Physical training took place out of doors unless it was cold and wet. On rainy days we pushed back the desks and one teacher played the piano while we danced. Other lessons were history and geography, nature study, knitting and sewing. If you made a garment Mrs Bown taught you to make a paper pattern from squared paper. For nature study you might take a flower to examine. During the First World War we picked blackberries but you were not paid as much as for those picked after school – a bone of contention.

Those who did not go home at dinnertime brought sandwiches, and the teachers made cocoa using a big black kettle which was kept simmering on one of the two open fires.

About 1919 I went to Athelstan, a boarding school in Weston for two years. Here we learnt elocution, French, German, Latin, dancing and algebra and geometry. We played hockey and tennis.

I later worked at the village school as a helper. I was paid £1 a week. Mrs Bown, the headmistress was paid £200 a year. She lived opposite the school.'

'The school I attended in 1915 was three miles from home, so I had to set out early to be there on time at nine. There was one teacher, a Mrs Townsend, and one big classroom, heated by a coal fire boiler, which was good if one sat at the front of the class, but freezing at the back. Desks seated two pupils and had lift-off lids with ink-wells in the top. The teacher set the seniors a lesson and drew a curtain across the room, which divided juniors and seniors. Our playground was rather small, and when the boys wanted to play football, the girls had to stand around and watch.

No hot water, in fact no water in the school, so we had to fetch the water from the well in the lunch hour. Lunch, by the way, was sandwiches, which we swapped. Windows were set high in the room, so no-one could look out and be distracted. On the way home from school we went across fields by footpaths in the summer and by the road in winter. By the roadside we saw the road men breaking stones, sitting on a large pile and using a big hammer to break them up. During the seasons, we used to pick primroses, go bird-nesting, pick wild strawberries, pick nuts and blackberries. In the winter it was getting dark before I got home as I had the furthest to walk; home to an open fire and a warm meal.'

THE CANE

'A lady now in her nineties was very ill as a child with diptheria but she recovered and the doctor gave instructions that she should eat "whatever and whenever she liked". One day she took a bite from an apple during class. The teacher was furious and whacked her palm so hard she broke the cane. This caused quite an uproar in Horsington and the rector had to intervene. The cane was not used in the school again.'

'Nynehead school had two teachers and the Head kept a cane named "Timothy" in a cupboard – this only occasionally made an appearance.'

GETTING THERE

'Village school life was so different, with girls and boys of from five to 14 years of age often walking several miles to school. The boys at Bishop's Hull wore hobnailed boots and stayed in short trousers until they left school to start work.'

'The children rode in to school with the milk when it was taken to Silver Street Dairies in Taunton (twice a day). They came back in the van after the afternoon delivery.'

'The school in Wiveliscombe, originally built as a Board school in 1877, served the local area for children from five years of age. Occasionally, children from outlying areas could be accepted. One lady speaks nostalgically of the days when she used to ride in to school on her pony Maggie, from her home in Brompton Ralph, a few miles away. Whilst she was in school, Maggie would be tethered in the field opposite, where she would patiently wait before taking the little girl home again. Pulsford Lodge, a residential home for the elderly, is now sited on the field which used to accommodate Maggie.'

'The village school was two and a half miles away across Exmoor and from the age of four, in the 1930s, I was transported there by one or other of my older brothers on the crossbar of his bicycle. We would meet up with other neighbours, all riding bikes. It was great fun and out in all weathers and with all the exercise we grew very strong and healthy. We also had lots of spills and mishaps – what happens when your little sister, sitting on the crossbar sideways, decides to put her foot into the front wheel? The road becomes strewn with bits of bicycle and badly damaged kids with teeth missing, cuts and bruises all over and with sprained ankles. Somehow we got to school, were patched up and taken home by car. As I progressed to the age of six I became the proud owner of a tiny bicycle, a hand-me-down from the older ones. We reckoned to meet only one car and the cyling postman en route to school, so what better way to ride than with my feet on the handlebars, or even standing on the saddle. We missed all this when eventually a school car was sent to collect us.'

'Children from Allerton attended the local school from five to 14 years of age, but during the late 1920s they were transferred to Wedmore school. A new bicycle was issued or they could ride their own and receive seven shillings and sixpence a year cycle maintenance allowance.'

'Older pupils were bussed to Wookey in "Charlie's old charabanc", an open-topped vehicle with wooden benches and solid tyres. The best seat was beside Charlie, blowing the rubber-bulbed horn. The same charabanc was used for Sunday school outings to Burnham.'

'Half past seven, a morning in 1938 in Rode. "Go down to Millard's and fetch two stale loaves for the sandwiches." We pass the war memorial on the green and see Mrs Moore with her enamelled pail trudging up Nutt's Lane after pumping her water from the well on the corner. Mr Gabb empties his ashes in the ruts of Marsh Lane. Mr Lambourne, the postman, with red bike, peaked cap and mittens delivers letters in the High Street. Why doesn't he ride the bike? We reach the door of the bakehouse. Cecil harnesses the horse for the morning delivery. The warm, sweet smell of new bread is every-where. Mr Millard, tall and thin, takes bread from the oven with his huge wooden shovel. He pauses to wrap the loaves in crisp kitchen paper and off we run to breakfast, overtaking Mr Holland, the gardener, striding up the middle of the road.

The school bell sounds louder on a frosty morning. Warm your hands on the wall of the brewery boiler before spending your half-penny on a roll in Miss Weaver's shop. Ah, just in time to carry Miss Gilson's case into school. She's rich. A new Morris Ten – GL 4749. There's Mrs Holland disappearing down her dark stairs to shovel more coke. – "All things Bright and Beautiful" again!'

MILK AND WATER

'I went to Wookey school. Went off in the morning and stayed there all day. Didn't come home until the evening and the road then was mud, water, grass and stones. We had to take sandwiches to school and then there was an old lady who lived up the road a little way from the school and she used to pump a bucket of water, wouldn't let us do it – she was afraid we'd break the pump. She brought out an old

134

enamelled cup, all chipped, and we all had to drink from this one cup. That was the only drink we had as there was no water then at the school.'

'We walked to school at Bickenhall, some of us long distances. We had a mid morning drink of cocoa. Teacher put the cocoa powder in the urn with the water and boiled it, it was probably too much trouble and time consuming to mix it in our mugs. We learnt quite a lot by rote, with teacher using the blackboard and we children with slates.'

'The schoolrooms at Saltford were each heated by a large black stove and in winter small bottles of milk (each with its little cardboard top which one pressed and inserted a *real* straw) were placed in water in a small galvanised bath and put on the stove to heat up.'

'Mrs Ballinger was the headmistress at Staple Fitzpaine school. It seemed a long day, particularly as we had to walk to and from school. We used to take sandwiches when I was very small and then eventually we had a lady who cooked the lunches; she was a Mrs Warren who came from Bickenhall. We also had school milk in those days and I can remember if you particulary wanted to, you could take in some money, I think it was about sixpence, and you could have Horlicks put in the milk.'

VILLAGE SCHOOLS IN THE 1920s AND 1930s

'I started school in the early 1920s at the age of four. I had to walk three miles each way to Nunney school from the village of Trudoxhill where I lived. The Marston children were luckier, they were taken in the "Marston Motor" which was not allowed to pick us up.

The school bell was pulled twice. My friend and I were often only at Nunney Catch when it rang the first time but had to be at school by the second time it rang or we were up in front of the Head for punishment. We were nearly always last to arrive.

We took sandwiches for dinner and made cocoa or Oxo on top of the coke stove in the big classroom. The rest of the dinner break was spent at Tom Tivey's Hole at Holwell or down at the castle or river in Nunney.

There was a school concert once a year and practices were held after school – after which we had to walk home, often in the dark.

Later I was given a bike to ride to school so that I could get home more quickly. I would then have to get two horses from their stable and walk them three miles to Gare Hill so that my father could harness them and bring home the load of timber pit props which he had cut in the woods.'

'I was born in Wincanton in 1923. Our house was opposite the school, but I was often the last to arrive. The school was divided into three departments, infants, girls and boys, the infants room being heated with a lovely open coal fire. We had to get into lines in the playground before going into the classroom, where we were inspected by the teacher for clean hands and shoes.'

'At West Hatch there was a village school attended by some 60 pupils, taught at first by two teachers and later by three. The old school is now the village hall. Every summer a local benefactor treated all the pupils to a seaside outing by charabanc – usually either to Weston super Mare or Weymouth. We were taken out to tea and it was a very exciting occasion. Parents could go but they had to pay.

At school the playground was divided by a high wall so that the girls played in one part and the boys in the other, and there were separate entrances for girls and boys into the schoolroom. At playtimes we played hopscotch, whips and tops and hoops.'

' "Off you go, and be careful of the bicycles" – returning to school after midday dinner at home. Yes, the bicycles were the only road hazard in those days, apart from the occasional horse and cart. It was the late 1920s and the village school was just around the corner from my home.

There I was, with my serviceable dark dress, white starched pinafore with frills on the shoulders and laced up boots. How I envied one of my friends who had a pair of black patent ankle-strap shoes!

I had started school in the infants at the age of four and at first played with sand trays and beads etc. After a while I went to the slates and chalk, then the pencils and paper and then nib pens with real ink!

The classes were not very large in number and we learned to read, write beautifully (what happened?) do "sums", scripture, history and geography. We had spelling tests, learned our tables and did mental arithmetic. The teachers were kind for the most part, though occasionally a sharp slap reminded us that we were at school to learn! We had games and country dancing – gathering peascods was a favourite I remember. We did drawing and painting, needlework, craftwork – cane and leatherwork, which was all taught by the teacher whose class you were in.

Our school life from four to eleven years was geared to taking the "scholarship". It was taken in March and if you passed you could start at the secondary school in September, to go on at school until you were 16 or more. If you didn't pass you stayed at the local school until you were 14 when you left and started work.'

'There were three private schools at North Curry, with about twelve pupils in each, which the middle class, farmers children attended, and the village school, which had four teachers and of course a certain amount of rivalry with the private school children! Lil admits to being a tomboy and used to go down to the rhines with the boys in the lunchtimes, inevitably they were late getting back, wet and dirty and for a punishment "Boss Williams" the headmaster would produce the dreaded cane. To counteract the pain of the blow, children would put a hair from their heads across their palms. The girls all wore white pinafores, some trimmed with broderie anglais, crochet work etc. All children walked to school, taking with them sandwiches for their lunch. If the teachers weren't looking they would toast them on the tortoise stove, but they were punished if they were caught! If the father of the family went home for mid-day dinner, the children missed out, and didn't have a cooked, hot meal in the evening, just a bread and butter tea, except at weekends! North Curry seems to have been fortunate, they had copy books, and didn't use slates. Even on school days, the girls were expected to do certain jobs, apart from helping in the house and tending the chickens etc. Lil had to strip willows by hand, one bundle every day of the week, and three on Saturday, before being allowed to go out to play.

Sundays, *nothing* was allowed. They would attend church, chapel and Sunday school, could read good books, but not even do any knitting or sewing. Lil remembers her father saying "Cards and dice and the devil's device; swords in the fire is God's desire."'

'I started at High Ham Church of England school when I was almost five years old and finished at 14 in October 1935. We had lessons until 12 noon with a break of 15 minutes. We went home for dinner, back by 1.30 until 4 pm, again with a short break. Lessons were arithmetic, English, nature study, geography and history. On Thursday afternoons was needlework, darning, patching, making simple garments – starting with a handkerchief and finally clothes for ourselves. On leaving school everyone made a handkerchief sachet in their own chosen colour as a keepsake. Our needlework teacher always ran a Brownie pack. We met each Saturday between 3 and 4.30 pm at her home. Cooking, washing and cleaning class were on Fridays. Aprons were provided and had to be washed at home; if we wore them dirty we were put on cleaning duties all day.'

'Brompton Ralph school was built in 1877 to replace the old schoolroom behind the church. By 1917, there were 44 pupils on the roll. Summer holidays were fixed to coincide with harvest so that children could help. During term, some boys over twelve could get permission to work on farms, others were kept away for potato picking. From school there were blackberrying excursions. In 1918, the school was ravaged by measles and whooping cough and was closed for two months by the Medical Officer of Health.

Discipline varied with headteachers. The strict teacher at the school in Brompton Regis made you "sit up straight with your arms folded behind your back while you listened to stories. Boys and girls sat in different rows and dared not speak to one another." However, they had maypole dancing together and dancing to a concertina played by one of the boys. Outside inspectors examined in needlework and religious knowledge and in 1933 Brompton Ralph school was commended for its "spirit of earnest and practical piety".

Children also had jobs to do. Joyce was paid a penny for collecting the milk cans from neighbouring cottages and bringing back milk from the farm, before going to school. Water for Brompton Ralph school and schoolhouse had to be hand-pumped from the well by the wash-house. In the early 1950s, one of the older boys was given a bar of chocolate each week for working the pump.'

'Up until the 1930s there were two schools in Mark known as East Mark and West Mark. I attended East Mark which was situated at the top of what is now Littlemoor Road, round the back of the church.

We were taught from a blackboard at the front of the class. There were no uniforms – we wore what clothes we had. The school building consisted of one large room divided in two and a small room for the infants. There was a small yard at the back and larger one in front. My mother also attended this school, probably from the age of five until she was 14, when she left and went into service in Weston. The school house, now known as "Old School House", is still occupied today. One of the teachers lodged with us for about two years.

We attended the church on special days such as Ascension Day, and for games we used a field at Mark House, now known as Mark College.

At the end of the year, before the Christmas holidays, we had a party. We each took a mug and plate and had lemonade, cakes and sandwiches. As presents we were given books with tables in, rubbers, rulers and pencils, all advertising things such as Rinso, Beecham's Pills, Oxo and various other things.

The school closed in 1932, after which juniors attended West Mark School and seniors went to Highbridge.'

'Some children started school as early as three and a half years of age, others did not start until five, it didn't seem to matter in the 1930s. The young ones were put to rest in the afternoon on a rush mat on the

138

floor – sometimes sleeping the whole afternoon. There were "quiet" times too, when other little ones were occupied with material to "fray" – making fringes on cotton cloth mats. Learning to write was started with chalks or crayons on boards.

Later on pencils were easy to write with, but if the points were broken they had to be sharpened by teacher. Learning to master writing with a pen with a nib dipped in an ink-well was far more difficult, and getting a crossed nib or a blot of ink on the book seemed to be an awful crime.

Always walking to school, no one liked to be late or to be marked absent. In the winter time children often arrived at school very wet and cold. The coats and shoes were put to dry around the huge radiators. If the weather was very bad, we were allowed to bring sandwiches for mid-day, our dinner time being from twelve noon to 1.30. We could buy a mug of cocoa for a ha'penny which was made for us by the "babies" teacher who always seemed to stay at school through the dinner time. The third of a pint of milk which was supplied at mid-morning playtime cost a ha'penny too at first, but later on a penny was charged.

Sometimes there was a visit from the school dentist, who set up surgery in one of the local halls. The charge was sixpence. An old-fashioned drill with no injection to stop pain – not all the children went to see him! Going to see the "nit-nurse" however, was compulsory and so was being measured for height and weight.

A few days absence from school without a note being sent, meant a visit from the attendance officer. Chickenpox, mumps, measles and other childhood ailments meant two, three or even four weeks away from school. There were some weird and wonderful remedies for children's illnesses. Children with measles were kept in a darkened room for several days. Whooping cough was supposed to be relieved by a "tarred" or creosoted piece of rope tied near or around the afflicted child.

The equipment in school always seemed to have seen better days, although there was great excitement over the arrival of new books. There seemed to be as many or more children to one teacher and one classroom as there are today.'

'When I grew up in the 1930s Wiveliscombe was a thriving market town, well served by a variety of shops. I attended the local junior school and remember learning and chanting tables, sometimes loudly so that the teacher could hear us when he was out of the room leaving the door open. We also learned passages from the Bible by heart, and I particularly remember learning the whole of the parable of the Good Samaritan. On the way home from school, in summer, I would

The first class of Burnham on Sea infants school in 1930. Learning by repetition, sitting in rows was most children's experience of early education right up until the 1960s.

occasionally stop at a sweet shop and buy a small dairy ice cream (home-made) in a half size cornet, which cost a ha'penny.'

'In the early 1900s at Brent Knoll village school, my father and my aunt used slates to write their school work on. The boys wore dark suits and Eton collars. The girls wore white pinafores over their dresses. All had lace-up boots.

In the 1930s when I myself went to school at Burnham on Sea, I too wore a white pinafore and lace-up boots. Instead of slates we had exercise books with various coloured covers. Our lessons were learned mainly be repetition. Times tables, history dates, Kings and Queens of England, the Woollen Towns and the Cotton Towns, even to the books of the Old and New Testaments. In our spelling class, difficult words were spelled out aloud over and over again, until the correct spellings were ingrained forever in our memory.

Our school had no gymnasium so our only exercise during school-time was marching and drill in the school playground. The boys went swimming once a week in the Marine Lake. On Friday afternoons the girls played hockey and the boys played football on pitches marked out on the sands.

Annually the school sports were held in Holt's field and many schools in Somerset sent teams to represent them, and to vie with each other for the silver cup which would be presented to the school with the most successes.

There were no school meals. Children who stayed to dinner brought sandwiches, or occasionally would run up the High Street to the fish and chip shop for two pennyworth of chips. I sometimes had cakes for dinner, purchased at the local cake shop at seven cakes for sixpence.

During our morning break we had small bottles of milk containing a third of a pint. Straws were provided. An extra bottle of milk could be had at lunch time if wanted. At one time Horlicks was given during the morning break. This was made in a large urn and distributed in distinctive Horlicks mugs. I think we paid about threepence per week for Horlicks.'

'I lived about two miles from school at Dunster and had to walk with a number of others every day – wet or fine. The main roads were narrow and lined with banks or hedges. At the edge of the town where the roads crossed a small stream often flooded the road. When this happened a man often appeared with his donkey and gave us rides through the flood.

At seven years old, boys and girls went to separate schools. We had to carry sandwiches for lunch, and in cold weather a kind teacher boiled a kettle on the old round tortoise stove and made us cocoa. All the children went to Sunday school and were given coloured attendance stamps illustrating Bible stories to stick in a book. In the summer we were taken for an outing in an open-top charabanc, either four or five miles to the seaside at Blue Anchor or to a farm at Holford Glen where we had a huge cream tea and ran sports in the field. At Christmas the WI gave us a party complete with gifts from Father Christmas. In the summer holidays a group of us spent long happy days on the beach. We walked across the marshes to the sea and sometimes took the moorhens' eggs with an old tablespoon on a long stick. A friend's mother came sometimes and then we picked winkles off the pebbles and laver.'

'As with most schools in the 1930s, boys at Nynehead were segregated from girls in the playground by a brick wall. The toilets were situated at the bottom of the playground and comprised wooden seats situated over the small stream. The stream was given to regular flooding and often the children had to be sent home when the water bubbled up through the wooden floor, and it had to be scrubbed and dried out before they could return.'

141

'We went to school in the next village from Sutton Mallet, either by walking across three fields or further around the roadway if we cycled. We had very warm coats and boots and leggings which all got very wet and muddy. We carried sandwiches for lunch and paid a halfpenny for a third of a pint bottle of milk which was heated in large water containers on top of a combustion stove. At one stage we were offered Horlicks or Ovaltine tablets also.

The highlight of the school year was our outing to Burnham for the day. Also every December was the school concert followed by a party with a huge Christmas tree in the classroom and a present was handed out to every child. The dreaded day was Dentist Day. We all had to go and his surgery was in the head teacher's house which adjoined the school.

We played many games in the playground, like Flick (with cigarette cards we collected from dropped packets – neither of my parents smoked and they never visited a pub, though a glass of sherry was special for Christmas). We played spinning top, hoops, marbles and many team and ring games such as Farmer's in his Den, In and Out of the Window, Oranges and Lemons, Here we go round the Mulberry Bush, and Snow on the Mountain. We organised ourselves, nobody stayed in the playground. The headmistress could see us from her kitchen window and the only other infants teacher sat by an open fire in the classroom.

I can remember sitting in the classroom and the announcement being made about war breaking out, and eventually the difference it made as quite a lot of evacuees were sent to us.'

SENT HOME FROM SCHOOL

'At Staple Fitzpaine in the 1920s Rev Coote would come in to give us a Bible lesson. If anyone wasn't well we had to take a letter from our mother and give it to Miss Munday earlier in the morning. When Mr Coote came in, Miss Munday would give him the letter and he would call us up to the front and if, say, I had a bad throat, he would ask me to open my mouth and have a good look at my tonsils, or something or another, and say "Oh yes, yes, I think you had better go home today and stay quiet, yes, that'll be alright, you go home and keep warm." I would run home as fast as I could go!'

GRAMMAR SCHOOLS

'At six years old I went to a small private school held in St Mary's vicarage, Taunton. The vicar, Canon Corfield and his wife the Hon Mrs Corfield lived in a large house, Blagdon Lodge. When he died

142

and the next incumbent needed the vicarage the school had to move to less good surroundings and my father decided it was time for me to move on. The evening before the local girls grammar school term began, my parents took me to the headmistress's house. How advanced was I, she asked? My father mentioned the names of two classmates of mine who, in a more orderly way, had sat and passed the entrance exam to the school. Oh, said the headmistress, relieved, splendid, that would do for me too. That was entrance for a fee-paying pupil into a grammar school in 1928!'

'With the closure of both the girls and boys grammar schools, both with their boarding houses, so much has gone from Ilminster. Now our older children are transported early each day, mostly to Wadham Comprehensive School, Crewkerne.

When I was at school in the 1930s, life was very different. Buses would arrive from Chard and Crewkerne and the train would steam in with a large contingent from Donyatt, to walk up Station Road, all converging in the Market Square. Then off to their respective schools in Silver Street (boys) and Church Walk (girls). A large number came by bicycle, in all winds and weather.

During the day, pupils could be seen walking to the gymnasium in Wharf Lane or to the school playing fields, via the recreation ground; all open country then (now two large estates).

On certain occasions, the church rang with the combined voices of both schools. At close of school, the town would be alive again with pupils going home and an orderly crocodile of boarders could be seen taking an after school walk, supervised by a mistress.

The schools brought much prosperity to Ilminster. Two drapers and outfitters supplied school uniforms, a bookshop supplied all school requisites and shops selling sweets, etc did a roaring trade!

Gone, gone, are those days now, but Ilminster will always be remembered for its dear old grammar schools.'

'During my schooldays in Rode in the 1940s the lord of the manor would bring sweets to encourage those of us taking the scholarship (eleven-plus) so that we could go to Frome Grammar School.'

VILLAGE SCHOOLS IN THE 1940s AND 1950s

'I travelled from Wiveliscombe to Taunton to school by train and later by bus. The branch line was well used and many mornings I ran the last few yards as I heard the train coming out of the cutting from Venn Cross into the station. On reaching Taunton station the pupils formed a crocodile in twos and walked to school with a prefect in charge, all in school uniform complete with hat and black woollen stockings. Coming home we had to cross the line to reach the exit side of the station. We usually ran to get across before the train moved off, but often the engine driver would blow the whistle as we were about to cross and together with the noise of the steam we shrieked and stood well back from the train as the driver and the fireman laughed and waved to us.

In needlework lessons we made underwear from scrap pieces of parachute silk, to eke out clothing coupons, and we made handbags and tea cosies from felt used for lining airmen's jackets. We dyed the felt to our chosen colour at home so that it was dry and able to be cut out for the next lesson.

In the early 1940s, a number of girls of Bishop Fox's School, including myself, helped to embroider a hanging for Wells Cathedral. It commemorated the school's founder, Richard Fox, Bishop of Bath and Wells 1492–94. The design included the Bishop's arms and motto, "Est Deo Gratia" (Thanks are due to God), which formed the school badge together with a pelican feeding its young. The banner now hangs in the Quire in the sequence of bishops' arms, in chrono-logical order. The wool used was specially dyed to be more resistant to fading.'

'At Allerton in the 1940s, the teacher would march into the classroom and say "Boys get out your Bibles, girls get out your knitting". As a result most of the boys learned to knit!'

'I lived on a farm a good two miles from my school at Withypool. To get there, I had to walk; part of the way was across open moorland, and part a narrow road between two high hedges. During the winter of 1947 this road was completely blocked for ten weeks.

When I started school at five years, there were about 30 pupils, I think, and during my first few years we had at least seven different head teachers – no one stayed very long, I don't know why. The infants teacher didn't change.

The school had two classrooms and an entrance at the front for the girls, where we hung our coats and sandwich bags (the sandwiches were usually jam). One door from the cloakroom led into the big room and a door from that room led into the infants' room. Another door from the cloakroom opened out on to a small yard with two toilets at the far end. The boys' entrance cloakroom was at the back, and their toilets at the back again.

The infants' room had an open fire for heating, while the big room for the eight to 14 year olds had a large round stove. We arrived at school one morning to find the then head teacher in tears. She had

144

put the pewter teapot on top of the stove to warm, gone back into her house, which was joined on to the school, then returned to find her beloved teapot a mass of molten metal – it had melted!'

'The rooms at St Thomas' Wells were very large, with the windows high up in the walls. There were up to 40 pupils in any one class. The only heating was an open coal fire or a coke stove, with the teacher's desk always in front of it! The toilets were an outside affair, usually frozen in the winter – but the school never closed, whatever the weather. Uniform consisted of a gym slip with blouse (cotton dress in the summer) and a navy gabardene mackintosh with gloves on elastic in the wintertime.'

'Schooldays became more interesting after the war at West Buckland. Instead of knitting socks and scarves for the Forces, we made jumpers and aprons for ourselves. I remember going to Bishop Fox's School, Taunton for inter-school sports, a visit to Bristol Zoo and an outing to a pantomime in Bath. Our headmistress started a Christmas Tree Committee – they raised funds by jumble sales, raffles etc and at Christmas every child up to the age of 14 in the parish was invited to a Christmas party at the school and given a present from the tree. We had a little plot of ground where we grew vegetables and sold them to the villagers. The school also had a quarterly delivery of books, and I used to collect and deliver books for the elderly in the village.'

'Limington village school in the 1940s only had one teacher, Miss Reeve, a strict disciplinarian but an excellent teacher. Children aged five to eleven were all taught in one room. We were given a solid grounding in the three R's, chanting multiplication tables regularly. School milk bottles were covered with cardboard discs with a per-forated centre for the straw. Two discs formed a convenient template for making woollen balls. During very cold weather, bottles of milk were arranged around the pot-bellied stove. I can still taste the lukewarm cardboard flavoured milk.'

'Weare school in the 1950s was one brick building with two class-rooms. Miss Watts taught the five year olds in the small room. Miss Dynes had three age groups, seven to eleven years, not easy to concentrate while others are trying to work. Our daughter was always busy answering the questions put to other groups. Children walked to school whatever the weather. Some brought lunch, but there were school meals. These came in metal boxes possibly from Burnham on Sea. An unpopular sweet was "cake and custard". Milk was free and each child in turn had the job of chalking up the number

145

of bottles required each day – "35 today please".

Children who took the eleven-plus exam found the day both anxious and enjoyable. At the halfway stage a school governor Mrs Norah Ham, arrived with a cloth covered wicker basket. She then gave each child a tasty titbit, which made it a special day. Those who passed went to Weston Grammar or Sexey's Grammar School at Blackford. The others went to Cheddar school.

The nature table was always well stocked. An oilcloth map of the world was rolled over the blackboard and displayed the British colonies (pink) which seemed to stretch from shore to shore. PT exercises consisted of tucking your skirt in dark knickers and climbing on the low school wall, running the length and jumping off and back to the start!'

FIRST DAY AT SCHOOL

'I remember my first day at school in 1959 very clearly because I was absolutely terrified: I was very much Mummy's girl and I could not bear to leave her.

The dreaded morning arrived and my mother took me to the coach stop a few yards from our house at Chilcompton. A friend of mine, Richard, was waiting too, but it did not make me any less nervous. My brother, Colin, went to the same school but as he was older, he rode his bicycle there.

I saw the coach coming round the corner, my heart was beating fast, I felt sick and the tears welled up in my eyes as the coach stopped and my mother kissed me goodbye. Then panic took over and I refused to get on; my mother just did not know what to do with me, she must have felt very embarrassed.

The driver was Scottish (his name was Donald) and he got out of his seat and came down the steps. I was rather upset by this time but he had such a way with children that he managed to coax me onto the coach. He put me in the seat right behind him so that he could talk to me on the way and this made me feel very special.

There were only a few of us on the coach and he had nicknames for all of us by the time we got to school. I still do not know why, but he called me "Snow White" and I loved it. I finished up looking forward to going to school so that I could see Donald every morning. I'll always remember him for helping me through those first terrifying days and I can hear him now, shouting, as the coach pulled up "Good morning, Snow White, and how are you?".'

THE WORLD OF WORK

A FARMING LIFE

Work on the land was the lot of the majority of Somerset's men and women, just as it had been for centuries, and, though a hard life, it had its compensations in this beautiful county. Farm work has changed tremendously since the introduction of machinery, but within living memory the farm year followed a pattern hardly altered over the generations.

FARMING IN THE 1930s

'Even into the 1930s in small and difficult fields, grass for hay was still being cut with scythes and turned and tossed with rakes and forks, often the hay being ricked in the field, the rick being thatched for weather protection and finally cut out with a hay knife for winter feed. Iron rods about six to eight feet long were inserted in new hay ricks to test for heat and guard against internal combustion. Even so, many a rick has been spoilt by overheating.

Corn harvesting was a long and laborious task, especially when tying sheaves after the scythe or reaper. "Stitching" (stooking) of corn was hard work, particularly in a wet season when it may have to be turned once or twice in the hope that the grain would not grow out. It was a sad sight to see the sheaves getting darker and the heads green. Even in a dry season it was said that oats should stand stitched to hear "the church bells on three Sundays". During the winter months the cumbersome threshing machine would be seen going from farm to farm.

Ditching was another important job in water meadows destined to be "let up" for mowing, thus making the best use of rivers and streams, this being done by the use of "fenders" (weirs) along the water channels. One of the nicest sounds of spring was the horse-drawn ring roller.

Many a winter evening was spent in the barn turning the chaff cutter and the mangold cutter, where at least one romance flourished.'

CHAFF AND MANGOLDS

'Growing up on our farm at Duddlestone near Taunton, we children helped with many tasks. One of the most enjoyable was working in

148

the chaff house. The chaff-cutting machine, mounted in a loft, chopped up straw and hay by way of very sharp knives fixed on a wheel. We were forbidden to climb the loft steps while this dangerous "beast" was in action. Through a hole to the floor below the small pieces of golden straw and silvery hay cascaded, making an ever growing pile. I thought this was magic as the sunlight caught the falling chaff.

Then we threw mangolds into the root pulper on the ground floor, producing lovely slices in white, yellow or red. The power supply for all the barn machinery was a fascinating stationary engine. No self-starter, just Father to swing the big handle round and round until suddenly it fired, a lever was pulled, the long driving belts sprang into life and everything was off with a thrilling clatter.

Eventually the engine stopped, a layer of chaff was spread out and covered with pulped mangolds just like butter. Topped by a further layer of chaff and all mixed together by shovel. Put into big baskets (or so they seemed to me) and carried down into the forbye or feeding passage; one basket for each cow. How they loved the mixture and how I remember the noise as they rattled neck chains and champered away at the juice feed!'

THE DROVERS

'Sheep were moved about the country by drovers who had no fixed abode but cadged food and lodging from friendly farmers.'

LOWER FARM, KINGWESTON

'I was born in 1909 at Lower Farm, once a coaching inn on the road from Exeter to Bath. My father followed my grandfather as tenant under the Dickinsons, who had purchased the estate from profits of Jamaica rum. My father ran 100 store cattle and 300 Exmoor lambs ready for Christmas. The rest of the 500 acre farm was arable, which meant a visiting team of threshers with a machine driven by a steam engine. At haymaking I drove a swarf-turner and hayrake and at harvest made stooks. Our two carters had their teams of plough horses; they worked from seven am to three pm with a short break for cider and hay respectively. Carters never went for their meal until their horses were fed and watered. Each farmworker had two ranks across ploughed fields where they grew potatoes, and milk was free. Wives coped with glovemaking at home as well as charring at the farms and bringing up their families. The slump in the 1930s forced my father to retire.'

149

STAPLE FARM, STAPLE FITZPAINE

'Tuberculin Testing of milk was first introduced about 1925 and Staple Farm at Staple Fitzpaine registered in 1927. This meant that milk was up to a set standard from healthy cows. On the introduction of electricity, cows were milked by machine, previously it was always handmilking. Instead of delivering milk in the churns, bottles were used, first with crinkly paper tops like little cake cases, then cardboard circles and this progressed to foil tops. To cool the milk it was put over a metal rack with cold water running down inside, this was taken over by in-churn cooling and later by bulk milk tanks. Red Poll cattle were kept as they were dual purpose (milk and beef) but have been replaced by Friesians for just milk production.

Most farms were "mixed" having cereals – oats, wheat and barley and sometimes clover seed. This was difficult to harvest as it did not ripen until October and by then the weather was often poor. Teasels were grown in the Staple area, a biennial crop which was very labour intensive. Cut by hand, wearing thick leather gloves, tied onto poles, then packed into large square canvas bags and taken to Hatch Beauchamp station for their journey to the mills in Yorkshire for use in teasing up the nap on the rolls of woollen cloth.

Summertime with its haymaking and later the harvest was a busy time for all the family. The farmer's wife spent afternoons cutting sandwiches which were then taken out to the fields with large earthenware bottles wrapped in towels to keep the tea warm. Cakes were made and all this was often dragged across the field in the baby's pram, taking the baby as well.

The cereals were cut with a reaper which started at the outside of the field and the men came along behind to stack the sheaves. As the binder progressed to the middle of the field the villagers came with their dogs and sticks to catch the rabbits as they ran out. The corn was then stacked, often on staddle stones to protect it from rats, thatched and left to dry. In February the threshing machine came and all hands helped with this work. Cider was often provided for refreshment, but when one man fell into the machine and was killed, thereafter only tea was provided. Lots of rats and mice would be running around and on one occasion a large land girl screamed that she had one run up her leg. However, she slapped her thigh hard and killed the mouse!'

A FARM NEAR DULVERTON

'We bought a farm near Dulverton on the edge of Exmoor in 1948. The house had no amenities. We had a small wash-house adjoining with a copper which was lit every morning to provide hot water. The water was pumped by hand from a well. We had an open fire in the kitchen and we carried water in and bathed in a tin bath in front of it. Each evening I lighted the oil lamps and we had candles to carry up to bed. We had a privy (a two-seater!) built over a stream near the house. Perhaps a child would be nervous to go out alone.

When we began farming after the war we had four cows, two black and white Friesians called Moonlight and Starshine and two brown Ayrshires called Daisy and Buttercup, which we milked by hand. We gradually increased until we were machine milking about 30 to 35 animals. We also had a horse called Mary who we used for carting mangolds and haymaking. Haymaking was hard work but fun in those days, when families and friends could picnic in the fields without fear of being caught up in the tractor or baler. The dried grass would be swept up and made into a rick which was later thatched to keep out the rain. There were no combine harvesters at that time. Corn was cut with a reaper and binder and the sheaves had to be put into stooks to dry and then built into a rick. The threshing machine came afterwards to thresh out the corn and tie up the straw into bales; a nasty, dusty job. The helpers were glad to be refreshed with cider which was made in a press on the farm.'

A SMALL FARM IN THE 1940s

'A small farm of 86 acres near Stocklinch was cultivated for dairying and arable crops by two brothers in the 1940s. There were nine cows, which were hand milked at 5 am by the light of a lantern.

The arable land was cultivated by traditional methods. They used a horse plough and walked thousands of miles behind the team. Sowing was done by hand as was hoeing and weeding. At harvest time they used a horse reaper, stooked the corn to dry and then made a rick. A steam thresher was hired.

Vegetables were also grown and the brothers think that kneeling in the fields contributed to their arthritis. Potatoes had, by law, to be grown during the Second World War.

One brother, when young, was a rick thatcher and worked for other farmers. He could carry two cwt sacks of winter feed into the lofts, climbing a ladder to do so.

There was hedging and ditching to be done too and the brothers are critical of present day standards. The roadsides were well cared for by a linesman.'

WHOA!

'In 1927 there were a few tractors at Pitney, though most of the farmers still used horse-drawn vehicles. One farmer in particular did have a tractor and plough and started off at the bottom of the field and away he went with a good straight farrow behind him, until suddenly the hedge appeared at the other end of the field. He called "Whoa, Whoa" to the tractor, but nothing happened and he went right through the hedge and into the ditch the other side before he stopped. Unfortunately there were some of his friends watching!

I can remember well, a line of ten men cutting a field of corn, each with their scythes. There was a wonderful rhythm about it and a swish as the sharp blades went through the stalks and then fell to the ground.'

THE FARM LABOURER

'Farmwork was long and hard, with low wages, although in spring and summer there were plenty of "perks". Labour was always needed at haymaking and harvesting. Earlier in the year it was mangold hoeing.

A popular source of overtime was cidermaking in the autumn; when the word went round that Farmer X was cidermaking there was no shortage of help. Workmen were often given a strip of ploughed ground to grow potatoes; this was communal, as on a farm employing four or five men each helped the other. Rabbits were a source of food. Hedges were allotted to the men to catch the rabbits and this fed their families and kept down the rabbit population. Another "perk" for the farmworker could be milk, swedes, or cattle cabbage, which in the days before balanced rations, were grown for the stock.

With most men their work was their interest and hedge laying and ploughing were works of art. This was in the workers' interest as a "good worker" was always well cared for. Ploughing was with horses up to the end of the 1930s in the majority of farms.

152

Haymaking and harvesting started very early in the morning and continued until darkness, tea being sent out from the farmhouse. Bread and cheese were distributed as the last wagon for the day came in. Cider was there, but rationed for obvious reasons. It was an accepted fact that the farmer with the best cider was never short of "strappers", as the volunteer labour was called then.'

'I was born in 1906 at Stogursey, left school at 14 and worked as a farm boy driving teams of horses – ploughing, haymaking and harvest loads. I was up at six am to walk to Woolston Farm three miles away, and had to feed and groom the horses by seven o'clock. Then I started work. It was bread and cheese for lunch, and cider. Over a thousand gallons was made on the farm, and it was strong stuff. At harvest time we had to "cut it, bind it, stitch it and stook it". Oats stayed out longer before cutting to mature the grain. Catching rabbits in the cornfield was a great game for the boys. I could throw and hit them, and still can, with my cap and stun them. Later it was rabbit stew for everyone and the pelts were sold for pocket money at sixpence each.'

'When I was aged about 15, in the 1930s, I went to work for a farmer at Blagdon, a small farm milking eight or ten cows. I had a weekly wage of about five shillings and lived indoors with lodging and food. When I became 18 they wouldn't pay me any more so I went to Marsh Farm and this was totally different as at Blagdon you got up at six-thirty to get in the cows and then do the milking but at Marsh Farm I was up at five am. Up out and get the cows in and milk. I stayed there until I was 21 when I was entitled to a man's wage but the farmer wouldn't pay this so I left.'

'We were eight in a small cottage at Dunster, and Mother worked very hard to keep us all well and happy. Father's wages were 27 shillings and sixpence a week and our rent one shilling and sixpence, coal one shilling a hundredweight.

We lived in a two bedroomed cottage with no bathroom or indoor toilet. The three youngest of us and the oldest girl slept in the large bedroom with Mother and Father. There were two double beds and one single in it. My two older brothers slept in the smaller bedroom. In the winter we went to bed by candlelight.

Our main meat was rabbit which we had roasted or stewed. It was very cheap and its full cost could be got back if the skin was sold to the rag and bone man who came round each week. Granny kept a pig in her back garden and when it was killed we were given pork and fat bacon. We had the fat bacon crisply fried with fried bread and potato for breakfast, stew for dinner and suet or bread pudding for tea. Father grew all our vegetables in his allotment. He worked very hard all the daylight hours except on Sundays. It was a very hard life for my parents, but we had a very happy family life which I still look back on with pleasure.'

'Most cottagers at Mark kept a little poultry or a pig to help the housekeeping as the farm worker often earned as little as 21 shillings a week.'

'Most of the local folk at Henton worked on the land, or on the railway (S&D) and the local council. Many women went hand milking twice daily. Owing to the Second World War many elderly men continued working although well after the age of retirement. It was quite common for veterans of the Boer War to be working alongside Land Army girls young enough to be their grand-daughters. As the 1950s progressed, the drift from the land and the villages became more marked. Those remaining in the villages increasingly commuted by bicycle, bus and later car to the factories and works in the towns.'

THE SMALLHOLDER

'My family farmed in a small hamlet called Nyland, approximately two miles from Wedmore, Cheddar and Draycott. The farm was part of a small community of eight dairy farms that were part of the Somerset County Council smallholdings scheme, that was originally set up for the returning soldiers from the First World War.

Being small dairy farms that were labour intensive, all the family had to help with the chores that are still part of any work with animals. Sunday mornings were always set aside for moving cattle and young stock from field to field.

During the winters the surrounding fields flooded and in hard winters it was sometimes possible to skate across the ice. Inevitably on one occasion in 1947, my sister and I fell through the ice and were saved by my eldest brother and one of the farm workers. We both ended up in a tin bath in front of the fire, being thoroughly scolded.'

'In the middle 1930s, in a radius of less than two miles of our village (Dunster) there were at least ten smallholders, the acreage ranging from one to 35 acres. Three of the largest were farmed by the two village butchers and a milkman. All the land was rented from the Castle Estate or the County Council. For someone with a love of the land it was difficult to obtain a field, nevertheless quite a number of farmers started in a very small way.'

HAYMAKING AND THRESHING

No matter the welcome given to modern farm machinery, nothing can erase the memories of haymaking in the past, when young and old joined in a tradition ages old. It was a social occasion, as well as hard work, lubricated by supplies of home-made cider and calling on the skills of rick builders and thatchers whose pride was reflected in their work.

A HAPPY SOCIAL OCCASION

'Haymaking and harvesting were always happy times in spite of the hard work. The grass was cut, dried on one side then turned with a rake or hay fork. When completely dry it was raked into rows with a horse-rake, loaded by hand loose onto waggons – as much as possible at a time – and taken to an experienced hand who would make it into a rick not far from the house.

It was the custom among neighbouring farmers to help each other as a field became "fit" – no wages were paid but everyone got their hay made! Young lads would come along in the evening to join in the fun and were always rewarded by plenty of cider, made on the farm, and a bread and cheese supper usually in the barn. These were quite social occasions and a lot of fun was had because one friend could tell "fortunes" and this provided great entertainment.

Corn was cut either with a trapper and hand-tied into sheaves or perhaps with a binder which would tie and throw out the sheaves already tied. They were taken to the rick-yard and made into a rick, then covered with a sheet (not plastic in those days), or even thatched with reed. Later in the year or the following spring the threshing machine arrived, this being driven by a steam engine, and it would do the rounds of the local farms. Threshing day usually meant cooked dinners for all the helpers mid-day – another happy social occasion! How did we manage without balers, combine harvesters etc? Of course farms were much smaller and so were the fields in those days.'

TURNING THE HAY

'I was born at Pear Ash Farm, Penselwood in 1905. Hay was cut with a horse-drawn mower. Village women would turn the drying swathes with wooden rakes. The hay was then carried by a "collector"

155

drawn by two horses to the elevator operated by a one-horse "gear" and thence to the top of the rick. A stone cider jar was always nearby for the labourers to quench their thirst. A well thatched rickyard was a fine sight. I remember the day the ricks caught fire. The fire brigade from Gillingham galloped up the lane, the engine drawn by two horses, and the pump was operated by three men on either side who endeavoured unsuccessfully to douse the fire.'

'In 1921, when I was seven years old, we moved from Minehead to the village of Alcombe a mile or so away. This is now a built up area, but then the roads were like country lanes and there was no school or large shops. It seemed like the depths of the country to me. I opened our back gate straight into the hayfield. The hay had been cut and the children were having a lovely time tossing it about and making houses in it. These were the days when it was important for the hay to be continually turned so that it would dry out completely before being built into ricks and thatched. The farmer had no mechanical equipment for tossing the hay so the local population were encouraged to play in it. We had many happy family picnics there.'

'At haymaking at Chapel Allerton the grass was cut with a mowing machine but turned with a rake into peaks. It was gathered by a

Harvesting on a family farm in a steep field overlooking the Aville Valley in 1946.

collector pulled by a horse. The hay was then forked up onto the rick. The rick was thatched with wheat straw and held down with split willow spars and long bramble stretchers. The turner came in after 1918 but most people still turned by hand. Bailers were introduced after the Second World War. During haymaking everyone helped each other and nobody was paid but the farmer's wife provided the bread and cheese and cider and the cheese would need to be made in time for haymaking.'

'Farming in the Corfe area betwen 1950 and 1957, I can remember turning fields of hay with a long wooden rake, as we had no "turner" to haul behind the tractor.'

BUILDING THE RICKS

'I used to go with father when he went ploughing with two horses, and helped on the rick when haymaking. Grandfather always told us "make sure to tread the hay firmly to make a good rick." A great event was when our first elevator took the hay onto the rick.'

'Farmers around Buckland Dinham would have extra help from villagers in the evenings to haul the hay to the rick by a horse and collector (later a tumble sweep), then pitch it up with picks onto the rick. When it got too high to reach, a ladder was put against the mow and one man would sit halfway up and take the pick from the man on the ground to place on top for the rickmaker. These haymaking evenings always ended with some hunks of bread, cheese and cider.'

'Before the Second World War there were thatchers and spur makers in most villages. Farmers put up hay ricks and corn mows to be thatched with reed. It was a very skilled job to thatch so that the rain kept out. The spars used to keep the thatch on were made from willow, growing along the road and ditches. These were cut every three years.'

'I can't recall the name of the man who lived at Lilac Cottage, Henton in the 1940s, but I do remember that he was the local spar maker and he was always sitting outside working when we went to school. We could hear him chipping away as he split and pointed the withy. Spars were like giant hairpins about two feet long and three to four inches wide, and by the start of haymaking he would have completed several piles looking like big brown igloos. Hay ricks in this area were usually thatched with reed cut from the rhines and dried. It was held in place by long thin withies which were in turn held firm by driving the spar over them, through the thatch and into the hay with a large wooden mallet.

Hay ricks varied in shape, size, quality and neatness and tended to reflect, in various orders of magnitude, those same characteristics possessed by their builders. Herb Boyer built the best ricks and was capable of making decorative dollies with the thatch at the apex of hip and pitch. As a boy I spent a lot of time "helping" Herb, and if he was milking down on the moor all I had to do was wait at the gate of Gully House. Herb had the most tuneful whistle I have ever heard and would stand at the back of his trap like some Roman charioteer, his whistle echoing from one end of the village to the other. As he went by I would run behind and without any change of pace or tune he would pull me into the trap with one hand, the other held forward with the reins at shoulder height.'

'At Chapel Allerton before the Second World War, Jack Herd made spars from willow and long stretchers were cut from the brambles to be held down by the spars. There was great competition to see who thatched the best rick. Thorns were removed form the bramble stretchers by passing them through a tool with a hole in.'

THE CORN THRESHER

'Before combine harvesters were in use, corn in the field was cut by a binder, producing sheaves of corn, which were then put into "stooks" (we called them "stitches"). These were left for about two weeks to finish ripening, and then were hauled and put into ricks, either in the corner of the field or in the farmyard; if the ricks were not under cover they were sometimes thatched to keep them dry.

Then during the winter the threshing machine was used. My father, who farmed at Isle Brewers in the 1930s, hired a machine from the next village which came with two men in charge. My father "borrowed" men from neighbouring farmers to help, and "lent" back to his neighbours when they needed help. There were casual labourers called "strappers" who followed the thresher hoping for work. About ten men were needed – to unload from the rick, feed the sheaves into the machine, make the straw ricks, bag off the corn into hessian sacks and take away to the barn, and clear away the chaff (the dusty waste from the threshing).

My mother supplied a midday meal, and as I remember as a small child there were large joints of beef and ham, hot potato, pickles, bread and cheese, and beer and cider, laid out on a large white wooden table in the kitchen.'

'Corn was carried by horse and cart to Bickenhall Mill Farm from West Hatch, up to about 1945.'

DAIRY FARMING AND CHEESEMAKING

⤝⤞

Somerset has a long history of dairy farming and, of course, her cheese is famed worldwide. Many a farmer's wife toiled long hours in the dairy to produce her own Cheddar or Caerphilly, exhibiting proudly at shows and markets.

MILKING IN THE FIELDS

'Until the war started in 1939, all farms were worked by horses; the first tractor appeared in Brent Knoll in 1940. Most village men were employed in farming, and in 1940 the Women's Land Army took over much of the young men's work. Wages were £1 to £1.10 shillings a week. Bigger farms had their own cottages where the farm worker lived and the wife usually helped in the farmhouse. All the village farms were dairy farms as the land in this area afforded excellent pasture. In the summer the farmers would go into the fields twice a day with their stool and bucket to milk their cows – mostly brown and white shorthorns. The churns were delivered to the milk factory at Brent Corner. Most farmers had orchards and made cider to keep their workers happy, and they kept a few hens and a pig or two, mostly fed on scraps from the farmhouse.'

'My father, who was a smallholder and milk retailer at Bickenhall, often had to walk through the village and then across four or five fields to milk the cows and then bring the milk back in buckets hanging from a yoke, this being done twice daily. Milk was delivered by bucket morning and evening, my sister and I often having to help deliver milk, in cans, to distant customers before school in the morning and then help with the evening delivery by collecting the jugs from customers.'

'I remember falling out of bed at 5.45 am to help with the morning

159

milking. Having harnessed Duke, the cart horse, and put the pails and churns in the milk float, we rattled down the lane to the cows. There were three of us, the cowman, his wife and myself squashed between them on the seat (board) fixed across the float.

The herd was usually waiting for us in the milking pen, but sometimes I was sent off to collect the stray ones. It was beautiful walking across the dewy field with the birds singing and the rabbits scuttling along the hedges. If I was lucky I might see a fox or a hare run across the field.

Then the milking. Leaning against a warm cow with my head pressed against the side of Primrose, and hearing the milk flowing into the pail, was a lovely experience.

Being a young, inexperienced milker I was given the "easy milkers" – not the cows that fidgeted or kicked, but the regular "hands" welcomed me, even if I was a slow milker. I milked only six or seven cows while they each milked twelve to fourteen!

I do not remember the cold, wet winter mornings, just the joy of being out of doors and being useful in the summer.'

THE MILKING MACHINE

'My first memories of farming are of when I came to live in Lympsham at Beck's Farm after gettting married. It is a very old farm and is mentioned in the Domesday Book. A milking machine had just been purchased and I learned to milk a herd of shorthorn cows tied up in yokes in the cowhouse, with much trial and error. We made clotted cream and butter for our own use and nothing tasted so good. After some years we purchased a milking bail which was used for milking the cows. Later we moved the bail to a permanent position in the farmyard. A big milk tank was bought and this was found more convenient as the milk tanker was able to collect the milk from the tank every day.'

'At Alston Sutton we bought our first tractor, a second hand "Fordson" during the war. My husband did some contract work for other farmers as more land had to be ploughed to grow crops to save shipping space.

We started machine milking our own milking herd during 1942 when we bought a "Gascoigne" portable milking bail. This was an improvement on hand milking but nothing to compare with the present day milking parlour. Our herd was Tuberculin Tested in 1939 and this meant if it was tuberculosis free we could get a little extra money for the milk. In those days the milk was transported to the milk factory in churns which were labelled so each farmer's milk

160

Dairy farming at Combe Florey. Many will remember the serious outbreak of foot and mouth disease in 1958 when herds built up over generations had to be destroyed.

could be identified. Now, all herds have to be Tuberculin Tested and the milk is piped into a big road tanker from the farm vat.'

CHEESEMAKING

'I remember going to my uncle's cheesemaking dairy at Buckland Dinham, my uncle carrying the milk in a large pail on his head, just having hand-milked (on a three-legged stool) the cows all tied with neck chains in the stall. I loved to be at the dairy the moment the curd was cut and salted – scrumptious!'

'Sunday at Mark in the 1920s was certainly the high day of the week when only the very necessary work was done, though the milking and cheesemaking had to be followed. Nearly all the young farmers' wives learned to make cheese and butter as soon as they married because there was very little organised milk collection and no factory cheese. All the Cheddar and Caerphilly cheese was taken by horse and cart to the Highbridge Cheese Market where dealers came from far and wide; many cheeses were packed between straw and sent loose in the trucks from Highbridge station.'

'My parents at Stone Allerton made cheese with their milk during the summer months. At one time they were ten or eleven pound truckles and some of them were sold in the open market at Highbridge. My father weighed the cheese before he left home to get a good idea then he took it on the horse and cart. During the school holidays my brother and I could ride with Father to Highbridge. We loved that. The weight was taken at Highbridge and the cheese put on a truck and pulled to the covered market. In the early 1930s my mother sold some of her own cheese out at the door but in the late 1930s things became more controlled. Cheeses were made bigger, 30 or 40 pounds or more. When the war came, there was no more Highbridge market. The cheese had to be graded and accounted for, it was taken into Wells to a store (collected from home).'

'In 1912 milk went to the milk factory at Bason Bridge. It had to be taken down to Mark in a churn on a pony and cart to connect with the horse-drawn milk lorry. Later on it was collected from a stand at the top of Back Lane.

In summer, cheese and butter was made every day up to the end of September, then the milk would be sold through the winter. Cheese was sold to a dealer. If we made Caerphilly it would go to Highbridge Market. In 1928 ninepence per lb was a good price for cheese. Some butter was salted down for the winter. Eggs were five or sixpence per dozen. Hens roamed the fields, foxes were not such a problem.

Milking started about six am, although Mr Teek would start at five. Father expected us to be down the moor before Mr Teek got back from milking, otherwise he would say "You could dance last night but you can't this morning!"

Most households down through Chapel Allerton kept a cow or two, less than ten and you were a smallholder. Only one person had a milk round. Most people kept a pig. Wheat for bread was ground at a water mill at Henton; the windmill at Ashton ground too coarse for flour.

In 1940 a farm labourer got a cottage for six shillings, a quart of milk a day and £3 a week. His wife helped with the milking and in the house and one of their daughters (they had eight children) helped look after my children. A cheesemaker got twelve shillings and sixpence a week and keep and the boy got £1.'

'A useful feature of our farmhouse at Breane was the lift (just a very solid platform hung on four chains) which was lowered from the cheeseroom at the top of the house through trapdoors in bedroom and kitchen ceilings, for taking the home-made cheeses (sometimes Cheddar and sometimes Caerphilly) up there to mature. Apples from

162

the orchard were also stored there – lovely old varieties like Tom Putt.'

CIDER MAKING

Long before bottled factory-made cider was being produced, most Somerset farms had their cider apple orchards and produced their own distinctive brew. A farmer who could not supply his workers with local cider was not one who would attract many helping hands at harvest time!

THE VALE OF APPLES

'Home for me was the Aville Valley, and Aville is a Saxon word meaning the Vale of Apples. This fruit grew in abundance in the orchards surrounding the farm. Some had names like Morgan Sweet, Quarnder and Lady Zudely. Tom Putt was a rich red apple but if you took a bite from it you quickly spat it out because it was very sour in spite of looking so inviting. My friend and I wandered through the orchard sampling an apple from every tree. This was an annual ritual and although we really knew the good-flavoured fruit from the not so good, we were young or naive enough to think perhaps they'd be sweeter than the previous year. The apples were for cider making, so that was the reason for growing Tom Putts and Kingston Blacks with their red skins and sharp flavour. There was a cider barn nearby and if I was thirsty I ran into the barn and hung over the cider barrel to catch a mouthful of the delicious golden liquid as it was squeezed from the apple press. At this stage the juice had not started to ferment. Many foreign bodies must have been on or in the apples as to harvest them the men shook the trees and raked the apples off the ground, regardless of what animals were grazing there beforehand, so I reckon this all added to the flavour. This really was "wine from the wood".'

CIDER MAKING TIME

'There was picking up apples in peck baskets in the orchards, making large heaps in readiness for being carted to the cider-press; the smell of the apple cheese with the juice trickling through the straw; and the first taste of sweet cider with the haymakers filling their heavy stone container jars.'

'The sound of barrels being rolled down the yard at Little Norton in the 1930s proclaimed that cider making time had come round again. Father was taking them down the road to the stream, where they were left steeping to plim for three days, to prevent them leaking. After which they had to be scrubbed clean. The water had to be collected in buckets from the pump which adjoined the cottage down the garden, some distance away.

Around the first week of October the whole family (there were seven of us) and various friends assembled in the orchards to pick up the apples, Horners, Kingstone Blacks, Jaiseys, Potato Apples, Lord Suffolk, Jolly Blades, and Little Norton Wonder. Those still on the trees were shaken down and we would stand clear not to be hit on the head.

The preparation of the cider press entailed forcing thick reed between the planks of the bed, after which it was filled with water to plim, like the barrels. Being three to four inches deep, it took quite a few buckets to fill it, there being no mains water or hose pipes at that time.

Baskets of apples were brought into the cellar and carried up the ladder to the loft. When the loft was full, the apples would be shovelled through a hole in the floor into a chute made of sacking, down into the grinder. The pulp was then transferred in wooden buckets to the press, where it was placed in alternate layers with straw. This was called the cheese. When the appropriate height had been reached it was topped with a large slab of oak, and gradually screwed down, very gently at first not to break up the cheese. After a few turns of the lever, the golden liquid would start to trickle, and then to a fast flow down into the collecting tub. This is what we as children had been waiting for, to taste this lovely sweet nectar through straws cut from the wheat. We thought it was heaven. Father had a beaker made from a cow's horn from which he quenched his thirst. It was always kept upside down in the cellar ready for use.

As the juice flowed into the tub it was dipped out with a baler into the waiting barrels (hogshead casks which held 52½ gallons) which were set up off the floor around the walls. A temporary bung (a piece of wood wound round with sacking) was placed in the bung hole, and it was left to "work". We could hear it "working" through the wall to our bedroom. After fermentation the bung would be rammed home and left until it was ready for drinking, when the bung would be replaced with a tap. A very delicate operation, it had to be done

164

The cider making begins – a farm cider press in action. (Photograph by kind permission of R.J. Sheppy & Son.)

quickly to avoid too much liquid being spilt.

After the last drop of liquid has been squeezed from the cheese (a very hard and difficult job needing two men to turn the lever as the cheese became more compressed), the pomace was sliced up with a large cutter and put out into the orchard where it attracted the pheasants. After feeding off this they became quite tiddly and were very easy to catch. We had some lovely roast dinners! This was kept a secret in the family, as had it come to the ears of the local squire, Father would have been heavily fined.

One year Father hired an engine from Will Sweet, a local smallholder, to help with the apple grinding. The fumes from this in an enclosed space must have been overwhelming, as Billy Bird who was in the loft shovelling the apples was overcome, and fell out of the loft onto the cellar floor. I don't remember that he was seriously injured.

Another incident was of a chicken being drowned in a tub of cider. I suppose it had perched on the edge to take a drink and had overbalanced. I wonder who had the chicken-flavoured cider? Various stories abound of items being put into cider to add flavour, such as pieces of beef, sugar, raisins, and even rats, though the last probably fell in of their own accord. The only thing Father added was beetroot to improve the colour.

Quite large quantities of cider was drunk during haymaking, as jars and small barrels were taken to the hay fields. It was much preferred to bottles of cold tea. There was no such things as thermos flasks.

165

Hot cider with spices and sugar was a favourite drink during the winter. Mum would heat it in a saucepan over an open fire. At the local pub a poker would be heated up in the blazing fire and then plunged into the mugs of cider, throwing up a cloud of steam.'

'Cider was made on our farm at Penselwood. Immediate neighbours would bring their apples for crushing. When our cider was finished the grinder and press, both horse-drawn, would travel around the area doing contract work.'

PIGS AND HARVESTERS

'Harry Brown used to live next door to me at Netherclay Cottage in Thurlbear and he had a lot of apple trees. Mr Quick used to come down and pick up these apples in a cart and take them to Hill Farm, and make cider with Lucy's father and Harry Brown.

When he'd made this cider, he brought it down in a barrel, and he'd push this barrel in the small gate and leave it in the orchard, for when Harry came home from work to put it away.

In a barrel like that, the bung's on the top. Well they'd usually have a piece of sacking to put in there, so they can pull the bung out of it. Anyway, Harry had an old sow out there; the sow pulled this sacking off and got the bung out and drank the cider.

So Harry goes down the yard next morning, where he worked and he said "What do you think? When I got home last night my old sow was as drunk as a pig!"'

'The school summer holidays were for the month of August only. Many children at Galmington helped on the farms. When John Aish was seven or so he and a friend would be sent to fetch cider for the harvesters at Penny's Farm. They carried an empty jar slung between them on a stick. This the landlord of the New Inn (now the Vivary Inn) filled with scrumpy and sealed with sealing wax. The men ate their bread and cheese in the fields and washed it down with the cider, handing the jar from man to man, tipping it up back-handed to drink. Some days the boys had to make two or three trips to the inn but Mrs Penny didn't really approve of alcohol. Hoping to set them on the right path perhaps, she'd catch the choirboys leaving the old tin church on Sundays and give them a drink of milk.'

'To the farm in summer would come the threshing machine, so big it occupied the width of the narrow lane to the village. The farmer dispensed his home-made cider from the press to the men, whilst he slowly became unsteady and incoherent.'

166

THE CIDER FACTORY

'The cider factory at Wiveliscombe, opened in the early 1900s, was one of the major employers in the area. Cider making began its short three month season in September. Hundreds of tons of local apples were delivered to the factory, no foreign apples were used. Some of the women working at Hancock's Brewery, on the opposite side of Golden Hill, would be given a temporary change of occupation. They were mainly employed on the bottling machines; the foremen were usually male and were allowed a gallon of beer a day. Wages had risen to approximately 37 shillings a week by the early 1940s, and overtime gave an extra shilling an hour.'

TRADES AND OTHER JOBS

There were many other occupations which were connected with the land, whether permanent jobs or seasonal, such as teasel picking for the Yorkshire woollen mills or collecting whorts or blackberries. Some were carried out by women in the home for extra cash, such as glovemaking. Somerset also had paper mills, brickyards, quarries and coal mines, though the majority of the latter were in North Somerset and are therefore now included in the new county of Avon. The following memories of the world of work are some indication of the variety of ways in which men and women endeavoured to earn a living, however meagre.

THE CHOICE WE HAD

'When he was young my father, like many more, worked in one of the quarries which surrounded Stoke St Michael. One brother drove a milk lorry, employed by the village milk factory, and he collected milk from the 26 farms around. My sister also worked there as a cheese-maker. Work as farm labourers was also plentiful, but there were few occupations for women. Another sister and other girls went to London, Bath and other cities to work for "better off" families; "in service" it was called. There was a corn mill, paper mill, woollen mill, saw yard and timber yard. These provided employment for villagers. Flour from the corn mill was delivered in large bags to local bakers.

There were also jobs in Shepton Mallet in the cider factory and shoe factory, but no transport was available, you had to get on your bike or walk five miles.'

COAL

'Radstock was the centre of the North Somerset coalfield and most men were employed in the pits. All had closed by 1960. I still have vivid memories of the coal strike of 1926. Whilst possibly not involving such a high level of hardship as in the larger coalfields there was deprivation in Radstock, alleviated by a series of picnic teas for miners' children. The cry was "Bring your own mug to the Rec (recreation ground)!".'

'The first time I visited Watchet I walked over the hill from Williton, on a grey day, saw an expanse of grey mud, a collier (The Rushlight) discharging coal, railway tracks, dirty wagons and coal dust everywhere. I went away and didn't come back for two years.'

'In the earlier years of this century there were a good many coal mines in North Somerset.

My grandfather, who kept a mixed farm, grew quite a lot of corn, particularly during the First World War. In those days corn was usually threshed in the winter, the threshing machine being driven by a steam engine. Steam engines were incredibly heavy and used a lot of coal and water in just one day.

Grandfather's corn took between one and two weeks, so he would send three men with four horses and two wagons to the pits for coal. Leaving before daybreak it was well after dark when the iron-rimmed wheels of the wagons and the well shod feet of the shire horses could be heard coming up the lane.

In the 1930s a steam engine went through the surface of the yard at my parents' farm in the Mendips, and was very difficult to move; eventually the horses pulled it out.

Once a year a man from the village would take his small lorry to the pit of Father's choice and bring us a load of coal. It was cut into rough cubes of about 18 inches or more. These were stacked in the shed and we would break one up as needed for the house. It was very good coal, but nearly impossible to crack if you did not hit it with the coal hammer on the correct side. It was also a very good way of getting very dirty!'

'I spent my childhood in the village of Coleford, seven miles from Frome. The village was surrounded by coal mines and limestone quarries, and my grandfather worked in the mine at Holcombe, walking the mile to and from work and in wintertime only seeing daylight on Sundays. My grandparents were strict Methodists and Sunday was sacred to them. They attended the Methodist chapel Sunday mornings and evenings and no work was ever done on Sundays.'

THE LIME INDUSTRY

'My father was born into a local family who lived at "Warren" on the coast just west of Watchet, in 1910. The family were in the lime industry. Alabaster, a low grade limestone, was quarried from the cliffs, taken to the clifftops and burnt in the limekilns. The lime was then transported from the kilns by donkeys who carried it in pannier baskets on their backs. From the jetty it was loaded onto small boats and taken to South Wales to be used in the iron smelters. The industry closed down in the 1920s.'

'In addition to a large agricultural work-force, the parish of Puriton had many craftsmen in other industries. During the early 1900s a flourishing salt-works was established. Deep bore-holes, drilled over 800 ft down into strata of rock-salt, were sunk and water pumped in to dissolve the salt. This brine mixture was brought to the surface and evaporated in large tanks over coal fires. The deposits of salt were then finely ground, packed by female workers, loaded onto railway wagons in sidings at Dunball station (now no longer existing) on the main GWR line, and despatched all over the country.

For over 50 years limestone was quarried from the Puriton hillsides, transported to Dunball where it was burnt in large kilns, crushed and ground into lime and cement, for the building industry nationwide.'

ON THE ROADS

'Another occupation was "stone-cracking" in the early 1900s. Charlie would set off each morning from Buckland Dinham on his tricycle to his pitch, taking his midday meal and his little stone-cracking hammer. There he would stand or sit by the roadside site cracking away the whole day, reducing really large stones to small ones. The stones were taken there on a big flat wagon drawn by horses from the quarry.'

'In 1912 the roads at Staplehay were made of flint stone quarried at Blagdon Hill which was delivered in loads at various places by the roadside. This stone was hand cracked by two men from the village.

The stone was very sharp and dusty, it was a godsend when the council switched to the grey Westleigh stone.'

'In the 1920s at Bishop's Hull, the stone-breaker still sat by the side of the road by his measured pile of flints. Wearing protective goggles, it was his work to crack the flints into smaller pieces for roadmending, using a hammer. The pieces were ground into the road surface by a steamroller. The stone-breaker sat on an old coat or piece of sacking on the grass verge, by him a straw basket with the day's food, and always a bottle of sweetened cold tea to wash the stone dust from his throat.'

'The triangle at the Yarrow end of the Abbots Causeway was composed in the 1920s of large stones, brought there by steam traction engines, ready for making up the roads, and very large stones were actually cracked there by men with pickaxes, before being laid down. The horses and carts wore this down to a hard surface rather to the detriment of the horses' feet and, also, anyone who had to walk to work or to church. On Sundays, ladies wearing long button boots held up their black skirts to walk through the mud or dust.'

'Father was lucky in the First World War. He had bad feet and ended up as cook for the soldiers at a recruiting station at Chelmsford. After the war he got a job working for Somerset County Council on the roads. I can remember him in the late 1920s, on his horse. The horse was a dappled grey called Prince. It was blind in one eye and had been in the war. The gang were repairing the road between Clewer and Cocklake – the tar spraying was only done in the summer. Father used his horse and putt to collect the stone or gravel from the old Shipham quarry, although often a lorry would empty out the stone in a bay by the side of the road, and he would collect it from there. He always wore a waistcoat and britches in the winter, with big hob-nailed boots.'

'The workhouse near Langport was for homeless people, and I remember my father telling how he went there with a horse and cart to fetch a load of cracked stone. He asked a tramp there who was breaking these stones with a hammer, what he got for doing this and he said, a bed for the night and bread. In those days the Council used to employ men with horses and wagons to haul big blue lias stones from quarries at Somerton and tip them along beside the roads. These had to be cracked to small bits to repair the roads. Here and there you would see steam rollers with their hut on iron wheels, parked for weeks. They rolled the stones in when spread. The drivers took their

170

wives and families with them, and very often babies were born in the huts. To show the hardship of those days, there was a man without legs who sat cracking stones, through all winds and weather, frost and snow. He would sit on a bag of hay and work day after day for little pay.'

'In the 1920s I drove a steam roller for Buncombe's of Highbridge. My wife and the baby came as well. We went as far north as Stone in Staffordshire and over to Suffolk, down to Southampton and into South Wales. Flint was used in Suffolk or granite was delivered by train. It took ten hours to get through Birmingham. Water could be a problem, as you had to be careful not to run out. Mrs Ham turned the wheel while I tended to the fire and the water. Ivy sat on the waste wrapped in a rug while we travelled. We towed a caravan as well as the water cart. In the early 1930s when we returned to farm, we kept house on £1 a week. Coal was one shilling and tenpence a cwt. You could buy a ton from the Earl of Dudley for 18 shillings.'

THE PEAT TURF CUTTER

'I was born in 1941 at my great-grandparents' small farm on the Somerset Levels at Chine Drove. My father's trade was peat turf digger so I spent all the school holidays helping in their peat field. This peat was used as a fuel on open fires. The season started in the spring when the large lumps were dug from the pit. These were split into three, then turned to dry, stacked in various ways – hyles, winrows, ruccles, rings – until they were dry, hard and about half the size. They were then stored in large ricks ready to be delivered by horse and cart to our customers. Also dealers came to buy them. We spent long happy days working in the sunshine, and when it got too hot to work we went to Dad's little tin shelter to have our sandwiches and a supply of lemonade for my brother and myself.'

THE PAPER MILL

'Watchet has always been a small trading port and up until the 1960s raw materials for the local paper mill, which was the largest employer in the district, also came into the port. I recall the old tramp steamers with the bridge and funnel amidships (as distinct from today's ships which have a large forward hold and bridge with accommodation at the rear) entering the port loaded with deck cargoes of esparto grass from North Africa and wood pulp from Scandinavia (often *The Gertrud*). Fuel for the paper mill was South Wales coal. This came across the channel in one of the mill's own boats. The most famous, of a long line, which I used to see battling in and out of the harbour in all weathers was the old Clyde "puffer", *The Rushlight*. Another was *The Radstock*.

Until the Dr Beeching era Watchet was on the branch railway line which ran from Taunton to Minehead. As children we would sit and watch the steam engines hauling the goods wagons from the harbour and paper mill.'

'Boys started work at the paper mill at Wookey at 13, working an eleven hour day. The apprenticeship for papermaker lasted seven years. Animal hides, bones, hoofs etc for making size were brought from Wookey station by a steam-driven lorry. The skin house, where the hides were processed, "Stank to high heaven", as did the men who worked there. During the Second World War the mill's felt-washing vats were used for washing army blankets, which were dried in the paper-lofts.'

'My father worked at St Cuthbert's Paper Mill at Wookey Hole. He had a bicycle to get him to work but many men walked from Coxley to Wookey taking a short cut across several fields.'

THE BREWERY

'Hancock's Brewery, founded in 1807, had become the largest brewery in the West by the 1880s and was one of the major employers in the Wiveliscombe area. Women were employed on the beer-bottling side. Their workday started at seven am and continued until five-thirty pm, with breaks for mealtimes which were marked by the siren in the Brewery Tower. Bottles had to be stacked neck downwards into units, which by a conveyor system washed, sterilised, filled and sealed them. They were then ready for crating, stacking and delivery to the local areas. Horse drawn drays were used until 1958 for local deliveries. The last horse, known as Prince, was very old by that time and had won the affection of many employees.

Local farmers recall the days before the Second World War when they would take their horse and "putt" carts to the brewery. The spent grain from the mash tun was dried out by a special drier, and could be bought for threepence a bushel. Hancock's home brewed beer and pale ale was considered to give the best grain, and was quickly bought up by the first arrivals. Any remaining grain was fed to the brewery horses. However, this practice had to cease during the war, when the grain was commandeered by the Government for conversion into cattle feed.

During the 1920s an annual event took place on 22nd December.

Mr Frank Hancock journeyed on horseback from his house in Ford, down to Wiveliscombe, and then walked up Golden Hill. Many of his brewery workers had their homes there, and would be waiting to greet him. This day was known as "Mumping or Begging Day" and every person he met would be given a two shilling and sixpenny piece. Male recipients were expected to touch their forelock, and ladies had to curtsey. He would also ask children to sing to him, and if they acquiesced, each child was rewarded with a sixpenny piece.'

THE MARKET GARDENER . . . AND THE HIGHWAYMAN

'The village of Merriott was once a thriving market garden area with a sail-cloth industry and farming community. Produce grown was mainly onions, peas, turnips and carrots. Merriott was renowned for its cabbage plants. My father carried on his market garden business here and took thousands of cabbage plants to Sturminster market and others. He told me the following story many times about his grand-father, who was a market gardener and poultry breeder.

Great-grandfather Eason's business took him, among other places, to Dorchester market regularly. One day, travelling home across Toller Down, the little leather bag in his coat pocket was full of sovereigns. Darkness was falling. Along the straight road where the BBC station now is, three men jumped out. One tried to hold the horse's head, the others jumped onto the wagon. Great-grandfather Eason knocked off the one in front with his whip. Then he whipped up the horse and hit back at the others, knocking one off. The other still hung on and he shouted to his man "Hit him with the stillers" (steelyards were a heavy iron rod with brass weights at the end). His man did this and the highwayman fell off. They came home and put the horse in the field. The next morning he went out to the carthouse. Suddenly he called his wife and daughters. They were horrified to see, lying on the back of the van, two severed fingers!

My husband has been a market gardener for nearly 40 years, growing acres of peas, beans and apples. All were harvested by hand and marketed in Plymouth, Bristol and Southampton. This has become a dying occupation with the advent of the supermarkets.'

RABBITS AND MOLES

'During the 1920s at Buckland Dinham, farmers in the village would shoot some 30 rabbits in a day, and a dealer named Grist would come out from Frome in the evening and pay sevenpence each for them.'

'Families were larger before the Second World War and at Nynehead

173

a family with as many as 13 children would catch as many rabbits as possible, which were taken into town and swapped at the butcher's for lamb or pork.'

'We took stout sticks into the fields where corn was being cut to catch rabbits as they ran from the corn, the excitement mounting as the standing corn grew less and less. I did sometimes catch a rabbit and hold it down with my stick but one of the men had to kill it. Most housewives in those days could skin a rabbit and the pelt was stretched on a board and saltpetre rubbed in. Traders came to the door and paid coppers for the cured skins.'

'In the 1950s, Mr Brock of Lympsham used to catch moles, and was paid one penny per tail.'

THE WELL DIGGER

'When father first came to Thurlbear at the end of the 19th century, he lived with Mr Hunt and was an apprentice helping to build wells. They dug them and then "bricked up" – and they put Mum down in the bucket once, before she was married to Dad. I think she had to pay a forfeit to come up!'

WASHING SPAR

'When I was a child in Cannington, before the First World War, the local women went to work washing spar, a very dirty job, in the nearby quarry. Spar is a bright, non-metallic mineral with good cleavage. It is akin to gypsum used in cement plasters, especially plaster of paris, and in some fertilisers.'

TIMBER, BRICKS AND BUILDERS

'At about six o'clock in the morning we used to hear the Snow's timber waggons go up through Glastonbury's High Street, on their way to collect the felled trees. Twelve hours later they would return to start their descent down the High Street. The waggoners were dressed in heavy leather breast shields and gaiters, the horses bedecked in their brasses, and when they started going down the waggoners put the iron brakes on the wheels, which caused sparks to rise all the way down the hill. A lovely sight, especially if the sun was setting in the foreground.'

'In the 1890s a brickworks was flourishing in Weare. Although the old buildings no longer exist, the old Brickworks House still stands and the descendants of the brickmaker, a Mr Day, still live in the house where they were born. His old ledgers show the price of bricks in those days:

600 perforated bricks	15 shillings
100 pan tiles	6 shillings
25 four-inch drainpipes	1 shilling and sixpence
25 red double roman tiles	£1 and sixpence.

The claypits are now a lake and other pits have been turned into Ambleside Water Gardens.'

'There was a brickworks in the village of Alcombe, and the children used to watch the trucks coming down a little railway from the quarry. Men would unload the stone and wheel it across the road to the brickworks. There were very few cars. People would rely on the brickyard hooter for the time, precisely at one pm and five pm.'

'On the north side of the village of Pilton was a large brick and tile works, where huge quantities of clay were dug by hand and machine from deep pits. Many highly skilled men were employed making best quality bricks and tiles, millions of which were transported all over Great Britain to build new housing estates during the 1930s, and exported from the wharfs at Dunball, loaded onto ships which sailed down the river Parrett to ports all over the world.'

'Father was demobbed from the Somerset Royal Engineers in the early 1920s and I left school at 14 to help mother at home. Father decided to risk all their savings and set up as a lone builder. The houses were the first speculative buildings in Bridgwater and many folk took a walk on Sunday afternoons to marvel at the semi-detached houses with bay windows!

The Council paid a subsidy on the stipulated floor area of each house. Father had a terrible time convincing the official measurer that the bay window should be disregarded.

We had a Sunbeam motorcycle and a sidecar and mother would ride with our dog, Tony, on her feet. They went to the various brickyards, tileworks and timberyards and Tony would disappear, but would soon come running when the Sunbeam engine started.

Thousands worked in the brick and tile yards and in the cement works at Dunball. We were told the Bridgwater scouring bricks went all over the world.'

THE SHOP

'In 1926 I went to Wells to live with a Mr and Mrs Cyril and their son and daughter. It was a shop and dairy in Sadler Street. I lived in and I slept there and every morning at six o'clock Mrs Cyril would shout out "Winnie" and I'd always say "Yes, ma" and up we had to get to come downstairs. Somebody had made the tea and we had as many cups as we wanted and there was always a seven pound tin of biscuits on the table and we could have a many as we liked because we never knew what time we were going to have breakfast. Then we went straight out and I used to start bottling milk.

Mr Cyril had a van and he fetched some of the milk but many of the local farmers brought it in by horse and cart. It was hard work there but it was very enjoyable, we used to have great fun. We used to put the milk up in a big tub and it ran down and you pressed the bottle in – there was a spring and it filled up and you took the bottle out and you pressed a cardboard disc in to seal it. Every other Sunday Mr Cyril's daughter and I used to do the milk round, because the men had their time off. This was in the afternoon and we pushed a three-wheeler trolley up St Thomas Street and to all the little cottages and delivered the milk.

When all the men had finished their milk rounds we used to have all the crates of bottles to wash and we just put them in a big tub on four legs and plenty of hot water and a brush and we used to put plenty of soda in and then just swill them afterwards in cold water. They were never sterilised.'

'I and a friend worked as assistants in a drapery shop in 1922, when we were aged 16. We walked to Shepton Mallet, three miles uphill, in time to start work at 8.30 am. Apart from halfday closing on Wednesdays, we worked till 7 pm Monday to Thursday, till 7.30 pm on Friday and till 8 pm on Saturday, all for the grand wage of 13 shillings and sixpence a month!

At about the same time, another girl was apprenticed to the village post office at two shillings and sixpence a week, where one of her duties was to make phone calls for members of the public.'

'When I left school at 14, it was the depression years and jobs were scarce. For me, there were practically no openings other than domestic service, but I was determined to find something better and eventually I was engaged in a drapery shop. I was overjoyed at my good fortune.

Days were long though, typically 9 am until 6 pm, and Fridays and Saturdays were much longer; it was usually past ten o'clock before I arrived home on these days. For this, I was paid three shillings and sixpence a week.

After my first month with a senior assistant, I was allowed to serve my first customer. Progress had to be earned, but I was soon helping the window-dresser and, some years later, I took over the job myself.

Sales were held regularly and were great events for both staff and customers alike. I remember the September sale of 1939, the town already full of evacuees. We did a roaring trade that day as the public, perhaps anticipating the coming austere war years, spent to stock their wardrobes.

The advent of self-service and checkouts was of course still some 40 years off, which meant that, leaving aside the extra work, assistants had to be familiar with all aspects of retailing, from stock control to serving customers. Naturally, it wasn't all hard work. For my first Christmas, I dressed as Santa and distributed gifts to children whose parents had paid to bring them into the Fairy Grotto. Yes, there were lighter moments.'

'In 1936 I was apprentice for three years to learn dispensing. The shop and dispensary were quite small with narrow shelves and tiers of small drawers. A chair was always by the counter and the door was always kept open. Most of the dispensing was done on the National Health, using a book of prescriptions supplied for this. We made up all our ointments, suppositories and quite a lot of pills. I was taught to make emulsions, liniments and embrocations. Reference books were the British Pharmacopoeia, its Codex and a little book called the Apothecaries Vade Mecum.

We opened at 8.30 am and closed at 5.30 pm with a half day closing on Wednesday. Supplies and drugs were brought from Bristol by Ferris & Co's van. Medicine was dispensed in eight or 16 fl oz bottles of mixture, not much in tablet form or ready packed as today. Bottles had to be accurately labelled and initialled as checked by the chemist, then enwrapped in white 'demy' paper – the folding was an art to be learnt – then sealed with red sealing wax. Pills and ointments were put in round cardboard boxes. All the bottles had to be washed and there was no hot water supply, I used to get chilblains every winter. Epsom salts, boracic acid, bicarbonate of soda, Glaubers salts and similar were weighed and packed in the white paper. We sold senna pods, poppy heads and pickling spices. In spring we stocked cotton bags of fertiliser which smelt horrible, kept in a cupboard under the stairs. When the sirens went in the Second World War this was supposed to be the safest place! Prescriptions were copied into a ledger with the day's date written in Latin at the top of the page.'

JOBS FOR WOMEN

'Before the Second World War there was little choice for work for girls as they left school at the age of 14 years.

Some girls entered service as a domestic in one of the large houses which employed quite a few staff. They usually lived in, worked long hours, and were at the beck and call of the family. From the lowly position of housemaid a girl could better herself and perhaps eventually become a cook or housekeeper.

To be a children's nurse or nanny could be a pleasant job if the family and children were kind and reasonable. Intelligence, some education and dedication were usually expected for girls seeking this occupation.

Later, hairdressing became a popular job for girls. Those who took apprenticeship in the better class salons were lucky, for some of the smaller salons used young girls as so much cheap labour and grossly underpaid them.

Office work for young ladies was becoming more popular between the two world wars. The advent of the typewriter created jobs in most offices for young women, and many learned shorthand to complete their skills. Shop work had always been available and was a favourite occupation for the majority of girls when they left school.'

IN SERVICE

'A lady now in her nineties remembers that after leaving school it was hard to find work, but she went to help at the "big house", where in addition to the chores she was "put upon to do a bakery round". The bread was piled into a wooden barrow with a basket of cakes on each handle and was trundled round Horsington village. A heavy task for a 14 year old.'

'Employment must, for girls, have been very limited in the 1920s and 1930s, unless the families were wealthy enough to pay for secondary education. The children of ordinary working parents left school at 14. It was very necessary for them to take any available job. Girls could work in shops or go into service in the houses of the well to do, or on farms or in business houses.

At 14 years old a girl lived in, and expected to start work at about 6.30 in the morning cleaning grates and lighting fires. She had to scrub the floors and passages on hands and knees and the outside steps, and clean all the family shoes.

These maids shared a bedroom and staff bathroom. In one household at Dunster there was a cook, who ruled the staff with a rod of

178

iron, a parlourmaid, housemaid and tweeny. The housemaid had to take my lady's morning tea not much later than 6.30. There were no vacuum cleaners. Carpets were brushed daily.

Permission was required to go out. The hours off were two hours each afternoon, a half day every week from 4 pm – 10 pm and half a day every alternate Sunday. When the family gave a party the staff worked from 6.30 to midnight.'

'My mother used to work in the dairy at the manor house at Staple Fitzpaine, and before I went to school she took me with her. Mother was making butter and as it was ready to be made up she used to spread some on a crust for me with her fingers. I can remember the water drops flying onto my face as she spread it so she couldn't have got it all out. I then had to sit on a stool with my crust until she finished the job.'

'When I was 14 years old I left school and went into service, which was expected of most girls then. The house I went to was on the edge of the village. There I had to cook and clean – no Hoover for the carpets, only a large broom and a dust-pan and brush – and how the dust settled on the furniture after the sweeping! I was paid five shillings a week and my food. I had to wear a white cap and apron which was starched with the tablecloths and napkins. The black-leaded stove in the kitchen was awful to clean. I stayed about two and a half years and to get more money came to Woolavington village to work as a house–parlour maid. The cook was a young girl like myself and we were very happy working together. It was a large house, fires on the hearth in some rooms and another black stove in the kitchen. Plenty of brass and silver to be cleaned and logs to be brought in for the fires. Our employers were very kind to us and to the poor in the village at Christmas time. I met my husband here, his father being the gardener, and the garden had all sorts of lovely fruit and vegetables. Our rooms were in the attic and it was very cold in the winter, when there would be ice in our water jugs. The village was small with two shops and a baker only five minutes away. Everyone knew each other and helped out when anyone was ill or if the children needed anything. The lovely old church has always been well cared for.'

'At North Curry young women went into service, not only in the village but further afield. Beattie's sister worked for a very fussy lady in the village who insisted that the quarry tiles throughout the lower floor of her house were polished with milk at least once a week. Ewbank sweepers were not available until later, so carpets were brushed on hands and knees with tealeaves to keep the dust down.

Lily looked after children and was paid £12 a year (which included her keep) when she was 14 years old.'

'In 1927 my father took early retirement and we came to live in Pitney. We had a "bull-nosed" Morris car – YC 23. The postman lived in the village and he had a car too – the only two cars in the village. There was no gas or electricity in the village. We had oil lamps everywhere. There was one maid who did nothing else but clean the lamps, about 30 of them. Every day she trimmed their wicks and polished the glass chimneys and the oil containers. They all sparkled when alight. There would be one in every room in the house and in the passages too.'

'One lady in Hemington remembers in the mid 1940s wearing a cap and apron while in service at the rectory and having to be in by 9.30 pm on her evening off.'

THE POULTRYWOMAN

'There are not many local people in Wiveliscombe who have not heard of the redoubtable Mrs Bessie Langdon. She embarked on her successful business career at the age of 15, in 1897. At that time, as a farmer's daughter, she sold eggs, but sought much more lucrative markets than the local ones. She found them in Bristol and London! This led, in 1909, to a contract to supply poultry and game to large London stores. Her egg and poultry business continued to expand, and during the First World War she bought a Ford motor van, the forerunner to the Tone Vale road transport fleet. She then opened an egg-packing station, sending lorries out to collect the eggs. More than 150 cases of eggs were packed daily, an astounding number, as each case held 300 eggs.

Despite her tremendously busy life she also married and raised a family of sons and daughters.

At the time of her death in 1959 she was chairman of B.A. Langdon and Sons Ltd, a director of Tone Vale Transport Ltd, and a director of Somerset Egg and Poultry Company.

Mrs Langdon's achievements would be quite remarkable even in these days of female entrepreneurial skills – how very much more so in earlier days! However, she is of particular importance in Wiveliscombe WI, who were delighted that she agreed to hold office as President during the years 1951 to 1954. Members who knew her personally, speak highly of her kindness and warmth, and of the efficiency and high standards which characterised her business career, which were also demonstrated during her Presidential years.'

180

'My mother Freda was brought up on an exposed farm just outside Mark village, within sight of Crook's Peak. Her father was rented the farm by Somerset County Council because he fought in the First World War. Granny said his bad temperament was caused by falling from a truck in France!

Mother left home at 14 to pick strawberries at Cheddar for a season, then looked after two children there and five years later came home to make cheese, gaining top price one week at Highbridge market for Caerphilly.

When we visited the farm I loved to see Grandfather taking a dented galvanised scoop to the brick-boiler in the kitchen. He would dip hot water and perch it on the wooden cover to rinse his hands before he ate anything. It was only recently I realised it was Granny's chicken-feed scoop!

In the 1950s we lived to the south of Mark Moor within sight of the Quantocks. We had a small black range in our front kitchen with an oven which I didn't see used for baking. As a poultry farmer, Mother would place a tray of egg shells inside the oven to become crisp and golden. She squeezed them into crumbs to feed to her laying hens for stronger-shelled eggs.

A telephone call would sometimes come to a neighbour, that day-old chickens were awaiting collection at Highbridge station. Miller-brooders were set up with their green felt interiors and cosy heaters lit, ready for Father's return with the tiny yellow fluffy creatures.'

ANY JOB HE COULD FIND

'Life was a struggle for many people in the 1920s and 1930s. There was no income support then, and my father was too proud to draw the dole. He would work hard and long at any job he could find. It had even been known for him to sit at the side of the road cracking stones for use in road repairs. In happier times he owned a horse and cart and worked a vegetable round, selling produce he had grown in his garden and allotment. He gardened early and late, even by moonlight or by the light of a Tilley lamp. He also hired his services as a furniture remover at the local auctions. When he needed a new horse, he once rode his bicycle 60 miles to Bristol to buy one and led it all the way back still riding his bicycle. In the 1920s the fishermen of Minehead made large catches of herring, and my father loaded his cart with buckets and baths full of the fish and sold them to the country people at 20 a shilling. These were salted in for the winter. He was affectionately known as "Shaver" and died when only 54, worn out by his life of hardship.'

ROPE AND HORSEHAIR

'In the 1940s, Messrs Donnes' factory was in operation at Castle Cary, making twine and rope. There was a rope walk and machinery was operated by water power; sluices, ponds, pipes and a water wheel were objects of interest. There were also once two horsehair factories, employing between 80 and 100 men and women. Preparing the hair was very dirty work, but the cloth when woven was used for furnishings and was very hard wearing. Fabrics are manufactured in part of the old factory to this day.'

A BOX OF FISH

'In the 1930s we moved to a bungalow overlooking the dunes at Breane. I noticed a large semi-circle of chicken wire and wondered what it was for. One day a little old man came trundling a wooden box on wheels. He prodded around the wire enclosure when the tide had gone out and a box of fish was the result – all sorts. After that I would run out with my pail and for one shilling and sixpence get a pailful of fish. Soon he didn't come anymore, but I noticed also about 20 or 30 stakes which were used to hang a baited hook. I soon got onto this – baiting before the tide came in and being quick to gather my catch when the tide went out, before the seagulls got there first. Skate, sole, dabs, conger and even salmon once! Fishing by seine net was another method used locally, but that was hard work.'

ENGINEERING

'William Sparrow Ltd have been established at Martock since 1867 as engineers and a bill head dated 1914 describes their many activities; "The Somerset Engineering and Waggon Works, boiler makers, brass and iron founders, millwrights, makers of agricultural implements, carts and waggons of every description, agents for motor cars, gloving machinery a speciality". During the 1914–18 war artillery wheels for gun carriages were made, 205 being made in a week to go to Woolwich Arsenal. They manufactured the first Dodgem cars and also made traction engines, one of which is still in use in Dorset. They made the truck and wheels for one of the first fire engines, made brick making machinery and iron spoke wheels with wood rings. They continue to prosper as Agricultural Engineers and suppliers of farm and garden machines and equipment.'

182

THE MASTER GARDENER

'My grandfather, Albion Case, was a self employed master gardener at Huish Episcopi and very much in demand at all the local large houses. He could lay tennis courts and prepared one for Dr Johnson of Langport. He also did work for the Stuckeys at the top of "The Hill", which later became St Gilda's Convent. He travelled to other parishes by pony and trap and was a master craftsman in the art of fruit grafting.'

CLOTHES, CLOTH AND GLOVES

'Gloving was a handcraft and means of earning a little extra money by the women in the area. The gloving van came round each week to bring the various types of gloves, ready cut out, and then collected them when they were completed. The tannery and factory was in Tancred Street, Taunton – now no more.'

'At Barrington gloving was (and is) done at home, a firm supplying the cut out materials and a special sewing machine. One villager, the mother of seven, was known to rock the cradle with one foot and manipulate the sewing machine with the other.'

'A retired District Nurse says "About 30 years ago I visited an old lady born in 1870. I found her waltzing round her room to the sound of the radio set. "Oh", she said, "I do dearly love to dance". As a young woman she would sit at her gloving machine right through the night to make enough money to go dancing the next night at Stoke, three miles away. A 90 year old who did a song and dance in her kitchen, she told me how she used to set off for Yeovil at 6 am with the gloves she had made and would receive about sixpence for a dozen pairs. Yet a younger woman, a farmer's wife, told me that when she married, her husband's pay was ten shillings a week and she was able to earn more than this by gloving – they ended up owning their own farm".'

'My great-aunt at Milborne Port had been an overseer at the local glove factory before the Second World War and also did outwork at home. She wore beautifully stitched gloves herself and we girls wore "shammy" leather gloves to chapel. Oh, the weary washing of those slimy horrors.'

'The old established firm of Fox Bros of Wellington, noted for their woven woollen cloths and manufacture of khaki and puttees,

183

employed many local women in their factory in Ford Road, Wivelis-combe. In the days before the Second World War some of the women worked as invisible menders. This involved correcting any mistakes made by the loom in the spinning and weaving process. In 1933 the hours worked were from six am to six pm with breaks for breakfast and lunch. Wages were seven shillings and sixpence a week.

Other girls were employed to pick out the "bits" from 25 yard long pieces of cloth, and were paid according to the number of lengths they completed. Outwork was also available, mainly on puttees, and was a very popular way of earning extra money, even by some who worked full time.

One married lady, who had worked for Fox for many years as well as raising her family, retired at the age of 70 in 1939, and was grateful to receive an occupational pension of one shilling and sixpence a week.'

'Before the First World War at Curland I recall my mother making shirts for workmen. They were hand-machined, no collar, just a white band; she stitched that on by hand. Long sleeves and cuffs and she would put a little gusset at the wrist and also in the tail. And she would make buttonholes by hand. She would get up and make one before she got us up for school – she would get a shilling for it. She would also make a woman's shirt blouse for which she received the same amount. I can remember her saying that there was extra work there but she said "Well, they wouldn't ask me to do it if it cost more." She made all of us children's clothes and brought up ten of us.'

'I was apprenticed when I left school in 1928, as a dressmaker to Mrs Edwards in Billet Street, Taunton. My first wage was four shillings and sevenpence a week; it went up to seven shillings and sixpence, then ten shillings, and finally one pound four shillings.'

SEASONAL WORK

'Teasel growing was quite an occupation in the Bickenhall area earlier this century. The seed was sown in springtime one year and the plant matured in the late summer of the following year. Women did a lot of the teasel cutting, the heads being tied in bundles of 50, dried and eventually sold to the teasel merchants who came down from Yorkshire each year and toured the area buying teasel, which was then transported to the mills in the North where they were used to bring up the nap on the best woollen cloth. The merchants based themselves at the Hatch Inn.'

'We all went cutting teasels in the fields for local farmers in the 1950s. We had a teasel knife to cut them; done up in bundles, they were strung up on poles. We all used to have a good old sing-song, but we had to remember to count as we were cutting – up to 40 or 50 a handful.'

'As a child, in 1941, I was introduced to whorting. Several adults and children crammed into a car which took us to Dunkery. Here we spent the day crouched over low growing bushes, tormeneted by flies, picking the small black round berries. Nearly as many were eaten by us children as went into our baskets and our mouths and fingers were soon stained blue/purple by the fruit. A quick movement often upset the container and the berries were difficult to retrieve. Woe betide anyone who ventured into another's patch of bushes too! It was a two mile walk back to Wheddon Cross laden with the day's harvest, which we took to the Sundial shop. The whortleberries were measured in a special quart pot and we were paid a shilling a quart. In the First World War payment was fourpence a quart.

I've been told that in the 1920s and 1930s (and probably before that) school holidays started when the whorts were ripe in July and families would walk to Dunkery and back, picking enough berries to pay for their children's boots for the coming winter.

Overstocking of the moors and hills, with declining bushes, would make this impossible today. Enough fruit for pies can still be picked if one knows where to look, and who can resist whortleberries and clotted cream!'

'I remember an old lady, at least, old when I knew her. She had been a cook in private service. Her husband was a carter, and earned 17 shillings and sixpence a week. They got a rent free cottage in return for him doing all the feeding and watering at the weekends, they also got free skimmed milk, and kindling for the fire. They had one child, and every autumn, mother and daughter walked up onto the Quantocks and picked whortleberries, they then walked to Taunton market, sold the "whorts", and that paid for the daughter's winter coat. She always said they were happy, and wanted for nothing, she always had a penny for the Sunday paper which was the weekly reading for the family. A 48 hour week was normal, and leisure time in very short supply.'

'In summer we collected blackberries. Everyone collected them and brought them to me, and my father before that. Early in the century they went on the train from Axbridge to Covent Garden or Manchester. In the 1920s Robertsons bought them and took them to Bristol or Paisley. I went around the villages, Mark, Weare, Allerton and Brinscome in a horse and cart until the 1940s after which we used a Morris Oxford. The berries went into cwt barrels which were then tipped into 3 cwt barrels to be collected by Robertsons and put in cold storage. From 1942 for 15 years or so we collected 15–18 tons a year. We stopped collecting when they went up to sixpence a lb.'

'At Queen's Farm in Tintinhull turkey plucking went on all year round, but it was busiest at Easter and Christmas, when there were turkeys and geese to pluck. At times there were five of us on duty. The farmer would collect and kill the birds and bring them into the old dairyhouse where they were wet plucked. After working almost non-stop for eight hours our fingers were very sore! This would go on for about two weeks before Christmas, always with a deadline to be met. Many a time we were still there at 10.30 or 11 o'clock to get the last one done. The farmer's wife would ply us with tea, home-made pasties and soup; working in such cold conditions those pasties never tasted so good.

One particular Christmas, one of the women helpers happened to mention that she had 14 turkeys waiting to be plucked by her husband that evening. On hearing this the farmer's wife suggested that she fetch them and do them at the farm. After much persuading, accompanied by a friend, the turkeys were fetched by driving them down the road with a stick. Having plucked and hung them a very irate husband arrived believing all his turkeys had been stolen. Very straight-faced all the women said how sorry they were at his loss. Without a hint of a smile the farmer's wife led him into the barn to show him all the turkeys that had been plucked that day. Seeing 14 turkeys hanging in a row he suddenly realized that they were his, much to the amusement of all the ladies who had followed him into the barn.'

WAR & PEACE

THE GREAT WAR 1914-18

⟨⟩

Somerset's young men were as eager as their contemporaries in the rest of England to join up and fight in 1914, as the war memorials in every town and village bear testimony. For those left behind life went on much the same, though horses were commandeered from the farms and the war effort included picking sphagnum moss for medical use and growing flax. Those families with men overseas dreaded the coming of the telegram bearing bad news, and the relief and delight which greeted the news "It's over" can be felt even today.

ALL THE YOUNG LADS

'I have lived at Meare a long time and heard both World Wars declared. In 1914, my young and much loved uncle, Richard Difford, persuaded young village lads and all his friends to join up. Sadly, most of their names are now on the village war memorial.'

CARRYING ON AT THE FARM

'The government commandeered a lot of horses, together with hay from the farmers, but expected the farmers to go on producing the same! Fortunately at the Cary farm at Buckland Dinham there were a couple of brood mares, so some colts were coming along to be broken in. Herbert Cary and his sister Daisy used to drive a float one a half miles in the afternoons down a lane to a field and milk 16 cows by hand, leave the milk in churns, unhitch the horse from the float and turn it out with the cows for the night, and then walk home. The next morning they would walk back (hearing the church clock strike six am), milk the cows again, catch the horse, and bring the churns back in the float to the farm, where the milk was tipped into a cheese tub with the rest of the farm milk.'

MOSS AND BLACKBERRIES

'Before I went to school during the Great War I went with an older girl, Louise Spiller, to the mission hut at Bickenhall and there were tables set up with piles of moss on them which had been brought off the hill. Miss Boyle from the manor house was setting everyone to take out leaves and prickles from the moss. I helped a bit and then got down and played. Sphagnum moss was used as a wound dressing in the war.'

'During the war in 1918 at East Coker, pupils were released three and a half days a week to pick blackberries for the war effort – they picked 492 lb.'

PULLING FLAX

'During the First World War there was a great demand for flax to make linen for parachutes and to use the seeds for oil; so the cry went out from the Government for farmers to plant this crop. This was an unusual crop for farmers to grow but many in Somerset undertook to do so.

An appeal was sent to the Teacher Training Colleges around London for students to go and pull the flax. I was one of them at the time and one day I found myself on Waterloo station boarding a train for Somerset. It seemed such an adventurous journey, so far from London. I remember arriving at Yeovil Junction station, where we were met by the country folk who had large cans of milk for our refreshment.

We were then taken to a huge field at Berwick, near Yeovil. In the hedge were one or two stone statues; I remember "Jack, the treacle eater" (I wonder if he's still there?). There, rows of bell tents met our eyes, and we were allocated spaces – eight students to a tent. As the days went by, lorries from neighbouring farms and villages came to the field to fetch us. We were then driven to the flax fields within a few miles of our camp – Odcombe, Brympton, Bradford, Stoke-sub-Hamdon, East and West Coker etc. In the fields we were instructed how to pull the flax, bundle and tie the bundles. We then had to stook it – six bundles to each stook – and it was left to dry. Later, it was gathered in and lorries took it to the factory in Yeovil. The flax had to be pulled and not cut for every inch of the plant was needed, from the root to the seed. Later, we learned, it was put into channels of water to "ret" the outside straw, leaving long strings of linen which were cleaned and woven into cloth. I remember we were very indignant when we learned that the students from the Royal College of Music were excused much of the hard work of pulling because it was so hard on the hands – oh! the poor hands – they were ruined!'

MULES ON THE COMMON

'During the war, as a little girl, I was fascinated by the long lines of mules camped out with the soldiers on the downs near Cannington.'

189

'Nynehead was a mule depot for the army. The animals were not under cover but tethered in lines in a field. One severe winter the field became a quagmire with the result that many of the mules got strangles – a disease somewhat like pneumonia in humans – and a great number died. The local vet was employed there almost full time and local men were pressed into service to bury the carcasses. Bones are still unearthed when ploughing that field.'

THE TELEGRAM

'One of my brothers was wounded at the Gallipoli landings and when the telegram came, my mother was too ill to open it and we girls were too frightened, so we sat and waited for my father to come home. My brother came home to recover, but before he was well again he was sent to France and two days later another telegram came.'

'DO AEROPLANES LAY EGGS?'

'During the First World War an aeroplane was quite a rare sight, so when a teenager, whose boyfriend was in the air force, heard a plane going over she always ran to the window to look out. Her sister of about five years asked "Do aeroplanes lay eggs when they come down?", obviously thinking it was a rare kind of bird.'

IT'S OVER!

'We were living at Rexton Farm. It was the biggest farm out that way but quite far from Stogumber so Rector would come out two or three times a year and take services in the farm dining room. He always came at Harvest and I remember decorating our dining room with vegetables and fruit. During the war, two lady pilgrims took the services and one of them gave me a religious book. From the time I was five years old, I walked the two and a half miles to Lydeard St Lawrence school. Some of the men from the farms had gone to the war and we heard terrible stories of life in the trenches and the soldiers being so hungry they would eat anything. There was no wireless or newspaper to bring news to the village but we were told at school the day the war was over. When I got home, I told my parents but they did not believe me at first, after all I was only nine years old.'

'The Great War saw Staplegrove playing host to a group of Belgian refugees. In common with other villages it sent its young men off to serve the colours in many parts of the world. One family in Staplegrove sent six sons and a son-in-law to France. At the end of hostilities 16 young men did not return. The lychgate at the entrance to the churchyard is to their memory.'

'In November, 1918, Lord Curzon was in residence at Montacute House. Telegrams arrived for him at the post office and on this particular morning Alice and a friend were to take the message up to the house. Having delivered it to the servant's hall, they waited to see if there was an answer, and were regaled with cake by the house-keeper in the meantime. Then the butler reappeared and said, "His Lordship says I am to tell you the war is over." At this news, the baker, who was delivering bread from his horse and cart, swept the little girls up, and they *galloped* down the drive to bring the good news to the village.'

COPING IN THE DEPRESSION

'Times were hard in the 1920s and although there seems not to have been too much unemployment in Galmington, there were some very poor people around. In cold spells the Parish provided extra blankets for sixpence each – when the weather warmed up the blankets had to be returned. Most of the men worked on the farms or at the brick-works, which were sited on what is now the Cornishway Industrial Estate. The 150 men employed there toiled long hours on piece rates. The yard itself was an eyesore with a 100 ft chimney belching smoke and fumes day and night. Two deep ponds had been created where the brick clay had been dug out, and in 1906 three children lost their lives there when the ice they were playing on gave way.'

191

'Though very young, I can remember the Depression years because I saw a man faint in the dole queue at Cheddon Fitzpaine. He fell into the road in front of us on the way to school, and we were told it was because he was hungry.'

THE SECOND WORLD WAR

The first bombs falling on Somerset heralded the beginning of years of black-outs, air raid warnings and disturbed nights. German bombers heading for Bristol and the South Wales coast passed noisily and menacingly overhead, sometimes bringing destruction to quiet farms and villages. The Americans came too, and made a lasting impression on the local population for their generosity – whether with sweets for the children or nylons for the girls! Those at home "did their bit" in the Home Guard, the Red Cross or other organisations, and women found themselves in demand by employers. Prisoners of war found a surprisingly tolerant reception. Perhaps what caused the greatest stir in many homes, however, was the arrival of the evacuees, those little refugees from the cities who brought new ways to their country hosts. Some were glad to see them go, but many others formed life-long relationships – and many evacuees themselves discovered a new world in Somerset they were reluctant to leave again.

THE FIRST BOMBS

'Thornfalcon's claim to fame was that the first bomb to be dropped in Somerset fell near the Nag's Head public house. Later a German airman who escaped by parachute from his plane, was apprehended in Thornfalcon by a farm worker, but he was taken in and given a cup of tea by his captor's wife.'

'The first bombs dropped in the Bickenhall area were all around our farmhouse (incendiaries). In spite of the fact that we had just come in from haymaking that evening and had our hayrick in the yard, and a thatched roof on the house, not one of the 20 or so bombs dropped on anything inflammable. I remember we laughed about it afterwards – there was a lovely smell of cooked onions in the garden where the incendiaries had dropped on the onion bed. The bombs were about six or seven inches long and just burned out. I believe a couple of land mines dropped at the top of Forest Drove, resulting in a large hole. This was June 1940.'

'The area around Milborne Port was a fighter corridor during the war. There were several small airfields dotted around and German planes were shot down. Bombs were dropped in Yeovil and Sherborne and some damage was done. One was dropped on the outskirts of our village, making an awful whistling sound, and one night incendiary bombs and flares were dropped near our house. Mother roused us and we ran up the road and hid in the ditch. One brother and I used to stay up very late to listen to Lord Haw Haw on the German radio and to watch the searchlights and ack-ack guns which were all around us on the hills. German bombers came over almost every night. We would lie awake and wait for the drone and when we saw the glow in the sky we knew that Bristol or South Wales was being bombed.

There was a total black-out at night, no street lights and car lights were very dim and shrouded. I often used to visit two elderly ladies who were very scared each night in case there was bombing.'

THE GERMAN SPY

'On the outbreak of war Nynehead Court became a nursing home for disturbed people and a German doctor who lived and worked in the village was found to be a spy, as radio receivers etc were found in his house.'

AIR RAID WARNINGS

'I was at school at Ruishton and air raid drill consisted of putting on gas masks and laying on the floor of the school corridor. At night the village constable would go round blowing his whistle if there was an air raid.'

'The planes flew over Brompton Ralph every night at about six pm on their way to Wales, mainly Cardiff. Searchlights sweeping around were quite blinding. Sometimes machine-gun bullets whistled past the window. Some people used to walk up to Raleigh's Cross to watch across the Channel – it was like a fireworks display.

We had to cover the lanterns when we went out to do the milking; you could only have a tiny light to see by, or you'd have the ARP

Wardens round. The Scotts had the only telephone. Brompton Ralph was too far away to hear the siren at Wiveliscombe, so when there was an air raid warning, a telephone message was sent to the Scotts. Mr Scott had to go round on his bicycle to check that no lights were showing, and give the alarm. Usually, by the time he was halfway round the village the All Clear would come, but he wouldn't hear that until he came home.

A landmine fell at Sandford Brett. It must have been on the same seam of rock as Truckwell, because the house felt as if the walls had fallen in. However, when I went down to look, only the windows had broken.

More frightening was the day the soldiers came to cook their meal at our farmhouse. You had to let them in. They went into a barn, where the straw was stored overhead, and used open petrol cookers. They spilt petrol over the yard and it caught alight; we were really frightened. Next day they moved up to Brendon Hill and we heard that bombs were dropped there so they must have shown a light that night too.'

'The nightly task of meeting blackout requirements became very tedious, as my family lived in an old rambling house at Wiveliscombe with uneven windows and sky-lights, and no light could be lit until they were all boarded up. My younger brother liked me to take him a few yards along the pavement at night. The darkness was a novelty to him.'

BOMBING WINCANTON

'Our quiet town of Wincanton was devastated in May 1944 when a German bomber was being chased and scattered its stick of bombs, some falling on farmland, but one hitting the premises of the solicitor's office scattering documents all over the town. The bank next door was also badly damaged, killing the daughter of the bank manager. This shocked the whole community, as local people could not believe that this little market town would be a target for air raids.

In the same year, an American Flying Fortress which had been hit by enemy fire in France and was badly damaged, flew over the town, but by the heroic efforts of the crew who managed to fly the crippled plane away from the town, another tragedy was averted. Sadly it crashed in flames near a farm, and the crew all perished.

Wincanton people were so grateful and a plaque was erected overlooking the scene of the crash to commemorate the courage of these brave men.'

194

Life goes on during the Second World War. People still need clothes and shoes even when rationed and on coupons.

195

UNEXPLODED BOMBS

'During the war Castle Cary was a busy place. There were evacuees billeted here, and soldiers – first the Grenadier Guards and then an American Medical Unit. A stick of bombs which did not explode was dropped here. Most were in South Cary Lane, but one landed in my father-in-law's field, not far from our cottages. This field was marshy, and when the Army came with all their special equipment to recover it, they dug a large hole but only recovered a fin. Then they went away on a course, which annoyed my father-in-law, as he and his sons had to fill in the hole. Presumably, the bomb has worked down for ever. Later, bombs were dropped on Castle Cary station, partly demolishing an inn and killing an engine driver.'

'Before the war a fourth reservoir was being built at the foot of the Blackdown Hills to supply Taunton and district. Work was abandoned as the men were needed for the forces, but I can remember the workmen going home on their bikes in the evenings, as I lived on a farm nearby. Mr Jones the foreman, brought his wife and eight children from Birmingham to live in a cottage close by.

As the war developed, American, Polish and British airmen and troops came to the Blackdowns, where there were three aerodromes and also army camps in the area. "Quants" became a practice range. At school, lorries of American soldiers passed by on their way, and sometimes threw chewing gum to us in the playground.

One awful weekend, a young boy from Angersleigh, Reggie Phillips, went to play with the Jones children, and wandered onto the reservoir, where they were blown up by an unexploded bomb. Three of the Jones children, Fred, George and Margaret, also Reggie, were killed. Fred lived long enough to tell his Dad that George had kicked something. Everyone was stunned who lived around. All four were buried in one large grave at Angersleigh, and I remember helping to take two baths of bunches of flowers, with a lot of roses included, to the service.

Rose perfume still reminds me of that day in June, and the loss of those young lives.'

AIR RAID SHELTERS

'In our garden at Othery was a walled saw-pit. My grandfather had been a wheelwright and undertaker and cut his timber from trees with a cross cut. As this was no longer in use, my father dug it out and turned it into an air raid shelter, equipped with double beds and everything we needed. It was covered over with soil and planted with vegetables to make it look like a garden. When the bombing was bad over Bristol, we were taken to sleep in the shelter. Later my father was requisitioned to go to London to repair bombed houses, as he was a master carpenter.'

'At the start of the war Dad made a dug-out shelter in our garden at Norton Fitzwarren, beside the greenhouse. I remember in the summertime my two sisters, brother and myself used to nip into the greenhouse, pick a cucumber and some tomatoes, take them down into the shelter and have a picnic tea! I don't think Dad ever found out where they disappeared to. We were lucky that we didn't have to use the shelter often during the daytime. We had an Andersen shelter in the house where we often slept at night when "Jerry" flew over en route to Bristol or Cardiff. We had a few bombs dropped nearby when Jerry was on the run from our Spitfires.'

'During the war at East Huntspill, as soon as the siren sounded we rushed out the back door, across the A38, and crouched down by the stone wall which surrounds the village green, absolutely petrified.'

THE LONG WALK

'Servicemen coming home on leave to the Minehead area would often have to walk the 24 miles from Taunton station, just for the weekend.'

BARBED WIRE ON THE BEACHES

'In 1939, as soon as war started, a gang of men appeared on the beach at Brean and began building concrete piles against possible enemy invasion. Concrete lookouts and gun emplacements were erected, and that awful barbed wire covered the beach where earlier we had played and bathed with such freedom, and very little supervision.'

'My father had his first paid holiday in 1944. Our family cycled to Sparkford station and took the train to Weymouth. The beach was partly obstructed with rolling barbed wire and soldiers were training in amphibious vehicles, I think they were called "ducks".'

AMMUNITION BY THE ROADSIDE

'I grew up as a country child at Woolston, used to walking the one and a half miles to see my grandparents and to the village school. The war brought dramatic changes to the countryside. Narrow roads almost always had quite deep ditches on either side, where in springtime we found masses of sweet smelling white violets.

It was necessary to store ammunition along our narrow roads, making footbridges across ditches and cuttings through the hedges for access to these stores some 25 yards apart. These camouflaged mounds were often galvanised covers resembling "pig huts" covering the ammunition. Nature has since restored the scene.

One Saturday, about May 1942, I was allowed to cycle with my mother to see Grandma at North Cadbury. We found the road from Woolston completely blocked with army lorries. There were countless soldiers about, who kindly lifted our bicycles across the obstructions. It was the first time I had ever seen black men. They were Americans.'

THE AMERICANS

'During the war the US army was stationed at Orchardleigh, so soldiers came to Buckland Dinham – with nylon stockings to offer!'

'Many Yankee convoys passed through East Huntspill, and when staying with my grandparents we would stand in the garden watching and waving to them, and they would throw us tins of meat, chocolate and chewing gum. My grandmother, mother and myself knitted many socks, pullovers, scarves and balaclava helmets for the men serving in the Forces, writing our names and addresses on paper and stitching it on each garment. We had several thank-you letters in return.'

'There was a Toc H club in Minehead, where many happy hours were spent with the soldiers. Many local girls married Americans. The Alcombe girls used to enjoy the sixpenny hops.'

'Brean Holiday Camp (before Pontin's) was filled with a contingent of American soldiers. The bungalow near to us housed British officers and their orderlies. There was a small wooden shack just along the road owned by "Old Kitch"; he sold stamps, cigarettes and sweets. Children found it very enticing! Unfortunately, he was found to be of German origin and was interned. The first six months of the war we had a lot of scares owing to German aircraft going over to bomb the docks at Cardiff and Barry. Many a bomb came whistling over us only to land in the mudflats.'

'I suppose the biggest impact on our lives was the building of a military hospital in the estate grounds at Bishops Lydeard. The wards

198

were built by young British soldiers mainly from the East of England. When they were sent abroad the Americans took over. Barbed wire barricades went across the drive and sentries were posted at entrances. Lorries bringing the wounded from the airfield at Dunkeswell thundered up the drive all night. The American soldiers were very friendly and generous to us children. They gave marvellous parties at Christmas for the school with lovely presents and sweets, and of course chewing gum. "Any gum, chum?" became a favourite saying amongst the more cheeky of us.

My mother often did some laundry for the nurses. She was envious of the beautiful quality of their clothes. I would have to pass the sentry and was always challenged with "Halt, who goes there?" when taking the laundry parcels back. Sometimes I would have to go right into the wards and was surprised to see real black men for the first time.'

'American soldiers were stationed around our farm at Whiteball. Their lorries were camouflaged under the trees on the road from Beambridge to Whiteball – no loitering on the way home from school or we were in trouble. There was a searchlight next to the railway line and we used to watch the enemy aircraft caught in the beam. An ammunition dump was in the wood at Werescote. These soldiers also guarded the mouth of the railway tunnel. My father kept pigs in a field by the tunnel, but he had to move them because they made noises at night and the soldiers fell over them in the dark. We wondered who squealed the loudest, pigs or men.

The soldiers used to drive their jeeps at such speed over Whiteball Hill that they were·unable to negotiate the narrow bridge at the bottom of the hill, with the result that there were frequent accidents and many American soldiers lost their lives. The porch of the cottage near the bridge was frequently hit.'

STRAWBERRIES ON TREES

'During the war there was an Army camp at Edington on the Polden Hills and the soldiers were often entertained by villagers. On one occasion the previous owner of our present house heard a young fellow saying to his pal, "There you are, I told you strawberries grow on trees." They were lying on the grass looking up through the branches of a heavily laden tree of rosy crab-apples.'

THE HOME GUARD AND THE ARP

'Father at this time was a Special Constable. The Home Guard were guarding each end of the village of Othery, when it was reported that a number of the enemy had gone by – our guards had failed to capture them!

'At the beginning of the war many of the men who were less likely to be called up joined the Local Defence Volunteers (later the Home Guard). Of these a selected few at Bruton were recruited into a potential guerrilla force, to come into action if an invasion actually took place. A hideout was constructed on Creech Hill and provisioned for 24 men for three months, and a smaller camp on the other side of the town. They were all men who had shot and trapped from their youth up. Their leaders were a farmer, a schoolmaster and a feed merchant. Their skills with a gun were such that, in training, they won competitions against regular soldiers. Every explosive device known was supplied and stashed away for the last ditch operation that was thought inevitable. Fortunately the invasion never came and on VE night an enormous "banger" was organised to get rid of all these dangerous toys. The noise was terrific and as fate would have it, the local piano tuner was standing rather too close and was permanently deafened.'

'During the war my mother and I were living with her father who was the vicar of Trull. One evening in the late summer of 1940 after the fall of France, when a German invasion was thought very possible, my mother and I were at a party in Taunton. During the evening and after mysterious phone calls all the servicemen left the party.

On the way home to Trull we passed Batts Park which was then an Army camp, later to be South Western Command, and were slightly alarmed to see trucks and buses full of troops – worse was to come.

Just as we arrived back at the vicarage the church bells started to ring. My grandfather who was in his mid-seventies and had gone to bed, sat up in bed demanding to know who was ringing his church bells? The Home Guard responded to the call of the bells with alacrity but no orders came through as to what they should do. By the morning everyone was stood down.

To this day I have never found out why the bells rang from the south-west and up to us. Could it have been an invasion exercise by the Germans? Or fishing boats wrongly identified as Germans? Or a Cornishman ringing the first bell by mistake? Whatever it was, my grandfather never forgot until he died in his nineties, the night his bells were rung.'

'My father was in the Home Guard at Nynehead and he kept a machine gun in a wooden box under the sideboard. We had a car, but there was very little petrol allowed for private use, though there was some for business and an allowance for his Home Guard duties. My husband's father was also in the Home Guard and he recalls having to cycle to the other end of the village with a message for two farmer brothers, telling them that there was an emergency call out because of a suspected invasion. The answer he received was "Can't come today, son. We have two ricks to thatch"!'

'The ARP had a post at the old church hall in Brean. A mock aerodrome was built across the river Axe at Brean, on the levels. This served the purpose of attracting enemy bombers on their way to Bristol Docks. The mock aerodrome lit up as the bombers approached. Consequently, thousands of incendiaries fell on Brean, and high explosive bombs, but there were no casualties.'

THE WOMEN'S LAND ARMY

'I joined the Women's Land Army in May 1941. Although a country girl I found the work was hard at the begining until muscles began to develop and toughen. Wrists soon became strong with the regular exercise of hand milking. Eight cows per sitting was considered a fair number. This also depended as to whether the cows were in full milk or drying off.

Not many farmers owned a tractor. Horses still pulled the wagons and carts and all machinery used on the farm was horse drawn. The milk was taken to the local milk factory loaded on the farm cart in churns.

We had a lady who listened to all our complaints and problems and generally looked after our welfare. She visited each farm every month to hear the farmer's report as to the progress of his land girl. Many of the girls came from towns and had no previous knowledge of the countryside. It was more difficult for them to settle down, and they often had problems.

A scheme was devised for land girls to take an examination at the Cannington Farm Institute near Bridgwater. This was to test their ability and knowledge of farmwork and to give them an interest and incentive. The tests were both physical and oral. Marks were accorded at the end of the day and each girl was assessed on performance of tasks given and answers to questions. A pass rate of about 70% was required and a Proficiency Certificate and badge presented.

In recognition of their land girl's efforts and ability in gaining the pass certificate, employers were asked to give the girl a rise of two shillings and sixpence a week. Most farmers were glad to do this.

In keeping with all agricultural workers, land girls were allowed an extra ration of cheese on their food coupons.'

'Having joined the LA in 1942, I spent the first six months sorting, bagging and planting potatoes, then was transferred to tractor driving on the Mendips. The hostel was three miles from a main road, and on our weekly late night pass we would cycle to Wells to the pictures. Afterwards there was an uphill climb – mostly walking – of six miles, and we had to be in by eleven pm! My working week consisted of 48 hours during wintertime and 52 hours summertime before any overtime, and as a top grade tractor driver I was paid £4 per week, less £1 10 shillings for board and lodging, which was deducted prior to receiving the wage packet. When I moved to the Exmoor area, I often had to cycle five or seven miles before starting work – with the same journey to be faced after a long day of ploughing or harvesting. There was severe winter weather in 1947 and I acted as fuel runner to the bulldozer driver who was clearing snow from roads and lanes into farms, and worked seven days a week for six weeks. I had a Tilley lamp for warmth as there were no heaters in the vans, and I was stationary for long periods waiting for the snow to be cleared. The branches of the beech trees were encased in ice, which made a spectacular sight in the glare of the sun. The following August I received a gratuity of £3 – for "devotion to duty during extreme weather conditions".'

'It was April Fool's Day in 1941 when I started work as a member of the Women's Land Army. Milking started at 5.30 am and being eager I arrived early on a dark and snowy morning.

I lived with the groom and his wife in a cottage where water was obtained from a well and there were no drains in the house. Later I

202

moved to a poultry farm where the hens were all pedigree and had to be trap-nested, that is a metal tag was put on their leg when they laid their first egg. We went round every two hours to release them and write their number on the egg. During double summer time, I was shutting up the hens at 11.00 pm and in tears as they would not always go to roost. We took the food round the farm in bins on a pony and cart. One day the pony bolted and knocked the gate post and the wheels came off the cart, which went bumping along the rough track wheel-less.

At the end of the war, all the Somerset Land Army assembled in Victoria Park in Bath and with three military bands to accompany us we marched past the Queen, who was then Princess Elizabeth, at the Guildhall.'

ON CALL

'The Red Cross at Cheddar were trained to be at the ready for any call of duty necessary. Having no headquarters, lectures were held in a ramshackle barn at the back of the local bakery, with the aroma of newly baked bread always present. Whist drives and dances were organised to provide welfare comforts for troops, and we took part in floats and parades for War Weapons Week etc.

The first aid post was at the local fire station; this housed ARP Wardens and Special Constables. Many German bombers passed overhead on the way to Bristol but apart from dropping the occasional strays, Cheddar had very little damage, though duties had to be kept and we were always on call.

Due to the blackout I remember falling in a trench of muddy water on the way home from a first aid lecture. I was lucky not to receive practice treatment from my friend.

Then came the arrival of evacuees, first from London's East End and later Bristol. We helped with receiving and billeting to various homes. The children caused many health problems. A sick bay was set up at Axbridge, and many skin complaints such as scabies, impetigo and ringworm were treated. Bandaged from head to toe and only faces and bottoms showing they looked angelic, but many times a potty was hurled at you from over the cot side and you had to duck! This and work at the local hospital kept us all busy.'

'I am Somerset born and bred and have lived in Wells for many years. I remember the late 1930s and 1940s well. I was a member of the St John's Ambulance Brigade and we did a variety of duties which increased as the war broke out. Between us we manned the emergency hospital which had been set up in the cellars of the then workhouse. Four people manned this every night. We didn't get a lot of sleep as the old men's ward was overhead and they seemed to be continually on the move, plus the heating pipes were in the cellars and they gurgled non-stop.

We also manned a field ambulance which would travel to the villages to set up a first aid post. Our team consisted of four women and two men. One of the team was a doctor who enjoyed his "tipple". I remember well the unmarked medicine bottle among our supplies which often seemed to shrink (doctor said it had evaporated). Our ambulance often used to run out of water in the engine and it always seemed to happen near a pub. No need to guess who volunteered to fetch a can of water, he always returned with a look of innocence on his face.'

'A mock invasion was held at Othery and a casualty post was manned by various helpers, including an ARP Warden with his whistle. My sister and myself were the casualties and when we were rescued I had to pretend my leg was injured and hobble at least 200 yards with my arm around my rescuer's back. He was much shorter than I and I was very embarrassed. On arrival at the casualty post I was splinted and bandaged. That was fun!'

'Miss Eliott who lived in Underhill Cottage at Stone Allerton owned a dormobile. Early in 1940 she had it converted to an ambulance. She asked me to drive it with her. Each night we took turns to drive to the first aid post at Wedmore, which was then the police station. We were on call from 10 pm until six in the morning. During the many nights we went we were only called once, when I was on duty. It was 2.30 am and it was the Good Friday blitz on Bristol. A night never to be forgotten.'

MORE WORK FOR WOMEN

'Women's occupations became more diverse during the war years. A NAAFI canteen was opened in the Town Hall at Wiveliscombe; members of the Armed Forces stationed in the town, and those who were convalescing in nearby Abbotsfield House, enjoyed the hot meals and light refreshments prepared by the cooks who were employed there. A Food Office for the issue of ration books was set up in the council chambers, and provided a few more jobs for women.

Rationed goods were brought in by train from Taunton to the local

GWR station. These were checked by a female employee before unloading for delivery to the local shops. This would normally have been a male province.

A small factory was sited at the bottom of the High Street where small parts for aircraft were manufactured. Women who worked there on the night shift from seven pm to six am on piece work, could earn more than menfolk who were on day duty at the brewery. These hours also left them free to come home, prepare the family breakfast, and see the children off to school!'

'I had about 1,000 breeding birds to look after, and a baby. We used all the unfit potatoes, boiled them up in the washboiler, and added oathusk from the mill. The birds went to Wiveliscombe by car, or to Crowcombe station. Eggs were packed in cases of 30 dozen, and six or seven of these went to Mrs Langdon's depot in Wiveliscombe, for rabbits, poultry and eggs. Cattle would be walked into "Wivey" market. Land girls were a great help; they would be dropped off daily from Crowcombe Youth Hostel.'

'Local women were bussed on to the Brendons from Nynehead to cut pit props from the wooded hillsides.'

THE CHILDREN'S WAR

'An influx of evacuee children swelled the numbers at West Buckland village school; many were very poor and at school they were given supplements in the way of cod liver oil, malt and free milk. Learning was very much the three Rs and reciting reams of poetry. To help with the "war effort" we knitted socks and scarves for the Forces; the latter were 60 inches long, a marathon job and a real bore. In the autumn we collected hundredweights of rosehips which were sent for processing into rosehip syrup, a valuable source of vitamin C. We recycled cardboard milk bottle tops, which were used to make table-mats or pompoms. We had regular gas mask drill, and the Home Guard played an active part in making sure the blackout was carried out properly.'

'My father had a shop and I can remember him having to cut out all those teeny weeny coupons out of the ration books and then at the end of the week having to count them all up in separate bundles. I used to help, and it was quite a performance.'

We were taken out to collect rosehips. We also picked a flower called betony, a purply flower, and I remember Mrs Ballinger taking us on a walk up to Neroche and picking great sackfulls.'

'At Brompton Ralph children collected hips, blackberries (presumably for jam) and whortleberries for dyeing.'

'Huish primary school was opposite the entrance of Yeovil Football Club with its famous sloping ground. It was a two storey, imposing building built in 1844. I attended the school (which is very near Westland Aircraft) from the age of six to eleven, when I passed the dreaded eleven-plus exam. Seventeen, I remember passed the first part of the exam out of a class of 45!

During the final year, 1942, we attended lessons in pupils' homes who lived near the school, taught by mothers and teachers, because of fear of a direct bomb onto the building. Nine people were in fact killed in the road where I lived when it hit a shelter, Preston Grove.

The three R's were the order of the day, drilling in multiplication tables starting the morning. We knitted socks, scarves and balaclava helmets for the troops. Break consisted usually of jam sandwiches and one third of a pint of milk. This milk frequently had to be thawed out by the radiators in winter. We all went home at dinnertimes, walking long distances. If I was late home for dinner it was because we went Brooky Way, a path behind Westlands, still there but not now on the Yeovil map. We always met all the Westlands workforce going back and forth to work on their bikes, no cars in those times.'

'I was six years old when war came in 1939. I had to ride my bike two and a half miles to school, sandwiches in a shoulder bag, and we also carried gas masks to and from school. They were in a box with a strap for hanging round your neck. I wish I could remember the number of times the mask fell out of the bottom of the box onto the road. Sometimes we would wear them – we must have looked peculiar riding a bike with a gas mask on. I remember lying in bed with my two sisters and watching the searchlights flashing around the sky. We could hear the drone of the bombers, little realising the death and destruction in the cities. Two bombs were dropped on Dunkery, and I remember all the dishes and pots and pans and everything movable went into a panic for about five seconds. Tanks and army lorries laden with soldiers would occasionally pass our farm on their way to the moors for training, and we would watch them from an upstairs window.

During the war the Ministry of Agriculture, Fisheries and Food compelled farmers to grow a certain amount of corn to "Feed the Nation". Then came the binder to cut the corn, and there were the rabbits to catch. It was ricked and thatched, then later the thresher would come and thresh the ears from the straw. It was good sport catching rats which had been living in the ricks.'

206

THE POW's STORY

'The German prisoners of war arrived at Bridgwater station at night and were taken in a fleet of coaches and lorries through the lanes to Goathurst. Fritz remembers wondering what sort of conditions he might be held in. Next day when he was able to look around he was relieved and pleased to find himself in such a pleasant place. The camp was situated in a beautiful area and they could even catch a glimpse of the sea. The huts were quite new and clean and conditions were good. He understood his was the first batch of Germans there and that Italians had been held there before. There were men from all three German services, army, navy and air force, but SS men were soon moved out elsewhere.

Fritz says his hut was the third one down the hill from the top on the east side. The first hut was the wash house, and his was next but one to it. They were treated well. They got the equivalent of a soldier's rations, so knew they were probably eating better than the local civilians. The camp was completely self-contained – even having its own bakery. At eight am they were taken off in lorries for perhaps an hour's drive to where they worked. Most work parties had 25 prisoners, an English foreman to supervise work done, an interpreter (usually German) and a couple of guards. Fritz's first job was on a farm near Cannington where they dug sugar beet and cleared ditches.'

'My father had a German prisoner of war to help him on his farm. At first he had to fetch and take him to his camp in Wellington after his day's work. After a while he was allowed to cycle to and from the farm. He himself was a farmer in his homeland, so the work was something he was accustomed to. Every day (Monday–Friday) he brought his lunch with him – iron rations really, the sort of things which only required hot water added to them. Mother and Father did not think it was very substantial food for a hard working man – and he was an excellent worker, and once we became less afraid of him he joined us at our meal table. He soon learned by sign language what work my father wished him to do.

At their camp in the evening and at weekends, with limited resources available to them, the prisoners made bracelets which consisted of coloured plastic-type string woven into a design and wooden toys which they carved with only the aid of a knife. These items they gave to us at Christmas. After the war the prisoners returned to Germany with promises of returning to see us when things and travel became easier – this never materialized but he did write to us, a very sad letter, which was translated by a local man who had married a German girl soon after the war was over. He said his wife was without a lot of the little things that we took for granted – elastic, cotton, pins, needles etc, so my mother packed up a parcel with these things plus others that were required and sent them to him.

It was some years later that quite out of the blue we received a letter from one of his fellow POW's that we had befriended during their imprisonment in Wellington, saying he often thought of us and wondered how we were.'

'There was a POW camp a few miles from our farm near Dunkery Beacon, and each day a lorryload of first Italian, then German prisoners, would be dropped off at various farms around. One Italian who worked for my father was a tailor by trade, so on wet days he would be indoors sewing, making skirts for us children. The last German POW to work for us didn't want to go home to Germany, so he made his home with us, worked on the farm, and stayed 20 years.'

THE EVACUEE'S STORY

'Early 1940 saw the arrival of evacuees from Lambeth in London, and whilst only 200 were expected, between 750 and 800 women and children arrived at Williton station to be billeted on local residents. There was tremendous consternation when they arrived but the difficulties were soon overcome and they were all found homes by the early hours of the morning.'

'My first sight of an evacuee was in the Market Square at Highbridge. Carrying gas masks in the familiar square brown box, they stood in total bewilderment, hundreds of them, having just got off the train from London. Many were crying.

Each child had a school satchel or brown paper carrier bag which contained their personal effects and clothes.

We did not have billeted evacuees in our village of Edithmead as it was considered too far from town and the schools, but we did have families privately evacuated, who rented empty properties or stayed with relatives.'

'Minehead and district was an area during the war years that received many evacuees, mostly from the London region and later from Hastings.

Several schools from East and West Ham sent their pupils to Somerset; the Regent Street Polytechnic boys were here for the duration and some of these lads married local girls, thus strengthen-

208

Evacuees leaving for the West Country. Despite the culture shock for both hosts and guests, most remember it as a happy and rewarding experience.

ing their ties with this area. The local schools had to adopt a tier system, our children using the buildings in the morning and the newcomers in the afternoon.

Many long lasting friendships were formed during this period and our family had three schoolgirls, then aged 11, 13 and 14. They still write at Christmas; needless to say they are now grandmothers, but have fond memories of the country life they spent with us. We used to take them for walks over our lovely hills and to the nearby villages.

The weekly rate of pay by the Government was eight shillings per child so you can imagine how my mother had to budget to feed three extra healthy schoolgirls. Luckily my father had an allotment so the use of home grown vegetables was a great help to make a nourishing meal to supplement the small weekly meat ration of one shilling and twopence each.

Minehead was a packed town during these years; the population was doubled, of course increasing the trade in the shops. We felt here that we were helping the war effort as we realised how lucky we were to be living in a safe area and not experiencing the horrors of the cities.'

'Tearful mothers looked on from outside the station railings at Becontree, near Dagenham, as their children boarded a train taking them away from the threat of German bombing in September 1939.

I was one of those children who boarded the train on 1st September. It was an experience that changed my life. I remember being on Becontree station, which is near Dagenham in Essex. The station was crowded with children, aged between five and 14 years. We all carried gas masks, and had labels pinned onto our coats with our names on.

We all felt very lonely. We didn't know where we were going or what was happening. No mothers were allowed to come onto the station, but we could see them waving to us from outside the railings, as the train pulled out on its way to Paddington. We had been given a quarter-pound of acid drops each to eat on the journey.

From Paddington, we all went to Bridgwater, where we were taken to a school and given a carrier bag containing a tin of corned beef, a bar of chocolate and a packet of biscuits. From Bridgwater, I remember being taken by coach to the church hall at Chilton Polden, where billeting officers were waiting to allocate us to different houses. We were all very tired and bewildered. I went to a farmhouse called Kosy-Kot, with Mr and Mrs V. White. I was parted from my twin brother. He went to a farm at Pedwell and I didn't meet him again for over a month.

I walked to school from Chilton Polden. It was held in the village hall at Edington, a walk of over two miles. We were all taught in one large class (ages five to 14). When the weather was cold and wet we were all very miserable.

I was very happy with the Whites and helped on the farm, feeding the calves, sheep, poultry, geese, ducks and turkeys. My parents came sometimes by coach to visit us. This was quite a problem for them because there were no signposts to show them the way, and everywhere was in total darkness at night because of the black-out regulations.

I was the only one from our very large London school who stayed in Somerset, and didn't go back after the war except for holidays.

When Mr and Mrs White went to farm at Longhouse on the Orchardleigh estate in 1946, I went with them and helped in the house and on the farm. I was married at Orchardleigh church in April 1950, and the Whites gave us a lovely reception in Lullington school. Mrs White treated me like a daughter, and we are still very great friends.

If it had not been for the war, I might never have come to Somerset and my life would certainly have been very different.'

'Born in London in 1939 soon after war had been declared, I was evacuated with my mother to Wellington at the age of nine months. We lived firstly in Rockwell Green, and I know for my mother it was not a happy time. The landlady left a lot to be desired and was not at all welcoming, but wanted to make all she could out of the situation. She stole all my baby clothes at one point. Soon after we moved to Buckwell in Wellington and my father joined us – he suffered from tuberculosis at the time, as did many of the population. I remember queueing to get my gas mask. Everyone was very solemn, nobody laughed and I was told there was a war on. It meant nothing to me. Luckily we never needed the gas mask and it eventually became a plaything, mostly to frighten unsuspecting little sisters.'

'On a day in 1939 the first train pulled into Taunton station with hundreds of children, some mothers and teachers on board. They were taken to Taunton Market, where they were met by dozens of volunteers; my job was runabout girl.

There was a great hush when the first arrivals came into the huge building. Mothers carrying babies, boisterous boys, shy little girls, all with gas masks over their arms and looking bewildered. Gradually during the day places were found for them in Taunton and surrounding villages with kindly householders. Every effort was made to keep families together. I became friends with many evacuees and laughed at their Cockney slang, they laughed back at our Somerset burr.'

'In 1940 my mother, my sister and I left south Buckinghamshire to get away from the real fear of bombing for a few weeks. After a wearisome train journey with a change at windswept Templecombe station, we trailed into the refuge of my great-aunt's house at Milborne Port, only to be greeted with the amazing news that a stick of bombs had fallen on the hillside the previous day, a German plane had crashed nearby, and Sherborne had been badly bombed. The amusing part was that Lord Haw-Haw had broadcast that Sherborne and Milborne Port had been wiped off the map.'

'I was one of 40 children evacuated to Cutcombe parish, from Bristol in May 1941. After a tiring journey by train and coach we reached Wheddon Cross in the late afternoon. Friendly smiles and a super tea awaited us, no signs of food rationing here! Some of us were billeted in the village, others on farms. We swelled the school numbers to nearly 100 pupils. Trestles and benches became our desks and seats. We explored the countryside in biology lessons and gathered sphagnum moss for the war effort.

Later I moved to a farm where much of the cooking was done on an open fire and drinking water came from a pump outside the back-door. There was a toilet upstairs, but for outside use an earthen closet was situated near the pond. Which was alright in the winter months as the water flooded through, but in the summer, *whew!*

Farm animals at close quarters were a new experience and I loved it. I learned to handmilk cows, before and after school, and in due course helped with the sheep at lambing, shearing and dipping. Pig killing day was an eye opener though and I didn't like cleaning the intestines for chittlings.

On winter evenings we played table tennis, card games and read, going to a feather bed by candlelight. Sunday evenings we sang favourite hymns accompanied by a harmonium. After two momentous years I went back to Bristol but returned as a land girl in 1947.'

'In September 1940, my granny, my mother and myself were evacuated by train from St Leonards on Sea to South Petherton.

We left our homes with just a suitcase each, not knowing where on earth we would end up. Some evacuees stayed in Yeovil, while the rest of us transferred to a bus. Some were off-loaded at Norton sub Hamden, but we stayed on to the end of the run.

We arrived at the Blake Hall in the centre of the village, where our hosts were awaiting us. It was rather like a cattle market, with people saying "I'll have you, you and you." We were very lucky, as we were billeted at the Yarn Barton before the property was divided into two. We stayed there for three years until my mother was remarried to the local postmaster.

Then began a very happy period of my life, as although it was war time with all the shortages, we were far away from the bombing.

The Blake Hall was very well used, as it is today, and I well remember going to dances, amateur shows and WI meetings there. As there was no television everybody joined in, and there was a very happy atmosphere. We were all able to go for country walks and enjoy swimming in the river Parrett, together with unpolluted blackberrying in the autumn. A really idyllic life.'

'My grandparents at Misterton had two boys and their sister also stayed with the families in our farm cottages. I know at times they were very sad. The little girl called Molly, who was five years old, cried every morning as she walked to school with us. She wanted her mummy so badly, and her brothers tried desperately to comfort her.'

'The day came for us to expect the evacuees. Several helpers prepared tea at Croscombe school. We waited and waited, but no one came. We kept sending to Shepton Mallet, hoping to meet trains, but

212

everything seemed hopeless. By the time they did arrive it was quite dark; our quota was a school of very small children from Camden Town. I shall never forget the poor little mites! They had been prepared to come three days before, but on the day of their journey had been on the trains since early morning. Their little faces were all stained with tears; they were tired out, their teachers and helpers too, so you can imagine how they looked. Most of them had all their possessions in a pillowslip, and they were very poor. They were too tired to eat or drink, and most were still crying. House-holders were waiting to take the number they were allotted, and it was heartbreaking to get them fixed up as quite naturally brothers and sisters did not want to be parted. After a day or two a few little ones were missing, and they were found wandering on the hills trying to find their way back home. Of course they were brought back. From time to time their parents came to visit them and naturally there were tears because they could not return home with Mum and Dad.'

'We had two boys. They didn't stay long. They wouldn't eat fresh vegetables and roast chicken, they only wanted baked beans and chips. They didn't like going to bed with a candle!'

'The evacuees from London gave us an insight into a different way of life to ours – the children of one family on being given an egg and bacon breakfast said they always had doughnuts and beer!'

'I had two evacuees, two little girls. They came to Sampford Arundel from London, Poplar, and they stayed a long time, then went home and the flying bombs came and they came back to me again. That's 50 years ago. One has kept in touch with me every birthday and Christmas. The other day she knocked on my door. I said "No" and she said "Yes!" I'd never heard anything of the other girl but last summer she knocked on my door. She hadn't altered a bit. 'Tis lovely to see them come back to you again.'

PORT GALORE

'Early in the Second World War a driver was instructed to deliver a lorry-load of port in barrels. Succumbing to temptation, he bored a small hole in one barrel and drank deep. During his journey he picked up two sailors, who climbed up among the barrels. Alas, the port began to take effect and at Watergore the driver cannoned into the bank, tipping the lorry. However, it righted itself and the driver continued, oblivious of the fact that his two passengers had been catapulted over the hedge into an adjacent builder's yard and a large number of barrels were flung into the road, many smashing open. Port ran everywhere, the drains could not cope and a nearby ditch was full.

People ran with containers to collect any remains and several barrels disappeared into the builder's yard. For some weeks afterwards men would disappear, sometimes for two or three days, to be found curled up under nearby hedges, sleeping it off! Certain gentlemen knocked off the lid of a barrel and drank direct from it, but one little man was too short, so his companions hoisted him up and draped him over the barrel. Alas, he fell in! There he was, up to his waist in port, legs in the air! When it was suggested he be hauled out someone was heard to say "No, leave 'ee be, let 'ee have a good sup". Happily, better sense prevailed and he was rescued.'

RATIONING . . . AND THE PIG

'One of the most memorable things about the war was rationing. Everything was rationed. I can't remember the exact amounts but we were allowed four ounces of sugar per person each week, two ounces of butter or margarine, an ounce of tea and you could get no more from your ration book. What wasn't on ration was on points and this included tinned fruit, dried fruit, sweets, biscuits, bread, etc.

Meat was by the money pound (£1). If your butcher loved you, you could sometimes get liver and sausages off the ration; you were *never* rude to the butcher.

Clothes were on coupons. You gave up so many coupons when you bought a coat, so many for a dress, etc. If you were pregnant you got extra coupons for the baby. One saved all the baby clothes and passed them on, thus providing more points for towels, sheets etc.'

'Occasionally we would go by bus to Yeovil and have a tea at the British Restaurant housed in the Liberal Hall, or have tea at the Cottage Cafe – bread and butter, jam, a cake and tea, four shillings and sixpence for the four of us, all helping stretch household rations. How we appreciated those treats.'

'When in my early teens, 1940–1945, life was so different. Everything was rationed – i.e. two ounces of butter, sugar and cheese per person per week. Petrol was also rationed, often people would exchange anything they did not want for foodstuffs.

I can remember queueing for hair grips which had become available at the chemist, also using shaving soap (not rationed) for washing hair and clothes, and joining darning wool for knitting. Misterton did have quite a number of bombs dropped, although doing no damage and a number were unexploded. Travel was quite difficult, everything had to be blacked out – bicycles had lights with just a dot of light, just to be seen. Houses had to have blackout curtains, being black, heavy, material especially made, and wardens would tour the area to see no lights were showing. Misterton had a number of evacuees housed with families until the war ended.

Men who were not in the armed services had to join the Home Guard and were called out on a number of occasions when invasion by the enemy was forecast. Also the fire services were on call and had to go to any city being bombed. Our fire service often went to Plymouth, Exeter and Bristol and had to stay for several days. We also had to knit socks, scarves etc for the Services.'

'My father owned our house at Milborne Port, set in four acres of land. We had four goats and mother produced cheese and butter from the milk, a Wessex Saddleback pig named Henry and an accredited poultry breeding station. This meant we got a special ration of fowl food and sent (by rail) hatching eggs and day old chicks all over the country. The garden had many fruit trees and a large amount of vegetables. We had four hives of bees and with chickens etc we were almost self supporting during the war. Food, of course, was rationed, and I can vividly remember longing for sweets. Soap was in short supply. We all gave up sugar in drinks so that it could be used in cake making.'

'During the war years the Alcombe Women's Institute purchased a canning machine, to can the surplus fruit etc for a small fee. There was also a Pig Club. Members got together to buy a pig, feed and clean it, then a local butcher killed it and the pork was shared amongst the members.'

'Every Saturday my friends and I would have to collect potato peelings from the hospital kitchen at Bishops Lydeard for the pigs. For this we had an old high sprung pram, without a hood, on which we would ride down the hills. One sat on the front edge with her feet between the handles and steered. One sat on the back edge to act as brake and the other rode inside. We could get up quite a good speed and once surprised a cyclist by passing him. We were always in trouble with our parents for wearing out our shoes so quickly and they questioned why there were bits of stone in the peelings. This was because we often tipped over and had to scoop up the contents from the road.'

'We were very lucky with regard to meat as Dad kept chickens, geese and a pig. The pig was so tame, my brother used to ride on its back. We called the pig Sam and I remember Mum saying that when it was time for the pig to be taken by lorry to Taunton to be killed, the men who came to collect him couldn't get poor Sam out of his sty and she had to go to the bottom of the garden with a bucket of meal, rattling the bucket as she went so that Sam would follow her. He followed her up the path and into the lorry. When, eventually, Dad had half of poor Sam back, the hams were salted by Mum and then cooked by her, but she couldn't eat any of it herself!'

CITY VALUABLES

'During the war valuable archives belonging to the City of London were stored in a specially constructed room under Sexey's Hospital, Bruton. Several old inhabitants have assured me that the Crown Jewels were concealed there but that, I fear, is a myth.'

THE MEETING OF THE GENERALS

'After the war, we were surprised to hear that the largest secret assembly of high-ranking officers and generals ever held, including Lord Montgomery and Lord Wavell, had taken place in the Knatch-bull Arms at Stoke St Michael in 1942. The meeting lasted from ten am to four-thirty pm, when the village was quiet and everyone was at work. The landlord and his wife were sworn to secrecy and customers were served as usual.'

VE DAY

'In 1945, at Norton Fitzwarren, we held dances, whist drives, concerts and skittles to raise money for the war lads. On VE Day it really was a celebration; the village hall was decorated and all through the village at every possible point there were trimmings of red, white and blue. We held a sports day, fancy dress and various other competitions with a tea party and dance in the evening. At the dance they announced the winner of the skittles for the men. Farmer Sidney King always gave a suckling pig and as he announced the winner, the pig would be brought in. On this occasion the pig somehow slipped out of his arms and ran around the dance floor, which was extremely slippery due to the french chalk having been put down earlier. There were howls of laughter from everyone – just imagine the poor pig. They had a hard time catching it and it was hard luck on the poor chap with the bucket cleaning up after it!'

HIGHDAYS & HOLIDAYS

SPORTS & ENTERTAINMENT

There may not have been much time for leisure activities, but people made the most of what they had. Villages could boast a range of clubs and societies and there was always someone willing to get up and sing or put on a show. Whist drives and dances were regular country entertainment, marathon nights that began at half past seven and continued into the small hours of the morning. There was sport too, particularly cricket, which brought aristocracy and working class together in a common passion.

MAKING OUR OWN FUN

'Life in Mark between the two world wars was full of hard work for most people, but despite the hardship of making your own living there was much fellowship and enjoyment of the local talent, and the sing-song around the piano, perhaps after a little cider drinking! It was a more contented way of life with the larger families making their own fun and putting on concerts and shows with the help of the church choir.'

'On Good Friday children and parents went out to pick primroses and bluebells to decorate the church for Easter. Whist drives were held in the school to raise money for school outings to places such as Weymouth or Minehead. Young people cycled to Taunton sometimes for dances, and going to church was also an excuse for going for a walk with a boyfriend! The Ruishton cricket team played on the Blackbrook field, which is now part of the M5.'

'At Stoke St Michael we had a village cricket team, football team and tennis club. I remember going to tennis matches at other clubs in a pony-drawn governess cart. Our tennis court was in the surrounds of the ruins of the Duke of Cumberland's shooting lodge.

There was a mixed choir and WI choir, and we travelled around giving concerts. A strong Dramatic Society entertained the villagers with concerts. Dances were very popular in the village and we also used to cycle or walk to neighbouring villages for dancing.

Mr Parker, a blind pianist from Radstock, used to walk to Stoke to play the piano for dancing, and walk back again afterwards. There was a British Legion supper and dance yearly. The nearest cinema was five miles away at Shepton Mallet and we often cycled there before other transport was around. There was also a male voice choir which became quite famous locally and in great demand for concerts. They broadcast three times on the BBC radio.'

'Wookey between the wars had a male voice choir, football and cricket teams, and a tennis and bowling club. There was a church, a chapel, a pub and the village club. A drama club produced plays and there was a village pantomime. There was an annual rook shoot, followed by rook pie.

The caves were part of Bubwith Farm and people were shown around by the farm workers. Illumination was by candles, supplemented by benzine, thrown on the lake and ignited. This produced light, but also flames and a choking black smoke, through which the guide would point out the features of the cave to his spluttering audience. The soot deposited on the stalactites is still visible. One guide used to tell his audience, "They stalactites be the result of constant dripping. Thik's the dog. Thik's the witch. Mind thee girt 'ead under 'ere!"'

'At Stocklinch in the 1940s the work was very hard but there was enjoyment too. The village hall was open every evening for the relaxation of the farm labourers. There was a billiard table, with a wooden top, which could be used for harvest suppers. Every week there was either a dance or a whist drive, and a flower and produce show was held annually and everyone took part.'

'Does anyone remember the Burmese Pageant we performed in Puckington village about 1933? It must have been in aid of a Missionary Society, and was preceded by a service in church. Everyone took part. There were Tamils, Chinese and Burmese – all dressed in Eastern costumes. Three of us represented Tamils and had to recite a dreary piece which started "Tamils from India we". Most of us changed and were made up in the rectory, but my father elected to put on his costume at home. Consequently, a lady visitor home on leave from India, was amazed to see a Buddhist Priest in saffron robes, complete with begging bowl, walking up a deserted village street in the middle of a summer afternoon.'

CRICKET AND TENNIS

'The village cricket team was very important to Staple Fitzpaine, and Lord Portman was very proud of his team and often invited County players to play against them. On one occasion, Mr A. Grabham had made 60 not out when Lord Portman sent his butler out to the wicket with a glass of whisky – not being used to it, he was out next ball!

Rev Coote was also a keen cricket fan. Staple had, I suppose, one of the finest cricket fields in the district, the most beautiful anyway. It was right opposite Staple Farm, you went down over a field, crossed a little bridge and into a big field which was lined with oak trees; and it was well maintained. We used to keep it hard rolled. I used to play for Staple Fitzpaine, which at that time was one of the best teams in the area. They weren't all local members, we had a couple of Taunton fellows playing. We had a mixed cricket match once when we played the ladies at Staple. The men had to play left handed but as I was left handed anyway I took up my position at right hand. The girls wouldn't have it and made me play left handed – the result was I made about 80 runs!'

'We had a lovely cricket team at Goathurst, lovely cricket pitch, pavilion – everything. Enmore had their team and we had a team here, and that was the local derby. Enmore consisted mostly of Coles, while Goathurst consisted mostly of Jenkins – Jack Jenkins, Sid Jenkins, John Jenkins. Lord Wharton used to come and watch, and R.G. Seymour, he was the estate agent. He was a good cricketer, an opening bat. To see all these teams arrive with their caps on, I'll never forget it. We didn't have very much but we were a darn sight happier then.'

'My father-in-law, John Cornish White, played cricket for Somerset and England in the years between 1909 and 1937. The newspapers called him "Farmer White" because he farmed at Combe Florey. He was a member of the England side when they played in the Argentine in 1927 and he also played against South Africa. He was vice-captain of the England XI on the Australian Tour of 1928/29.

During the time he was away, his father looked after his farm for him. He was away from home for six or seven months, playing in Ceylon en route for Australia. The team only received expenses during the tour. On his return he was presented with a silver salver, inscribed to record the appreciation of 10,000 subscribers, to commemorate the tour. After retiring from cricket he became secretary of the Quantock Stag Hounds and hunted with them regularly.'

'We had quite a good cricket team of village men and boys at Kilmersdon, and the pitch was in the recreation field by the school. We had matches with other village teams and visited other teams also, namely Downside School, Radstock, Norton St Philip, Rode, and many others. We served teas at our matches and wives and friends of the players helped. When it rained everyone rushed to the cricket pavilion, but what a squeeze. We were also fortunate in having a tennis court in the Rec where friends from Haydon joined Kilmersdon people for matches, and there was also a tennis court on the vicarage lawn and two courts in a field opposite the vicarage gates.'

FROM MUMMERS TO RADIO

'As a child growing up in the First World War, I remember running with other children to welcome two lady minstrel mummers to Crowcombe. Mrs Florrie Barrat, who played the accordion, and Mrs Barnett, would stand by the garden gate, or be invited into the kitchen, where they sang old ballads and carols.

Later my father bought the family a crystal wireless set for £4. All the children loved Uncle Mac on Children's Hour. Parents would send in their children's birthday, and where to find a hidden present. A time of great excitement . . . real magic. Years later we sold the old wireless for £7.'

'When I was young, few people had radios and there was no television. I can remember as a child in Dunster going with my brother to get a new cat's whisker for our crystal set. Four men came to fix the aerial for our first valve set, which cost more than a new car.'

'In 1922 the first wireless set reached Chewton Mendip. A momentous occasion! A most costly item in those days, it was acquired by a Mr Curtis who lived in a house called Homedene. So rare and exciting was it to have such a set that he invited members of the village to special listening sessions: on one day the farmers and their wives and on the next the farmers' children. Some children also went with their parents and Hilda Emery, then aged ten, remembers going with her mother. Everyone crowded round and the four headphones belonging to the set were placed in a bowl on the table so that everyone present could hear the sounds emitted. It appears, however, to have been something of a disappointment for the sound was very unclear and crackly. Hilda recalls hearing music and Mrs Hayes a speaker but beyond that no more detail could really be distinguished.'

'I was given the job of fetching the wireless accumulator from Gammons in South Street, Wellington, and making sure that I didn't spill it. The radio was a wonderful invention. There was Tommy Handley, Just William, and we all rushed in every night on the dot to listen to Dick Barton, Special Agent.'

OUR FIRST GRAMOPHONE

'In the 1920s when we were living at Wookey, my father bought our first gramophone. It was one with a big horn and we only had a few records because they were rather expensive in those days, but my father used to like highbrow music.'

GOING TO THE PICTURES

'In the 1920s treats like silent films came to Stratton on the Fosse. They were shown in Downside College gymnasium and just now and again my father would take me along to see such stars as Charlie Chaplin, Harold Lloyd and Buster Keaton. Oh, how I remember their hilarious antics. They "brought the house down", drowning out the brilliant piano playing of Edna Savage, the resident pianist. We didn't even notice the hard old chairs we had to sit on. Later came the first of the talkies – *Goodnight Vienna* with Richard Tauber. I have never forgotten that night and all my life my secret dream has been to waltz the night away at a Viennese Ball, the glittering chandeliers spinning about me as I swirled around to the glorious strings of the orchestra!'

'My great passion for the cinema began at a very early age. Back in the early 1930s silent cinema shows were held in the schoolroom of the Methodist chapel, South Petherton. The first performance began at approximately 5 pm, and we queued excitedly, waiting for the doors to open. Then there was a mad surge forward followed by a sudden halt as we paused to hand over our penny entrance fee, before rushing to our favourite seats clutching a halfpennyworth of sweets.

We then waited with bated breath in case the equipment was in one of its taciturn moods and refused to function. This invariably happened, but it usually decided to co-operate after much coaxing by the projectionist, Mr Fred Allen. In retrospect I realise he must have been extremely fond of children, otherwise he would never have subjected himself to the ordeal of coping with 40 to 50 noisy children every week, plus temperamental equipment.

The films were mainly "cowboys", our favourite, and we could always distinguish the "goodies" from the "baddies" as the "goodies" wore the white stetsons. When the noise became unbearable, usually from the boys, who always sat at the back, Mr Allen would stop the film and threaten not to start it again unless we behaved.

Before our performance ended a queue was forming for the second house. We all scuttled off like little rabbits to our various homes, mainly two up two down cottages, to dream happily of being rescued by the hero in the white stetson.'

THE VILLAGE BAND

'Buckland Band consisted of six brass instruments, a B flat bass and two drums, the mainstay being its euphonium. Practices were held in the schoolroom, and on one winter evening the euphonium player had such a good supply of wind he blew out the lamps and left the band in darkness! On a special occasion when the band were playing through the streets of Frome, the drummer, when reaching Badcox, went up Broadway, and after a few minutes realised that the rest of the band were playing up Nunney Road! This drummer was also in trouble one sunny day at Orchardleigh House Fête. As he led the band to the stand, he hitched his foot in a croquet hoop and fell across his drum! The men were very proud of their dark blue uniform trimmed with braid, and caps with "B.B.B." on the front.'

GOING TO THE SEASIDE

'My mother lived at Greinton near Street, and she recalled the excitement as a child of the rare outings to the seaside. With the smallest children in the pram, she and her mother walked several miles to Shapwick station to catch the train to Edington junction and from there to Burnham on Sea. The walk home was not so much fun.'

'It was summer 1941, and we were going on holiday, 24 children, three assistants and one matron from a children's home in Shepton Mallet to Burnham on Sea for two weeks. The idea was for us to take over an empty school and use the facilities.

Clothes were packed into pillow cases, as were towels, and other household items that would be needed for us all. Us older girls (I was

13 at the time) had helped stitch sheets into sleeping bags which, along with one blanket and the mattresses from our beds, were to be our sleeping arrangements on the floor. The great day arrived and we travelled on top of the mattresses in a huge lorry, talk about luxury.

Each day we walked to the lighthouse and then played in the sea. The tide always seemed to be in. We also joined the Salvation Army Beach Crusade and joined in all the choruses with gusto; I bet they never had such an enthusiastic audience. Having tea on the beach proved very rewarding as some kind soul always paid for us to have an ice cream or sweets.

The highlight of this holiday for me was when we all attended the beach concert party "Freddy Fay's Follies". I was up on the stage in the "Talent Time" singing and dancing away. I was Shirley Temple and Deanna Durbin all rolled into one although I was plump and wore those awful silver framed spectacles. I won half a crown for my efforts – great wealth.

Nowadays when my grandsons come on holiday we always go to Burnham for the day and the cry goes up "Tell us about when you came here when you were a girl, Grandma, and sang on the stage." So off I start again.'

DANCES

'Mother would often tell us of the thrilling serial films she and Father went to see when they were courting. As children we attended the Saturday afternoon matinees. We would cycle to town and leave our bikes against the wall of the picture house. No one would dream of taking them in those days.

During the Second World War, dances were held in most village halls on Saturday nights. Blackout restrictions insisted that all windows were covered, and the wooden frames covered in thick blackout paper fitted close to the windows so no light could escape. Also this meant that no air could get in or out and the interior of the hall when the dance hotted up was very hot and stuffy.

Special dances were held on such occasions as "Wings for Victory" or "War Weapons Week". These dances usually went on to 2 am. We all had to cycle home afterwards.'

'Before the Second World War, and for a while afterwards, entertainment in the villages was often a whist drive/dance. As the dancing began as soon as the whist tables had been cleared, it was a good way of making certain that everyone was there at the start.

In the 1950s we put on our most glamorous long dresses for dances held in the cider factory at Wiveliscombe. These had to be timed for when the cavernous building was not required for apple storage. We climbed the rough wooden steps, threw chalk on the unpolished floor so that we could dance, sat on upturned beer cases, and when nature called, we used the buckets behind a tarpaulin erected at one end. In dances like the St Bernard's Waltz, we were asked not to stamp too hard as the floor was not safe.'

CLUBS FOR MEN AND WOMEN

'Prior to 1914, Litton was a little picturesque village at the head of the Chew Valley, comprised mainly of farmers and their employees, served by a butcher, a grocer, two pubs, a church and a school. Farming literally relied on "horse power", was laborious and depressing, with a work force which was poorly paid but usually housed.

Meals were often contrived from nature, rabbit pie or jugged hare regularly on the menu. Prudent housewives pickled and preserved everything in surplus. Pig's offal costing about one shilling, was painstakingly processed and fed the family on chitterling faggots and brawn. The only form of cooking was a coal or wood burning stove. Times were extremely hard, especially for women. They led a very pedestrian life centred around the local community.

The Great War shattered this peaceful tranquillity. Young men left for the front, two never to return. Women were forced to involve themselves in tasks outside the home. Thus stimulated, they yearned to broaden their horizons. In November 1922, the mistress of Manor Farm convened a meeting, resulting in the formation of the Litton Women's Institute. Unfortunately there was no village hall for meetings.

A Men's Club had been inaugurated in 1921, leasing, with reservations, the redundant village school which closed in 1916. Rule One read, No Ladies Please. A temporary, but unsatisfactory arrangement was negotiated with perhaps a hint of male chauvinism.

Happily the situation was resolved when in January 1925, Mr Henry Middle donated two derelict cottages to the WI. The ladies worked like beavers raising funds to transform the cottages into their very own WI hall, which is still the focal point of village activities today.'

'Puckington WI was started by Mrs Darby of Mavis Farm. She was President until her illness in 1949 but took a keen interest in village affairs until her death. The WI was held on Wednesday evenings. There were many young people in the village at the time and the meetings, held in the village school room, were conducted very like school proceedings. The register was called and each member answered by stating her favourite object, eg flower, scent, proverb, poem, recipes, etc. The answers required were entered on the Annual Programme. Most members brought knitting and busied themselves during the half hour's business and the talk. The tea hostesses brought their own paper and sticks and laid the open fire (the coal was already outside the hall). During winter, fires were lit an hour and a half before the meetings. A kettle had to be hung on this fire to boil water for tea. We paid twopence each for this and a cake. Next morning the room had to be cleaned and the grate done as there was usually another "get-together" that evening. The social half-hour was a must. Games, competitions, quizzes or a short dance was the usual thing. A raffle – for quarter pound of tea or similar – was also held. The speaker's hostess was a different person each meeting and the thank you vote was obligatory – despite any previous protests. Sadly, owing to people leaving the village, the WI closed a few years later.'

'Employment within Hemington parish was almost equally divided between agriculture and mining with a few men working in the quarries. Turners Tower once dominated part of the parish. Largely built of stone, it was reduced in size after it was struck by lightning in 1910. The tower had large rooms on two levels and it served as a men's social club as well as a doctor's surgery and a barber's.'

'In our teens in the 1950s we joined the Young Farmers Club at Exton. There were many competitions to enter, public speaking, debating, handicrafts, quizzes, cookery, to name but a few. We competed against neighbouring clubs so many friends were made, and many weddings have taken place in the YF circle, my own included.'

EVENTS TO REMEMBER

Some occasions could not be classed as entertainment, but they broke the monotony of country life and left a lasting impression – such as being taken to watch the Suffragettes march by on their way to London before the First World War, or the day the circus came to stay!

DISCOVERING THE BOAT

'A boat was discovered by my father, George Wall, whilst clearing a rhine beside Shapwick Road close to what was then Shapwick station. No nuts or bolts had been used in the construction of the boat – it had simply been hollowed out of a large tree trunk. Preserved by the damp peat, the boat had lain there for thousands of years until its discovery on 15th September 1906 and it was removed to an outbuilding of the station hotel for safekeeping. The discovery became something of a "fairground" attraction in the area and created considerable interest among local people.'

THE SUFFRAGETTES

'My mother recalled how, before the First world War, her schoolmistress at Greinton took all the children to the road to watch the Suffragettes marching to London.'

COUNTING THE CARS

'On Wincanton race meeting days we sat on a low wall and noted the make of cars (if we could) and number to see who collected the most. Cars in the 1920s were a novelty in Templecombe.'

'Horse racing days were exciting and I used to sit on the doorstep of our house in Wincanton writing down the registration numbers of cars coming from the racecourse. We were lucky if we managed 20. Imagine trying to do it today!'

THE CIRCUS

'It was in the summer of 1935 when the travelling circus paraded through Hatch Beauchamp on its way to Taunton. Mr Chipperfield, deciding to find a resting place for a day or two, lighted on the "front field" at Willcocks Farm in Station Road, then in the occupation of Mr Thomas Hunter. In return, he put on several exciting performances at which the family always had the best seats.

There were performing lions and tigers in a big caged enclosure, in an enormous marquee. There were equestrian displays of all kinds, as well as tumbling clowns, with acrobats and dancing girls, not to mention plenty of rousing music, and a call to the show on the barrel organ.

However, when it was time to move on, Mr Chipperfield asked Mr Hunter if he could leave his caged lions and tigers in the orchard for a few more days, with their keepers. So the excitement continued, with daily roars at feeding times, when they were thrown huge chunks of meat, all brought in on the railway, and fetched thence by many willing hands. One can only imagine the panic of the domestic residents . . . the milking cows, the working horses, the pigs, sheep and hens, all living side by side with wild animals in the quiet village of Hatch Beauchamp in the mid 1930s.

There came a surprise parting gift for the farmer's daughter who received a box of small tortoises to distribute among her friends, as well as a promise that whenever Chipperfield's "set up shop", any of the family could claim free seats for evermore. I wonder if they ever did?'

ROYAL OCCASIONS

Coronations and Jubilees were celebrated with gusto in Somerset and have left lasting memories, as have visits by the Prince of Wales to his Duchy of Cornwall lands. Many people still treasure momentoes such as Jubilee mugs given to them at town and village parties which involved the whole community. Memory can even reach back to the death of Queen Victoria, who was mourned as 'the dear old lady'.

THE DEATH OF QUEEN VICTORIA

'My first memories are of a period following the death of Queen Victoria in 1901, when everybody wore mourning for over a year. My mother was still wearing a long black skirt which had a deep band of crepe round the bottom. I hated it, but was consoled by my mother explaining that she wore it "out of respect for the dear old lady, Queen Victoria who had passed away." At that time Dad was the chairman of the Babcary Parish Council and all correspondence – notepaper and envelopes – had an inch wide black border (my brother still possesses one of the original envelopes). Dad bought Mother a jet brooch and earrings, and a jet watch chain for himself. I have these items still.'

THE PRINCE OF WALES 1934

'In July 1934 a great event came to Stratton on the Fosse. His Royal Highness Edward, Prince of Wales, visited us during his tour of the Duchy of Cornwall estates. At mid-day all the schoolchildren assembled in the paddock field belonging to Mr Bryant's farm in South Street. There we all were – boys in their Sunday best, hair tidy for once with the help of lard, and we girls dressed in our best frocks, ribbons in our hair, frantically waving Union Jack flags to welcome the Prince. Lined up in rows, straight as could be expected of excited children, he passed along the ranks accompanied by Nurse Byrne, our District Nurse. She was a tiny lady who always reminded me of a perky little sparrow. Well, that day she was looking so proud, having been given the honour of walking beside His Royal Highness, when suddenly one of our classmates fainted. She fell into a crumpled heap upon the grass. His Royal Highness could not help but notice the incident and whispered to Nurse, pointing to the unfortunate Gwen. Nurse Byrne hurried across to attend to her ailing "chick" as she was bid and helped the now dishevelled and embarrassed child to her feet.

At the end of the day we were all given a commemoration mug. I still have mine which I greatly treasure and I remember with such clarity my grandmother's remarks on that day.

"Yes, my child," she said, "Prince Edward might eventually become King, but mark your old granny's words . . . he will never be crowned!" I was too young to ask her why, and sadly she did not live long enough to see her prophecy come true.'

'The schoolchildren from West Hatch were once taken to the main Taunton road, walking to wave our flags for a visit by the Prince of Wales to his Duchy property at Curry Mallet. This was Edward, the King who eventually abdicated and was never crowned. We were a bit fed up at having to stand and wait for two hours on a very cold day (the story was, afterwards, that the Prince had been celebrating the night before and had overslept). Any royal visitors to the Taunton area slept on the royal train on a siding near Taunton.'

THE JUBILEE 1935 AND THE CORONATION 1937

'Hay waggons were used in the villages to transport the local people to the Harvest Homes, Coronations, Jubilees etc. Firstly waggons had to be washed and often painted, the harness cleaned and oiled and brasses cleaned to shine like gold and extra ones brought out for this special event. Next was the decorating of the waggons with ivy

G. R.

ALLERTON.

Silver Jubilee Celebration

6th MAY, 1935.

COMMITTEE:

Rev. W. P. Putt. Messrs. Duckett, Teek, Wall,
Watts, Webber, Woodward, Sully.
Mesdames. Putt, Watts, Wickham, Webber, Adams.
Miss Tucker.

Secretary: Mr. J. Binning.

Oliver, Printer, Axbridge.

The Programme for the Allerton Silver Jubilee Celebration of 1935. Included on the list of sports for the afternoon was 'Musical Chairs on Horses'.

entwined in the lades and spokes of the wheels, also flowers from the gardens and sheaves of corn. The farm horses must have wondered why they were getting so much attention, being brushed and spruced up and their hooves oiled. The quietest horse was always chosen because he could cope with the brass band music and flags which decorated the field entrance and large marquee. "Topper" was the mare my father chose for these grand occasions.

The Jubilee of 1935, King George V and Queen Mary, is the one that stands out vividly in my mind. We children always helped and oh! what fun, "simple fun" in those days. I was nine years old.'

'I recall the Silver Jubilee of King George V and Queen Mary in 1935. At school we designed Jubilee samplers in our drawing lessons and some of the girls used our designs and stitched and sewed at colourful samplers to be kept for posterity.

A big celebration was held in the village of Edithmead. Being a small hamlet with very little in the way of facilities, it did not even have a village hall in which to hold functions. Whist drives were sometimes held in the village and these took place in some of the larger farmhouses, using all downstairs rooms and the overflow being put in the scullery.

However, behind the back of an old rambling house called The Homestead there were various outbuildings and to existing cow stalls a large wooden building had been built on which was used for rabbit breeding. Appropriately, this was called The Rabbitry. After all rubbish was cleared away and tarpaulins hung to hide the adjoining cow stalls, it made quite a roomy place to set out the Jubilee lunch.

Oil lamps were hoisted and tied to the wooden beams and village ladies decorated the walls with paper trimmings and evergreens. Above the uneven concrete floor, trestle tables groaned under the weight of home cooked hams and large pieces of prime beef. Pickles, chutney and home grown salad vegetables jostled with the many loaves of freshly baked bread. Local farmhouse cider and ale were used to wash down the splendid repast.

After the meal the celebrations continued as sports for young and old were held in an adjoining field. During the evening a band played for dancing in the Rabbitry on the uneven concrete floor.'

'Memories of the 1935 Silver Jubilee celebrations are still vividly recalled by many local inhabitants.

Celebrations began at 7 am with the firing of a salute by the Somerset Yeomanry, followed by a morning service at St Andrew's church. Everyone over the age of 14 in Wiveliscombe had been invited to a special lunch at 1.30 pm. The WI were very proud to have

Many towns and villages organised events to mark the Coronation of George VI in 1937. This fancy dress parade formed part of Henton's celebrations.

been asked to organise the arrangements for this. They served 1,400 people with a superb meal on the first floor of the cider factory, which had been converted into a dining room for this joyous occasion. Joints of meat figured prominently on the menu, and Mr Frank Hancock, of brewery fame, was one of the skilful "carvers". To add to the conviviality, beer and soft drinks were also provided by the brewery.

Lunch was followed by recreational sports, and all children under the age of 14 sat down to a splendid tea in the recreation ground pavilion. Jubilee mugs and books were then distributed to 361 delighted boys and girls.

The youngest WI member, at that time aged 16 (and who is currently a member), had the privilege of planting a tree to commemorate this grand occasion.

The festivities continued well into the evening in the cider factory, and huge bonfires were lit at 10 pm at adjacent Withycombe. It was indeed a day to remember, and similar celebrations followed two years later in Coronation year!'

'In Brompton Ralph, King George V's Silver Jubilee was celebrated with a sit down dinner in the hay barn of Scott's (Cridlands) Farm. The beef for it was cooked in the village bakery. Later there was a dance in the old schoolroom (now the village hall). There was another dinner and dance for King George VI's Coronation.'

'All the parisoners of Sampford Arundel had a celebration lunch in several sittings in the barn at Sampford Farm. The ladies were waited on by the young men of the parish and the men had the ladies as waitresses. All wore red and white striped aprons. Then we had sports and the children had a tea. All the children were given Silver Jubilee mugs.'

'The Silver Jubilee of King George V was a great celebration for West Hatch, as was the Coronation of George VI two years later. Sports, tea parties and a huge bonfire were held, with a village social and dance in West Hatch school. Each schoolchild was given a mug on each occasion.'

'Alston Sutton's celebrations for the Coronation in May 1937 took the form of sports for all ages in a field near to Weare Hall, then tea was served in the hall followed by a dance in the evening.'

THE CORONATION OF ELIZABETH II 1953

'The whole village of Meare joined in celebrating the coronation of Queen Elizabeth II. A carnival would pass through the villages, ending up in a field at Millbatch. At school playtimes, groups of children huddled together, whispering secret plans.'

CORONATION OF HER MAJESTY QUEEN ELIZABETH II.

The pleasure of the company of

....

is requested at a

Coronation Party

to be held at
The County School, Main Road, West Huntspill
on Wednesday, June 3rd, 1953, at 5.30 p.m.
"GOD SAVE THE QUEEN"
Transport available if requested.

An invitation to a celebration party at West Huntspill on the day after Queen Elizabeth II's Coronation in 1953.

233

My group decided on a "Maypole" tableau which we displayed on a trailer and tractor. A long wooden pole was cemented into a container on the trailer and was painted red, white and blue and our parents helped with the costumes. The village shop soon ran out of red, white and blue crepe paper and ribbons. Greatly excited at the sight of all our work, we clambered onto the trailer for our ride to Westhay for the judging. Our hearts fell as we did not receive the expected prize but we later discovered that we had been entered in the wrong section. In spite of that, we all had a wonderful day.

In a large marquee the elderly were given lunch, the children a mug and a sumptuous tea and at night, to round off the proceedings, the villagers enjoyed a dance.

Few people then owned television sets but a van equipped with TV was procured so that people could watch something of the celebrations in London.'

'Wells City Council gave all the schoolchildren a tea party at the Bishop's Barn. We had orange squash and iced buns and were each given a coronation mug.'

'The Queen's Coronation in 1953 was celebrated in West Buckland with a party for the children up to the age of 16 and each child was given a souvenir coronation spoon. Our WI celebrated with a pageant at Gerbestone Manor.'

'At Corfe, Mrs Sword invited all members of the WI to her house to watch the Coronation on her television – the only one in the village at that time.'

'A TV set was set up in the village hall at Exton on the day. Food was provided and anyone could stay all day. During the next few days there was a fancy dress party, and a comic cricket match with sports for the children.'

'My grandfather, Walter Wheller, was the first person in Huish Episcopi to own a TV set. His sitting room was packed on Coronation Day.'

'At the time of the Coronation of Queen Elizabeth, TV was a comparative novelty but we were able to watch at my parents-in-law's home. Several other people came to watch too. In the evening there were bonfires up on Exmoor.

There was a single track railway which ran from Taunton to Barnstaple stopping at every station. One day we heard that the

Queen and the Duke of Edinburgh were going to Barnstaple to visit a china factory, so we went across the fields to where the railway went through a cutting. The train travelled quite slowly and the engine driver leant out of the cab and said "Third coach back". Our little son, who was about three years old, had a Union Jack to wave but unfortunately the blinds were drawn.'

THE VILLAGE YEAR

From January to December, the village year ran a familiar route through celebrations and remembrance, May Day to Harvest Home, Pancake Day to Christmas, perhaps even Egg Shackling to Punkie Night! Weddings, of course, took place at any time, but were always enjoyed by the community and some local customs kept up. Empire Day, once celebrated on 24th May by every schoolchild in England, has now gone the way of the British Empire it represented, and the hiring fairs which once represented the high spot of the year have lost their status, but other annual celebrations go on today.

WEDDINGS

'It was the custom at Edithmead to tie the gate of the house to confront the newly weds when they returned from the church service. I recall my parents tying the gate of our house when my aunt and uncle were married. The same thing happened on my wedding day when a lady in the village tied the selfsame gates as I returned from church.'

'Marriage was usually preceded by a long engagement. In those days the bride would save up a "bottom drawer", comprising gifts for her future home and oddments given her by her employer. Wages were low and it therefore took a long time to save up. The man usually worked on a farm and had to wait for a cottage. When the wedding day dawned, the bride in her best dress and hat and the bridegroom in his Sunday suit, went to church with their families. The service was followed by a cold meal at the bride's parents' home. The happy couple would return to their cottage and be back to work the next day.'

'One lady tells of her wedding which took place at St James' church in Taunton at eight o'clock in the morning, in order to be back for milking. When asked when they went on honeymoon, she replied that she was still waiting for it. They have, in fact, celebrated their golden wedding.'

SHROVE TUESDAY

'When I was a small child in the 1930s and 1940s, my grandparents lived in an old watermill at Croscombe that had been converted into two houses.

The original mill house was much as it had always been but my grandparents lived in the bit that had been the mill. It was a rather spooky place to a small child, with a living room and large scullery on the ground floor. In the scullery were the open-tread mill stairs to the first floor, where there was one bedroom. A narrow dark passage led to a dark, steep, stairway to the top floor. There were three bedrooms and a wide corridor across the whole mill, including the next door neighbour's bedrooms. In one of the bedrooms there was still a trap door and hook, where mill sacks were hoisted up.

It was the stairs I found most frightening. I hated the open-tread, wide, mill stairs and always sat on the top step and edged down them on my bottom, legs like jelly!

We lived at the opposite end of the village to the mill, but often visited Gran and Grandad. I vividly remember Shrove Tuesdays when all my mother's large family turned up at Gran's with various offspring. My grandmother had been a cook "in service" and she was an excellent cook.

She would stand with her big black iron frying pan, while the young ladies caught up on all the gossip, and the children raced around the old mill, hiding and frightening each other.

Gran seemed to have her own recipes for pancakes. This involved putting currants in some of them. They tasted wonderful, eaten the moment they were cooked, taking it in turns to have one. Sometimes one of the younger ladies took over cooking, but Gran's always tasted best.

I can't smell pancakes without being back in those days, when whole families got together for simple pleasures, and my grandmother took it for granted all her family would turn up for their pancakes.'

'The Somerset and Dorset Notes and Queries of 1890 describes Egg Shackling.

236

About 50 years ago, on Shrove Tuesday "it was the practice in smaller village schools for pupils to bring an egg and deliver it into the hands of the master or mistress on arrival. At the end of morning school, all the eggs (having been previously marked each with its owner's name) were laid side by side on a corn sieve, which being placed on the ground was 'shackled' or agitated to and fro until the shells were cracked." The child whose egg was the last to crack and was removed unbroken, won a prize and was installed as the hero or heroine of the day.

The reasons for this custom were queried and it was asked whether it was simply to give the teachers a cheap way of keeping Shrove Tuesday by eating pancakes or was it in a mild manner a way, among the rising generation, of "giving up a small modicum of animal food to one who was, in by-gone days, almost as much a spiritual master as the priest himself?"

The word "shackle" is a local term for the noise made by a collection of small stones or marbles shaken together. The word survives in "ramshackle" and is derived from the Anglo-Saxon "sceacan" – to shake.

Somerset Men in London (1920–21) stated that the owner of the first egg broken was given a farthing, and the winners received prizes. The custom continued regularly until 1915, when eggs became too precious to be used in this way. "Only last year, however, I read of it being carried out in Shepton Beauchamp". When the older children went to Shepton Beauchamp they took their eggs with them and they were sometimes cracked before the shackling. One lad ate four on the way home!

Another local custom was that Barrington children had hot cross buns on Good Friday but Fivehead children had an orange.'

THE CLUB OR FRIENDLY SOCIETY

'On Trinity Monday, bells would ring out at six o'clock in the morning in Long Sutton, followed by a service for the Men's Friendly Society. The Society Walk would follow and later dinner in the evening. All the village would enjoy the fair on the green.'

'There was a Henton Club and the men used to wear a blue silk sash and carry a staff with flowers and a brass plate on the top. They had a church service in the morning and then they walked through Henton with a band playing in front and had cider at different farmhouses. When they came back they had a meal in a marquee in what is now the Jubilee Field and after that they used to walk partway up Yarley, up as far as Manor Farm, Worth. Then there was a dance in the evening.'

'Witham Friary has a Benefit Club (known as Witham Friary Friendly Society) which is one of the oldest in the country. The subscription was one shilling and threepence a month and the sick were paid seven shillings a week. Every Whit Tuesday the Society held a celebration – a parade through the village, headed by a brass band, followed by a service in the parish church, with afterwards a dinner at the village inn. The rest of the day was spent in various amusements, the whole village making it a holiday.'

MAY DAY, MAY FAIR AND THE HOBBY HORSE

'My mother used to walk us in to Wells May Fair in the 1920s, which was a great day. It was held where the bus station is now and it was called the cattle market, where people would bring cows and horses to be sold. There used to be a lot of gipsies and they would run the horses up to what was the Wells Blue School, and trot them up and down for the people to see what they were like before they bought them. Then they all used to go in the Mermaid – the men used to go in the pub and the women would sit outside on the pavement with their babies and children. They would feed their babies there and have their glass of beer. But there was never any bother. There was generally a policeman around. It was one of the highlights of the year, was Wells May Market, and the big fair up in the market place.'

'There was a May Queen held at Wookey in the 1920s and the young ladies used to dress up in white with a lot of flowers and go up to Colonel Perkins house where they had big lawns. I remember one May Queen was Miss Queenie Chapman, who did a lot in the village.'

'Looking back to childhood days in Minehead, the most eagerly awaited event was the annual reappearance of the Hobby Horse, in May. Heard in the distance, the music itself was exciting. Deep-toned drums and accordions accompanied the "Horse" as it pranced its way from its winter "home" at the Quay. Yes, we knew there was a man inside, but it was still comforting to hide behind the nearest grown-up at first sight of the grotesque mask with the feathers atop, and the swishing rope "tail". We neither knew nor cared that it might be part of an ancient fertility rite to welcome Spring, or a fearsome creature made to frighten marauding Danes! All that mattered was that the

Hobby Horse would be cavorting for three evenings (and the hope of slightly delayed bed-times!).

In my grandmother's day, young children (dressed mostly in white) would walk in the early morning of May Day to White Cross on the edge of town. They would dance around a maypole, and the Hobby Horse would be there also, to welcome Spring.

The ancient custom still continues, though now the children are missing! The Hobby Horse (with the occasional wild, exuberant shout), plus drums, accordions, etc passes my house at 5.30 am on May Day, on its way to White Cross. The route is the traditional one used for hundreds of years, and as the drums wake me, I am five years old again!'

EMPIRE DAY 24th MAY

'Empire Day at Burnham on Sea's infants school was celebrated by grouping around the tall flagpole on which the Union Jack had been hoisted for the occasion. We sang patriotic songs, *God Save The King* (George V), marched around the playground and then at twelve o'clock were given a half day holiday and allowed home.'

'On Empire Day at Saltford school the children dressed up in various garments depicting the countries of the British Empire. We sang songs and the National Anthem. The vicar would say prayers for the "heathen" children in some of these countries.'

'At Dunster we marched down to the boys school and staged a celebration of England. One of the songs we sang was *Hurrah for the Red, White and Blue.*'

THE FAIR

'We all looked forward to Bridgwater Fair in the 1920s and a ride on the Golden Dragons with the steam organ. At Carnival, mother would prepare a ham tea for aunts, uncles and cousins who would arrive on special trains from Wales. We all turned our coats inside out (so there were no pockets for fireworks to go into) to see the squibbing in the High Street, where there was a competition between rival gangs. There was a huge bonfire on the Cornhill by the Blake statue, but this was discontinued when the street was paved.'

'On one occasion in the 1920s, to the great excitement of Walton village, an aeroplane came to our field behind the school and for five shillings people were taken up for a quick flip and a loop-the-loop.'

'The circus used to travel from town to town, and I remember seeing the elephants walking up the hill at East Huntspill.'

'Before the First World War the annual Babcary fete took place on the last Thursday in July, the school having broken up for the month-long holiday the previous day. All village children met at the school and chose a partner with whom to parade. The Keinton Mandeville brass band arrived at 1.30 pm and the children would line up behind it in pairs. Three loud thumps on the drum and the procession started. First it went to the rectory and the rector came out to greet the bandsmen and children. Then the procession started off on its long journey through the village streets which were lined with cheering spectators. At last back to the field where the fete was being held, and it was a sight to delight every child's eye.

There were swings and roundabouts, coconut shies, a machine on which men could test their strength, stalls of many kinds selling gingerbread, sweets and nuts, popcorn and fruit. There would be an ice cream cart where an ice cream cornet could be bought for only a ha'penny. In the huge tent, tables would be laid out ready for tea. The children would sit outside on the grass to have theirs. Following tea there would be various kinds of races for the children and a competition for the best bunch of wild flowers bearing the name of each flower. There were pony races and other competitions for adults which continued until it was getting dark, then there was dancing in the tent to music from the band. What a lovely happy day!'

'Tor Fair in Glastonbury was the highlight of the year. Before the First World War it was a hiring fair where farm workers were hired for a year. Almost all the local villagers would attend and there would be no work on the farms that day, except for feeding animals and milking cows. Most of the money for spending at the fair would have been earned from picking the luscious blackberries which grew in abundance on the moors.'

'The Harbour Water Sports Day at Watchet in the 1940s was of keen interest to young and old. The harbour dries out at low water leaving a large expanse of mud where the "Mud Sports" were held. Beginning with football matches and other games, they would evolve into swimming events as the tide came in. People from the surrounding district would crowd into Watchet, filling the esplanade, pier and pleasure ground to listen to the town band playing popular music on the esplanade and watch the event keenly contested among rival clubs. The arrival of White Leggs Fair on Bank Holiday was a great attraction.'

The village fair at Buckland Dinham c1925.

'October brought Kingsbrompton Fair Day. Everyone came from miles around to meet friends and pay the yearly cart, baker and blacksmith's bills. Meat and pickles were provided to all who settled their grocery acounts.'

'There was a village carnival every November in North Curry, with decorated bicycles and carts, but the big event was Curry Fair, with roundabouts and gallopers, swings and side shows. All the young people working away from home tried to get back for the fair.'

THE FLOWER SHOW

'Dad was a keen gardener. He became a member of the Norton Fitzwarren village club and was secretary to the Flower Show, which was a day we all looked forward to. Flags and bunting were across the road all through the village and skittles were played throughout the week. The first prize for the men was a pig, second prize ten shillings and third prize a fowl. There were children's sports held the same day as the Flower Show on a Saturday. In early years there were horse events – races for cart horses and ponies, and a ball race with horses. In 1937 they held a motorbike football match. There was always a dance in the evening to finish off the entertainment week. At the dance they would announce the winner of the skittles.'

'Winsham's first Flower Show Queen was in 1936. Eleven girls entered the competition and the girl selling the most penny tickets was the Queen. She was crowned, we were all given a dress and we rode through the village on a horse-drawn wagon. The village came alive that day, finishing with a "Bop Hop" in the village hall.'

'When I was young the Huish Episcopi Flower Show was held in a large marquee in the memorial field, where now part is the Huish car park. It was always a lovely day out as besides the Flower Show, there was Townsend's Fun Fair with roundabouts, swings and stalls, selling gingerbread and mint humbugs.'

'Time was when we held a Garden Fete on the vicarage lawns at Kilmersdon. The vicarage was on the top of the hill and there was such a lovely view of the village from the lawn. Some of the fetes were held to raise funds for the village church. The farmers' wives always took over the produce stall, selling home-made butter, cheese, cream, new-laid eggs etc. Teas were served on the lawn, tables decked with pretty tablecloths and bone china cups, saucers and plates. There were sensible teapots holding about six cups in each, and two dear ladies from the village shop would sell ice cream cornets and wafers and home-made lemonade.'

THE HARVEST HOME

'East Brent is famous locally for the founding of the "Harvest Home" movement in Somerset. This was originally a great village celebration; the women made Christmas puddings (in August!), farmers and businessmen subscribed enough for the men to have a free lunch, the women and children received a free tea, and there were sports and jollifications. This was, and remains, the high point of the year in East Brent, with a meal for 600 in a tent.'

'Edithmead is a hamlet with a small population of a few hundred souls. But not to be outdone by the larger neighbouring villages, I can recall in my early childhood at least two Harvest Homes being held in the village.
A huge marquee was erected and long trestle tables displayed a tempting harvest lunch of home cooked hams, beef, cheese and pickles of all kinds. This repast was washed down with local cider and ale.

242

The village ladies entered the decorated hoop competition and there was fancy dress for the children. Sports too were held after lunch and skittles and tug-of-war for the men. A four piece dance band was engaged to play for dancing in the marquee during the evening.

I do not know why, but no further Harvest Homes were held in Edithmead after the early 1930s.'

'As a young girl growing up in a Somerset village in the 1930s and 1940s, entertainment was made by family and friends in the village.

The highlight of the year was the Harvest Home. We started with a church service, singing all the well known harvest hymns, then we all filed back to the local farmer's field where there was an enormous marquee which was laid up for the harvest meal.

Mountains of cold meats, salads, crusty bread and drinks were followed by apple pie and cream or trifle, all made by the ladies and we were allowed to eat as much as we could possibly pack in! A silver band played to entertain us. After the meal and all the speeches from the various guests and dignitaries, we looked forward to the children's sports – not easy with such a full stomach. About four o'clock it was back to the big marquee for a lovely tea of home-made jams, local baker's bread and cakes. At six o'clock the pony sports started in the next field; we loved all the excitement. Of course we all enjoyed the roundabouts, dodgems and many amusements and sideshows which entertained us on this fun day. It was also exciting to see it all move in on site and then packing up and moving out several days later. At eight thirty in the evening the big marquee became alive with the music of the silver band and the final event of the day, the dance, and as a special treat we were allowed to stay up very late.'

'No account of Batcombe would be complete without a mention of the Harvest Home. This yearly event took place in a large tent, and prior to 1914 was surrounded by a fair, with swing-boats, sweet stalls, coconut shies and skittles in the old waggon house, which was spacious and open at both ends so that the waggons could drive straight through.

Within the tent were tables and forms, every farmer's wife vying with the rest to make her table the most attractive. All the "best" china was laid out. Children from the school next door would be excited with the draymen's calls and the showmen's shouts. The brass band from the next town played from tea-time until day-break next day if "the hat" was passed around about 2 am.

After tea the trestles were taken away, and the forms placed round the edge of the tent, to the delight of the small boys who would rush outside and thump every "bulge" showing on the exterior of the tent. The band played, lights flared outside, and there was the smell of grass trodden down with dancing feet.

We sang the *Galloping Major* while the more prudish went outside, *Underneath the old Umbrella* was also a favourite, and no evening was complete without *Widdicombe Fair*.

The girls wore their hair with curls piled high, young men wore gloves. We all did the Lancers, sometime the "big" families making the whole set. Dancing "Up the Sides and Down the Middle". Those were the days.'

PUNKIE NIGHT

'In the 1934 edition of *The Somerset Countryman* it was stated that Punkie Night was probably only celebrated at Hinton St George, but, in a modified form, it provides an evening entertainment for village school children now. Its origin is obscure. One tradition is that the women of Hinton St George, being accustomed to attending Chiselborough Fair on St Luke's Day, for the purpose of purchasing red cloth for their cloaks, on one of these occasions returned home without their husbands, who remained behind. "The hour growing late, the good wives waited up but there was no sign or sound of their husbands and to illuminate their paths in the darkness the women pulled mangolds from the field, scooped out the flesh from within, perforated the outer skins and inserted lighted candles, then walked the three miles across the fields."

"A less likely version 'is that the husbands, having refreshed themselves unwisely, collected mangolds in Lopen" and made lanterns. The custom may be 200 or 300 years old.

"Children of the two villages continue to do the same with mangolds, decorating them with geometric designs or representing the village cross, ships, animals, Adam, Eve, Buy British, Bless our King, Britannia Rules the Waves." They generally preferred the face of a man, who had a pipe or cigarette in his mouth and spectacles on his nose.

Children paraded up and down the village, calling at some houses asking for additional candles. They sang:

  It's Punkie Night tonight
  It's Punkie Night tonight
    Adam and Eve won't believe
  It's Punkie Night tonight

as they waved the punkies, suspended from a piece of string.

244

The Somerset Countryman, in London in 1954, suggested the origin of the name came from America, where pumpkins were used. A local WI revived the custom.'

BONFIRE NIGHT

'Bonfire building at Wells was started at the end of September and added to till 5th November. Paper was always kept dry and added on the night. Lanterns were made out of mangolds. Fireworks were always kept in pockets and coats, along with the matches, but I never heard of anyone being badly hurt!'

'Our house at Walton Farm originally had a thatched roof. My grandfather Barnes got very worried on Bonfire Nights as the local lads always made a large bonfire on the cross, which was opposite the house. On one November night, afraid that the sparks might set the thatch alight, he went over to them at about eleven o'clock and said it was time the fire was put out. They took not the slightest bit of notice but knocked off his bowler hat and kicked it into the bonfire!'

'We always had a big Bonfire Night in the 1950s with all the children in the Bickenhall district coming to us as we had a huge garden. We had hot drinks and potatoes cooked in the bonfire. I had visitors one day and one said "You always get a welcome in this house although there are no handles on the cups".'

ARMISTICE DAY

'To the best of my knowledge we only came out through the front door of Henton school on Ash Wednesdays and Armistice Days when we went as a school across the road to the church.
During the 1940s the eleven o'clock service on 11th November was always held outside at the war memorial by the gate. Miss Ashley would play a small harmonium positioned on the path and a very feeble and meek Mr Maver would take the service. In those days Henton did not have to share its vicar with Wookey and Coxley but we did have to share Mr Maver with his telescope which stood on the lawn at the vicarage.'

'On Armistice Day in Dunster we marched to the war memorial from school and held the two minutes silence and had a solemn service. At that time all the people stopped whatever they were doing for two minutes at eleven o'clock on 11th November. The whole country was still.'

'In the 1950s at Wiveliscombe, the brewery siren sounded at 11 am and we all stood for two minutes silence.'

CHRISTMAS

'The morning in November in the 1920s when my mother announced "I think I'll begin the pudding tonight" meant that Christmas preparations were beginning.

What child today could be dragged from TV or even homework to stone raisins, grate suet or chop candied peel? Basins were greased and once the puddings were made, Father was roped in to help tie the basins down.

At a late hour all was ready for the morning when the big boiler would be hung on the crook over the fire and Father's main task of the day would be to see that the fire was kept going to ensure the puddings boiled constantly.

Later that evening we would be allowed to taste the tiny basin of pudding that had been filled for that purpose.'

'How long it seemed from one Christmas to the next, and how eagerly children looked forward to it – putting up decorations on Christmas Eve such as bunches of mistletoe entwined with coloured paper, getting the stockings ready for Father Christmas to fill.

During the early years of the century the "Mummers" would pay us a visit in the evening and entertain with songs which they had composed about "doings and happenings" in Babcary during the past year – stories of people's experiences and local gossip (some of which I feel was libellous!), but no names mentioned. These men, usually about five in number, would play small musical instruments including a melodeon, tambourine and triangle. Their faces would be pasted with some black stuff and white marking which I thought hideous and somewhat frightening. After being regaled with cider and mince pies they would move on to other houses.

The stockings tied with ribbon of different colours to identify ownership, were hung on the bannisters as we went to bed, but sleep did not come easily, and we were awakened very early by carol singers below our bedroom windows. We were only allowed to have the stockings when daylight came because of the danger of candle-light. It was so exciting to search into the stockings to find an apple, orange, sweets in small packets, nuts, a new penny, a new hanky, and of course a sugar mouse (no Christmas stocking would be complete without a sugar mouse!). There would be one nice present – a book or a card game. It does not sound very exciting these days, but it was really wonderful to us. Then the Christmas dinner! Dad always

246

brought home a big, fat goose (how else would the goose grease be obtained for our chest colds?). As soon as the plates were filled and passed round the youngest child would say grace and Dad would say a special toast for "absent friends" – some of our older brothers and sisters who were now away from home.

And the rich fruity pudding! A huge one set alight with brandy and hiding in itself several silver threepenny pieces for those lucky enough to find one in their portion.

Everything went quiet after dinner. Card games were played and new books read while Mother and Dad had a good rest. A really, truly Happy Christmas.'

'My first memory ever is of Pitney when I was a very small child, the Christmas of 1916. My father was away at the First World War, in the Navy. My mother and I and my nanny were invited to Pitney House for a long Christmas holiday. Our home was on the edge of Sherwood Forest near Nottingham. The journey here was a long one and quite an adventure; eventually we arrived at Long Sutton & Pitney Halt station with the Pitney House carriage waiting for us. That Christmas was magic. A large party was given for me. My nanny and I waited at the nursery window watching the carriages roll up the drive. We had jellies and trifles and little sandwiches and biscuits for tea (no icecream in those days!). After tea the Christmas tree in the hall was lit by proper candles and decorated with glass ornaments, sparkling in the flames of the candles. We sang round the tree and we played games in the dining-room (the tea had all been cleared away). A fiddler came and played music for us. It all had to come to an end and nanny and I watched the carriage lights departing down the drive.'

'The Cary family at Buckland Dinham in the 1920s kept their Christmas presents until all members had finished work on the farm, and then in the early evening the tree would be in the middle of the drawing room with all the presents piled underneath. Everyone formed a circle and holding hands sang "Here we go round the Christmas tree . . . on a cold and frosty evening" to the tune of the mulberry bush song. At the end of the verse, they would stop, and several parcels be given out, each person making a pile by the chair. Then some more singing and stopping, this continuing until finally all the presents were given out, followed by the grand opening and rustling of paper.'

'Our family drank Fry's Cocoa in the early 1930s at Winsham and saved the coupons which were inside the lid. Before Christmas my mother would count up the coupons and send them to Fry's cocoa factory. In return came a large box with all sorts of chocolate bars, even novelties to hang on the Christmas tree. My father hung them on a bunch of holly so that little fingers would not help themselves.'

'During the 1930s at Dunster we would go carol singing. About 20 of us, the choir from our church, set out to outlying houses of gentry during the week before Christmas. We had three violins and a small organ with foot bellows. As many as could plus the organ were transported in the lorry lent us by a local builder, the rest in private cars. Our visit had been announced beforehand and we were invited in to sing before the host and friends who had gathered there. Having sung our carols, the cook came in with a tray of hot mince pies and the butler with sherry. We must have visited about ten large houses.

On Christmas Eve we stayed nearer home and toured the village carrying the organ by hand. We stopped on street corners or near a cluster of houses – very little traffic around then. We carried torches and lanterns, but after a few practices we knew all our words, which I have never forgotten. On this occasion coffee and mince pies were served in the hall by the non-singers. All this was curtailed during the Second World War, and how we missed it. Even now Christmas does not seem the same to me without our carol singing.'

'Carol singing was exciting. Imagine a gaily decorated horse and dray with harmonium precariously balanced, accompanied by carollers with bobbing lanterns. Anyone knowing Pilton and its steep hills will appreciate the magnitude of this undertaking, and that success depended on enthusiasm and a prayer!'

'Christmas was always family celebrated, the week before always a hectic time for shopping locally. In our stocking was usually a sixpence, an apple and orange and sweets, with perhaps a doll or toy. We enjoyed Christmas night with the family dressing up and singing songs and carols around the piano. On Boxing Night we always had a dance in the village hall at Stoke St Michael.'

'When Len was a boy, before the Second World War, the children and the church choir in Crowcombe were taken carol singing in a cart drawn by a white pony. After which Joe Keeting, who lived in a cottage at the bottom of Flaxpool Hill, led the singing in the church house. Joe, who was totally blind, played the hand bells by feel. He laid them in a row on a table at the end of the hall, and never made a mistake.

Nellie Stevens once worked as a kitchen maid in Weacombe House and Combe Sydenham House, near Williton. At Christmas she blacked her face and, with some of the other staff, went upstairs to amuse her master's dinner guests. Nellie, who played the accordion and sang, was quite a star turn. On one occasion the master brought one of his guests downstairs to thank the staff. The guest was Winston Churchill. He shook hands with them all, and said "Why, Nellie, I would never have guessed it was you." In later years Nellie used to love to tell the tale of how she entertained Sir Winston Churchill.'

YOU DIDN'T LOOK FOR LUXURIES

'We never had turkey at Christmas. I don't think anybody had turkey in those days, the 1920s and before, never heard of a turkey. Mother had chicken. And we never had crackers or a Christmas tree, no, nothing. Mother used to put things in the stocking and you'd go to bed .and you was so excited you wouldn't sleep and about twelve o'clock Mother would bring the stocking up. You'd pretend to be asleep, this was me and my sister, and then you'd wait a bit and then suddenly you'd wake up – but you hadn't been to sleep – and "Mum, what time is it?" "Oh, you go to sleep", but we used to take the things out of our stocking, which was an orange and a few sweets and a doll and perhaps a few chocolates which my aunts used to send down. But that was all, not like today. Mother always used to buy us a doll at Christmas. We didn't have much for Christmas but we had lots of pleasures, all sorts of games, ludo, snakes and ladders. We used to walk round Goathurst village and sing carols and we used to take Dad's lantern. And if you were lucky, if you called on someone, like down the rectory, you might have a mince pie. That was a luxury, but you didn't look for luxuries, you had your own happiness, your own pleasures, it was lovely.'

Index

253

254